HOPE
BEHIND THE
HEADLINES

HOPE
BEHIND THE
HEADLINES

SHIFTING
CULTURE
IN HEALTH
AND SOCIAL CARE

LIZ WIGGINS JANET SMALLWOOD BRIAN MARSHALL
with contributors

Endorsements for Hope Behind the Headlines

This is a kindness of a book. It offers rich and deeply personal insights from leaders about how we can all learn to improve health care. The honesty of the contributions stands out – exhilarating, poignant but most of all: helpful. There are patterns but no recipes – so there is lots of room to see ourselves in these accounts from different health care contexts. It is both practical and inspirational; I found it offers moments of clarity in the oft bewildering fog of ideas and activity that envelops this subject. Wonderful.

Andy Cruickshank, Director of Nursing,
East London NHS Foundation Trust

Hope is such an important ingredient in healthcare and needed more than ever right now. This inspirational book offers hope in abundance and also practical ideas about how to shift cultures to be more conducive to providing the quality of patient care we all want to see. I applaud the leaders who have shared their stories and encourage all of us involved in health care, including politicians and policy makers, to take the time to read them.

Professor Dame Sally Davies, Chief Medical Officer, England

This brilliant book takes an enormous topic and cleverly crafts theory with real life experience from senior leaders working in the NHS. For any leaders grappling with shifting culture, read this book as it provides invaluable insight into what matters to people in times of change.

Cathie Cowan, Chief Executive, NHS Forth Valley

Media headlines always attract attention, often creating negative energy and false perspectives. This book offers hope, a raw and beautiful concept that helps build personal resilience and commitment to the life-giving, life-augmenting and life-saving organisation we hold dear in its 70th year, the NHS. The fact it is co-created between academic and professional colleagues 'in the moment' means all those who want to improve systems and care experience should read it. It celebrates the very best in humanity, it is a different type of book that I am certain will make a difference to all who read it and live in the hope it offers.

Dr Ian Bullock, Chief Executive Officer, Royal College of Physicians

This is a book I thoroughly enjoyed reading and did so, cover to cover. I became immersed in the leaders' experiences – their highs, their lows and their learnings. It provided me with much needed time to stop and reflect about what leading improvement in health is all about. Hope and belief shone through, providing a timely reminder that health, like leadership, is at its heart all about people.

Bridget Turner, Director of Policy,
Campaigns and Improvement, Diabetes UK

The authors provide relevant and accessible insights from theory, vividly illustrated through the stories and reflections of people leading change in the challenging context of modern health care. *Hope Behind the Headlines* invites readers to see their role as leaders differently; as powerful participants in the ongoing work of change and improvement.

Will Warburton, Director of Improvement, The Health Foundation

This wonderful book really does offer hope. At a time when the media is full of gloom and doom about the Health Service, this book tells the stories of those in the front line who are making critical improvements in services and care, right here and now, and shows how they are doing it. Make sure you get a copy.

George Binney, Programme Director, Ashridge Executive Education at Hult International Business School and Author of *Living Leadership* and *Breaking Free of Bonkers*

Leadership in any organisation in times of uncertainty with changing priorities is a challenge but leadership across NHS organisations is particularly demanding. This book offers evidence-based narratives on the key components of leadership in complex organisations. These accounts, combined with current leadership research, provide thoughtful, practical examples on how to enhance the leadership process for the benefit of individuals and organisations. *Hope Behind the Headlines* offers a refreshing insight into the intricacies of shifting cultures in complex and large organisations.

Professor Rosalynd Jowett, Dean of Health Sciences, University of East Anglia

Honest stories of leading change in the complex health and social care system with a delicate dusting of theory; there's a lot to learn and reflect on for anyone who wants to improve health care, but most of all I was filled with hope for the future, because commitment, integrity, passion and compassion ring out from the voices of these NHS leaders.

Dr Mark S MacGregor, Associate Medical Director, NHS Ayrshire & Arran

This heartening book tells the stories of those many leaders in health and related sectors who continue to care, to struggle and to lead in the face of a wide range of complex and competing demands. I was moved by the compassion and bravery of these leaders in sharing their worries and insights which give me hope and faith in our capacity to move closer to achieving our aim of a fair, efficient and equitable health service.

Dr Helen Crimlisk, Deputy Medical Director and Director of Undergraduate Psychiatry, SHSC & Psychiatry Module Lead, University of Sheffield

Whilst media stories swing wildly between cutting edge innovation to the gloom of a personal tragedy or a disastrous performance statistic, there is never much focus on how well the NHS does at just getting on with it. What comes across in the stories contained in this volume is that it isn't the action plan, the Gantt chart or the spreadsheet that ultimately bring about successful improvement. Instead it's the people, their relationships, their gestures, how they treat each other and how they respond to each other that is the powerful change agent. For all those working in the NHS and trying to make a difference, this book is a reminder that it is worth it, that others have faced what you have faced and got through it, and the NHS and the individuals concerned are better as a consequence.

Dr Nigel Sturrock, Regional Medical Director, Midlands and East, NHS Improvement

A stimulating combination of gripping real-life stories and bite-sized theories. I felt as if I was right in those tricky organizational situations alongside the protagonists, who show how good things can come to pass whatever the surroundings. The situations they describe stayed with me long after I finished reading.

Professor Gill Coleman, Ashridge Executive Education, Hult Business School

First published in 2018 by Libri Publishing

ISBN: 978-1-911450-16-0

A CIP catalogue record for this book is available from The British Library

Cover and book design by Carnegie Publishing
Reprinted in 2019 by Halstan UK

Libri Publishing
Brunel House
Volunteer Way
Faringdon
Oxfordshire
SN7 7YR

Tel: +44 (0)845 873 3837

www.libripublishing.co.uk

Acknowledgements

The volume in your hands represents a great deal of collective thinking, inquiry, learning, challenge and support. It has been a truly collaborative endeavour. There are therefore many people whom we would like to thank and acknowledge.

First, we would like to thank those senior health leaders including Anna Burhouse, Mark Cheetham, Clare Dieppe, Ruth Glassborow, Paul Gowens, Hilary MacPherson, Dave Raw, Hiro Tanaka and Anna Winyard who were willing to share their experiences and take the time to write their stories, on top of busy clinical, leadership and family commitments. Their gesture in doing so represents true courage, real generosity and a deeply felt desire to help others working in a system that you, and we, care about. Their willingness to "put themselves out there" by sharing their experiences, with the intention of helping other leaders to improve quality of care for patients, service users, carers and staff, is something we applaud, appreciate and admire.

These senior health leaders' ability to lead, to be brave, to experiment and to then tell their stories and share their learning has not been a solo endeavour. It has been made possible because of the numerous conversations that have taken place on the GenerationQ leadership programme with other participants on the same cohort, as well as across cohorts, with coaches, in action learning sets and with the wider faculty team. We would therefore like to thank and acknowledge every single leader who has taken part in GenerationQ for all each one of you has done in your own work as a leader and all that you have contributed to these particular stories told in this volume.

Thirdly, we would like to thank the Health Foundation who commissioned, and have then funded, GenerationQ since 2009. It has given us as faculty a deeply satisfying source of work from which we ourselves have learned and gained enormously. It has also enabled us to get to know some truly fabulous, deeply committed people. Further thanks to Jennifer Dixon, Will Warburton and Frances Wiseman for their willingness to support our desire to disseminate some of the GenerationQ learnings more widely by supporting the creation of this book and its companion volume, *Beyond the Toolkit: Leading Quality Improvement in Health and Social Care.* A particular thanks to Frances for joining us in our thinking and creation of this volume.

Project managing a team of senior NHS leaders and authors with multiple commitments is not for the faint hearted, but Sue Jabbar has done a truly wonderful job, staying calm and being organised as versions of stories went to-ing and fro-ing. Our thanks as well to our faculty colleague Howard Atkins for his support to us and some of the Fellows. Zoe Cavell at Ashridge Executive Education has been a delightful guide as we navigated our way through the legal complexities of copyright and ownership. We cannot thank her enough. Our thanks as well to our publisher, Libri, in particular to Paul Jervis for his confidence in what we had to offer and his patience as we worked out what the book was really about. James Baylay has added a wonderful visual element to the words which we believe really enhances the experience of reading the book, so thank you to him too.

Lastly, our thanks to our families, friends and colleague for putting up with the amount of time and energy it has taken to pull the book together and for joining us in many conversations over the years. Our hope is that some of the inspiration and learning from this book will help our wonderful children see that they have choice as they enter the world of work and organisations. Each of them has been, and continues to be, our inspiration.

Thank you all.

Contents

Preface

This year, I reached my silver jubilee of working in the NHS. There was no bunting or commemorative mug, but I can reflect on a career of which I am proud and have largely enjoyed. I have met some amazing staff, patients and families and I have learned a great deal. I am now in the privileged position of leading collaborative work nationally to develop leadership capacity to improve the quality of patient care in our health and social care systems. This work includes sign-up to a strategic framework[*] which commits national organisations to changing the regulatory and oversight environment to help to enable greater local improvement in care.

The framework emphasises compassionate and inclusive leadership: paying close attention to the people you lead, understanding the situations they face, responding empathetically and taking thoughtful and appropriate action. Importantly, it means progressing equality, valuing diversity and challenging existing power imbalances. At the heart of this framework and the shared improvement endeavour sit issues of culture and leadership.

This book is therefore relevant, timely and useful. It is full of stories of leaders of health and social care in the UK and their efforts to shift their local cultures to be more conducive to improving the quality of care. The stories illustrate the challenges and hope contained in every individual's acts of leadership, and remind us of West's words (2016) that "every inter-action by every leader, every day, shapes the culture of an organisation".

---

[*] https://improvement.nhs.uk/uploads/documents/Developing_People-Improving_Care-010216.pdf

The emphasis on real-life stories makes this book all the richer. In the opening chapters it also offers the reader relevant and accessible theoretical insight. Importantly too, the book invites personal reflection. Written with a spirit of what Professor Don Berwick (2013) calls "all teach, all learn", this book aims to evoke and encourage us all to reflect on our own thoughts and behaviours, to enable us all to take effective action in our daily leadership work.

The stories and theories within the book underline the importance of relational leadership skills, which doesn't always get the recognition it needs in our health and social care system. Stacey (2012) suggests some of the best leaders are those who are connected and "channel the vitality of the 'real' organisation to achieve the goals of the 'formal' organisation", and Schein (2009) suggests senior leaders have the potential to be effective change managers but they are more often drawn to the expert role. When I reflect upon my own context, there is still a way to go to achieve the mindset and capabilities to ensure a supportive, enabling regulatory and oversight environment. Local leaders report that the current system is too focused on assurance over improvement, on the short term over medium term, and describe how many of the national messages are still overwhelmingly about "grip", "pace", and of "strong leadership". There is still insufficient under-standing or acknowledgement of the behavioural and relational aspects of improvement and change in health care. I continue to ask myself what it will really take to shift cultures across health and care. How long before leadership behaviours are described as consistently compassionate? How long before the senior leadership reflects the diversity of the population served and offers diversity of thought, and what will it take to help get there?

However, as I read the stories in this book and the underpinning theories, I have renewed hope that we will see the necessary shifts in culture. The storytellers evidence their own practice of what Berwick describes as "unconditional teamwork", to communicate, share, show up and never worry alone, and the personal risks this can involve. The different style of leadership illustrated in their narratives may sound curiously "soft" to some, particularly when health and care services are facing unprecedented, urgent pressures. If this is your response, I urge you to reflect on your own assumptions about the nature of leadership that the current context and challenges are calling for.

It has been such a privilege to be part of the peer group developing this book, and a growing network of leaders committed to continuous improvement and the relational and personal leadership this requires. I would like to thank the authors and the contributors for their generous work to develop *Hope Behind the Headlines* and importantly, the Health Foundation for its commitment and investment in the GenerationQ Fellowship programme, and the Fellows themselves.

I deliberately chose to write this short preface in the hallowed halls of the British Library in London. It somehow felt appropriate to read the chapters of the then unpublished *Hope Behind the Headlines* in this impressive space, which is home to a collection of well over 150 million items in most known languages. Since 1662, legal deposit has existed in English law which ensures that the nation's published output and legacy is collected systematically and made available to future generations. I look forward to this book joining the 3 million new items added every year, and to the encouragement it offers to us all, and future leaders.

As we enter the 70th anniversary year of the National Health Service, this book offers some optimism that the health and care system that my son experiences in his lifetime will be truly compassionate, and that we will have found ways to scale the hope that this book contains and achieve the quality of care that our staff, patients and communities so rightly deserve.

Suzie Bailey

Director of Leadership and Quality Improvement, NHS Improvement

January 2018

Introduction

The opening ceremony of the London 2012 Olympics was designed to celebrate and showcase to the world British history and British culture. It included reference to a national, dearly loved and highly regarded institution which employs more people than any other organisation in Europe, and continues to be regarded with admiration in many other countries. That institution was the NHS. Hospital beds, with actual nurses pushing them, and real patients in them, paraded with pride to music and then morphed to form the logo of Great Ormond Street Children's Hospital. The NHS, launched by the then minister of health Aneurin Bevan in 1948, is an asset of the people for the people with the guiding mantra of care to all, free at the point of delivery and based upon clinical need and not ability to pay. Such is its place in the national psyche it was worthy of inclusion as something particularly British and important.

And of course, although people talk of *the* NHS, as if it were one homogeneous organisation, it is in fact made up of multiple organisations. In NHS England alone, there are 44 Sustainability and Transformation Plans (STPs), 137 acute trusts, 17 specialist trusts, 56 mental health trusts, 35 community trusts, 10 ambulance trusts and over 5,000 GP practices (Keough 2017). We are therefore wary of making generalisations, recognising that there will be local variations.

Yet, in the current context of growing demand for services and further constrained resource across the whole of health and social care, newspaper headlines seem to talk increasingly of missed targets, failures of care, avoidable deaths, people waiting on trolleys in A&E. Governance and assurance processes too tend to focus on what is not working, the near misses, the never events, complaints. Deficit talk can easily dominate. Amongst commentators and policy-makers looking at the health and social care system, some talk of concern, others of a stretched system under pressure, and some talk of crisis. A similar range of views is evident if you talk to those working within the system or using the services.

Our intention in writing this book is to offer an antidote to any despondency and to shine a light on some examples of what is being achieved and what more might be possible. The intention is to inspire, reassure and encourage other leaders, without pretending it is all easy. As such, this book is a gesture of hope.

We, the authors, have many years of experience, working in the NHS as organisation development practitioners and as leadership developers. The idea for writing this book emerged from our work as members of the faculty team who design and facilitate a leadership programme for senior leaders from across all four countries of the UK. The programme is the Ashridge Masters in Leadership (Quality Improvement), funded by the Health Foundation and branded GenerationQ. The Q stands for Quality. Over the past eight years we have had the privilege and delight of getting to know, and learn alongside, one hundred and twenty-six truly remarkable yet also ordinary people. The participants, or Fellows as we call them, represent the full gamut of professions and skills needed to keep our health and care services running: nurses, allied health professionals, surgeons, clinicians, managers, paramedics, pharmacists, GPs, commissioners and policy-makers. They all share a common purpose – to care well for patients and service users – as well as a desire to learn how to do it even better. It seemed a waste that only we were able to enjoy hearing what the GenerationQ Fellows were doing and learning as we read their assignments and Masters theses. Hence the idea of collecting and publishing some of their stories in this book.

In their stories, the Fellows share how they have sought to shift the culture of their local environment to be more conducive to providing high-quality care. They describe their own acts of leadership, some of which may have seemed small at the time, yet which often had unexpectedly significant consequences. The stories are of progress as well as some setbacks, of trying different approaches, of experimenting, of building relationships, of having different conversations, of connecting with others and being willing to be personally brave or vulnerable to challenge and shift the dominant way of doing things.

We imagine that many of you reading this book will be leaders, or aspiring leaders, in either health or social care. Our hope is that in reading the stories you will feel others have been in similar situations to yourself, and that the stories will stimulate and encourage you to see new ideas, insights and possibilities for action in your own role as a leader. We promise no silver bullets, quick fixes or generalisable truths. The health and social care context is far too complex for that, and each local context will be different, each meriting a specific approach. Our invitation to you is to enjoy reading the stories and, as you read, notice what strikes you as important or interesting. What catches your attention or curiosity? What challenges you? What do you disagree with? Some stories may resonate with you whilst others leave you cold. Whatever your response, what questions and insights does your reading elicit for your own leadership?

A few words about how you might choose to read this book.

The first four chapters set out some of the informing thinking and research about context, culture, leadership and change to which Fellows are exposed on the programme. Each chapter also includes some short reflections and examples in the Fellows' own words, to illuminate how they applied them to their own experience as leaders. We hope that these ideas and frameworks may also be relevant and helpful for you, as well as giving you an insight into where the Fellows are coming from when you read their stories. And, if theory and concepts are not your thing, you might choose to turn straight to the first story, Chapter 5.

The stories are written by the Fellows themselves, and they provide a rarely heard account of what it is like to lead in practice, "warts and all". Each story represents the perspective of one individual. They each share their experience of what actually happened when they were making moves to shift the culture where they worked. As such, the stories represent their truth, their learning, their inner dialogue about what they thought and felt, what they did and why. And, as we will all recognise, whenever any of us recount what happened at work, our accounts are always partial as we choose what to share, what to leave out. The Fellows' stories are therefore not attempting to represent the truth or definitive answer of "what actually happened" as some objective, scientific account.

Care has been taken to disguise the identity of the organisation and individuals within each story, to avoid any risk of unintentionally offending others. We trust that the stories evoke an empathetic and generous response in the reader, as they were written with the intention of being helpful to others who may be in similar situations. As the stories are written by the Fellows, expect the writing styles to be different and to reflect their individual voices.

The book is in four sections:

- Section 1, *Framing*, comprises four chapters offering insight into ideas and concepts. You might choose to skip this section and turn straight to Section 2 where the stories begin and perhaps then return to it later if theory and research is not your main interest.
- Section 2, *Tempered Tenacity,* comprises five chapters each of which is a Fellow's story. The stories have in common the theme of persistence and resilience.
- Section 3, *Bridging the Divides*, comprises four story chapters. The theme in common is that of fostering connection, co-operation and collaboration across boundaries.
- Section 4, *Constructive Resistance*, comprises two story chapters both of which illustrate leaders standing firm to protect something of value.

We end by offering our own closing reflections. In addition, you may be interested in the companion volume, *Beyond the Toolkit: Leading Quality Improvement in Health and Social Care.* This explores the leadership implications of introducing quality improvement. The main thesis is that understanding the technical requirements of QI is necessary but not sufficient: a leader also needs to be able to adapt QI methods to meet the specifics of their context, and to have well developed relational and personal leadership skills. As with *Hope Behind the Headlines, Beyond the Toolkit* includes stories written by Fellows who were on the GenerationQ leadership programme, sharing their experience and learning.

Liz Wiggins, Janet Smallwood, Brian Marshall

January 2018

Framing

In this first section we offer four chapters that set out some of the informing thinking and research about context, culture, leadership and change to which Fellows are exposed on the programme. The chapters also include some short reflections and illustrations in the Fellows' own words. Our intention in writing these chapters is to help you understand where the Fellows are coming from in their stories, and encourage your own reflection on what it means to lead. It is also to set you up well for enjoying reading and learning from their stories.

In Chapter 1, *Reframing Contexts,* we explore the current context for leading and working in the health and social care system, and examine some of the current challenges. We examine the importance of staying connected to your core purpose and the idea of relative potency. We also encourage you to be the leader you are with more self-awareness and skill, rather than trying to force yourself to fit into the straightjacket of an idealised model.

In Chapter 2, *Shifting Local Culture(s),* we explore the notion of culture and examine why this matters to leaders, staff, patients, carers and all of us as members of society. We examine the subtle but important distinction between *the* culture, singular, and the lighter, more malleable and flexible idea of local cultures. Importantly, we explore the difference between shifting local cultures versus the dominant discourse of changing culture.

In Chapter 3, *Thinking Differently about Organisations and Leadership,* we draw attention to the way local cultures are impacted by local leadership. We explore how two contrasting ideas about leadership are rooted in very different perspectives about the nature of organisations. We examine the dominant discourse, or mainstream practice, in the NHS which all too often sets up leaders to be lonely heroes and has unintended cultural consequences. An alternative perspective, based on complexity thinking, sees leaders as in charge but not in control. This is a view that emphasises the unpredictability of much of organisational life and sees leadership as a relational activity, involving working with others, rather than a solo performance. This is a view that Fellows in the programme have described as at first discombobulating but ultimately liberating.

In Chapter 4, *Making Moves*, we turn our attention to the dynamics of relationships, conversation, power and politics. These four elements rarely get explicitly explored in organisational life, and yet they are key to the practice of relational leadership. As a leader, rethinking your approach to each of these can offer insight into specific moves you can make that might shift your local culture to be more human, relational and conducive to high-quality patient care. Many of the leadership moves or gestures that you will read about in the Fellows' stories arise from the approaches and insights shared in this chapter.

CHAPTER 1

Reframing Contexts

A few words to start

In the introduction to this book we have already mentioned the challenging current context for health and social care, not least the growing demand for services and constrained resource. In this first chapter we will illuminate some of the themes we hear as contributing to this context, in terms of their implications for leadership. However, in doing so we are mindful of the risk of potentially amplifying the sense of challenge.

It therefore feels important to remind you of our intention in writing this book: to offer an antidote to what some may experience and describe as a system under pressure, perhaps a system even in crisis. Our intention is to offer hope, to shine a light on some examples of what is being achieved and what more might be possible. The intention is also to inspire, reassure and encourage other leaders, without pretending it is in any way straightforward or easy.

We encourage you to read on, to acknowledge what makes the context challenging and yet also be encouraged to reframe the context to one where hope is alive and improvement to the quality of care is possible.

The context for leading in health and social care

There is a rather over-used acronym that originated first in the US military, but is now used regularly in management literature, to describe the context for leading in all sectors in the 21st century. You may well have come across it. The phrase is VUCA which stands for **V**olatile, **U**ncertain, **C**omplex and **A**mbiguous (Stiehm and Townsend 2002). It pithily, if inelegantly, describes the macro global context which makes leading in most organisations a challenge right now. Sudden dramatic shifts in the realm of politics, economic crises, technological breakthroughs, terrorism, environmental disasters and the socio-economic challenges of mass migrations, exclusion, ageing populations and poverty are features of the macro level context. Together these create an environment where planning and trying to predict the future become harder, if not impossible, so the job of leading has arguably become more stressful and anxiety provoking. In our experience, many leaders in all sectors, not just in health and social care, are questioning right now how to lead well and successfully whilst, at the same time, holding on to the essence of what it means to be human, for themselves as individuals, and for those whom they lead.

Talk to almost anyone working in health and social care, and people describe the current context as particularly tough. In addition to the macro level context described, there is talk of the unexpected and unpredictable happening all the time – key staff are off sick, there is a major incident, the CEO suddenly goes when you had just begun to build a good relationship, there are conflicting demands from further up the hierarchy.

It feels important to acknowledge some of the themes we hear as contributing to this, much of which will undoubtedly be familiar to you. In particular, we draw attention to those aspects of context where there are often unintended consequences that are contributing to the creation of cultures that are not always conducive to patient care and improving quality. We mention these because the Fellows' stories are, we hope, a counter narrative to what might otherwise feel daunting and depressing. The stories are evidence that shifts in culture to be more conducive to high-quality care *are* possible.

Financial austerity and the widening gap between demand for care and available funding

A common theme we hear from health leaders in the programme, as well as in the mainstream and medical press, is the constant pressure for further efficiency savings at the same time as increasing demand for services. The NHS in England, for example, has responded to the pressures by aiming to make £22 billion of efficiency savings by 2020 (Lafond et al 2016) whilst the reality is that by the end of 2016, 57 percent of trusts were in deficit (Charlesworth et al 2017). In the 2015 Comprehensive Spending Review, the government committed additional real terms funding for health in England of £4.5 billion by 2020/21, but this equates to an increase in NHS funding of just 0.7 percent per year in real terms. This is the lowest increase in real terms since the creation of the NHS in 1948, and comes at a time when demand for health care services is estimated to be increasing at around 4 percent a year and public funding for adult social care has fallen in real terms. This creates an inevitably challenging climate in which to work, with constant uncertainty and anxiety about funding levels and availability of resources to deliver existing services, or to support improvement and innovation to deliver further efficiencies and improve the quality of care.

The demand for quick fixes

It would be all too easy to lay the blame for short-termism at the feet of politicians who need to be re-elected, or senior executives who want to keep their jobs. Yet it is of course more complicated than that and at least in part a consequence of the significant gap between resources and demand. All of us, as a society, are perhaps also colluding in avoiding the difficult choices about what we are collectively prepared to pay for and how. Leaders in health and social care are increasingly telling us about the impact and perils of short-term thinking. One leader who tells the story of doing fabulous work in improving patient experience doubts that she would now be given the time and space to achieve what she has in recent years. Another says,

> In my view, we don't appoint poor leadership teams, it's just that we don't let them do the job they need to do in the way they need to do it. We are obsessed with turnaround and quick fixes and when the fix doesn't happen fast enough we change the leadership team. To me, it's a form of madness.

The challenge of finding and keeping good people

The likelihood is that wherever you work, there are vacancies that you are having trouble filling. The causes and indeed the solutions are complex. The impact on those trying to lead in health and social care to maintain service levels, let alone improve them, is significant. One leader described the impact in his context:

> There is a steady stream of junior doctors leaving the country to practise elsewhere or leaving medicine altogether. 51 percent of Scottish foundation doctors left medicine after their second postgraduate year in 2016. This, along with other factors, has led to a significant shortage of consultants and GPs. These shortages are felt everywhere but in small district general hospitals like ours it is felt

*even more. We are currently sitting with 30 percent consultant
vacancies and nearly 40 percent of GP positions unfilled. This has led
to an unprecedented reliance upon locum doctors who, recognising an
opportunity, have slowly increased their rates. We have some locum
doctors earning a fortune each a week. They work hard and yet this is
hard to stomach when the constant refrain from senior management
is that there 'is no money' and that we all need to 'tighten our belts'
and change how we work to save money. We have a £20 million CRES
(cash releasing efficiency scheme) target but an £11 million locum
spend. It is understandable that our permanent staff get frustrated
and wish to know that we are doing everything that we can to recruit
more permanent staff.*

Leading in the eye of the media

After tragedies, the response of the emergency services is often, and rightly, given great praise. Ground-breaking treatments too may feature in the news. However, evidence suggests that there is a significant shift towards negative coverage of the NHS and social care on TV, in print and on social media. Well publicised investigations into tragic failures of care at specific institutions impact public perceptions about the care and safety of the NHS more generally. Some argue that the freedom of information acts have further fuelled the increase in negative NHS stories, as it is relatively easy to write yet another story about missed A&E waiting times and the closure of wards, services or hospitals. "What would the Daily Mail report?" is a question that senior teams regularly ask themselves when making decisions.

Leaders can face a barrage of negativity, threats and emotional manipulation stirred up by social media campaigns. A GP surgery was forced to reduce opening hours because of lack of doctors. The receptionists were verbally abused in the supermarket after a local hate campaign on Facebook. A clinical leader at a public meeting was confronted by members of the public wearing Nazi t-shirts, claiming that he was a Nazi because they did not like the proposed decision to close some services. Another clinical leader described attending an open board meeting at which members of the public put pairs of baby boots in front of each board member, claiming these were the babies who would die if the local maternity services were shut and moved to the nearby town. There is also significant research (Ashforth and Kreiner 1999), that constant negative comments about any organisation we work for has a detrimental impact on our pride, motivation and well-being, with long term implications for the mental health and well-being of leaders and staff, as well as their ability to connect with and lead others.

Providing a counter-narrative to the mainstream was part of our motivation for writing this book, hence the title *Hope Behind the Headlines*.

The rise in the language of deficit and blame

We all recognise the need for investigation and assurance when things go wrong. Yet overplayed, this dynamic can contribute to a climate of fear and threat. The rational desire to investigate problems, to learn from them and institute new improved policies and procedures to make sure they don't happen again is vital. However, the way this is sometimes done can create a dysfunctional psychological pattern of persecutors and victims. This pattern is easy to fall into when people are stressed, anxious or feel that they need to find someone else to blame for fear of finding that they themselves will be blamed or scapegoated. It can create a toxic culture where negative feelings of anger, blame, fear and anxiety predominate.

Keeping perspective

Given all of this, it can be hard to hold onto perspective and to frame the context as one where hope is alive and improvement is possible. Alternatively, you might also fall into the trap of grandiosity, believing that you can sort it all. To "split" into the polarities of hopelessness and grandiosity is a natural human response to challenging situations, but neither is healthy or sensible in the long term. In our work with the GenerationQ Fellows we often speak of the need to find an alternative, a place where as a leader you can hold the tension and not collapse into either extreme. Finding a place of relative potency (Lapierre 1989) is where you can acknowledge the level of challenge and see possibilities for action without feeling that it is all about you stepping forward, rather heroically, and taking all the responsibility to fix things.

In our experience, several things can help to find this place of good-enough balance. One is recognising that the context in which you work is multi-layered. There are aspects of the current context for leading in the NHS which can create a sense of gloom. At the same time, we all know it isn't the same everywhere. There isn't *one* NHS context or *one* NHS culture. There are at least as many contexts and cultures as there are organisations, departments and teams and some of them are brilliant: full of hope, taking initiative, learning and improving, supportive, even joyful.

To believe that improvement and change for the better is possible also requires hope. We have learned through working with the Fellows that hope can be kindled by staying connected with a strong sense of purpose and sense of your own humanity, as well as experiencing it vicariously through hearing others' stories.

In the very first workshop of the programme we invite Fellows to participate in a simple exercise which you might want to try for yourself with colleagues. In small groups of three we ask them to share stories of their own experience of either being a patient, or being alongside a family member as a patient. We invite them to share the best of experiences and the most troubling; not to interrupt as others tell their story, rather listen attentively, and listen not just for the facts but for the emotions as well. We then ask them to reflect together on what they have (re-)discovered is important to them as a patient, to in effect stand in the shoes of their own patients. The exercise is apparently simple and yet always profound. Years later Fellows often talk of this as being a pivotal moment for them, allowing them to reconnect with the sense of purpose in their work, to get back in touch with why they joined the health or social care service in the first place. It may surface buried emotions of sadness and anger, or relief, gratitude and joy. It serves to connect people differently too, as they see and experience their own and others' humanity and vulnerability, both of which we believe are essential for leading well.

Leading is also about (re-)learning to listen well and connect with what is important to others. We are always struck by the quality of conversation when the group engages in this exercise. The conversation slows; there are fewer interruptions; there is space for pause and silence. William Isaacs (1999), a writer on dialogue, describes such moments of connecting as "sacred". In the process, GenerationQ leaders are sometimes dismayed when they realise how easy it is to lose touch with their own sense of humanity, and the human needs of others, in the day-to-day hurly burly and pressure of getting the work done. As leaders, they often come to recognise that they may have also lost sight of the needs of staff, evaluating people rather than helping them feel valued and cared for. One leader poignantly reminded us when we last did this exercise, "Hurt people hurt people". A senior anaesthetist went on to share his story with the group:

> The parents of a terminally sick baby had been on the ward for several months but had gone home for a rare weekend's respite. The baby suddenly took a turn for the worse and we desperately tried to keep the child alive in time for the parents to return and say goodbye. Despite our best efforts, we were not able to do so. The parents had no complaints but the whole ward team was distraught. The next day, the sister asked me to talk to the nurses involved as they were so upset. I was surprisingly honest in my response: "We all need to have someone

to support us through this. I am really devastated as well and feel too emotional and drained to do it for the team. Can someone else help us?"

Everyone was too busy. I'm still carrying this hurt around and look at me, I'm still talking about it even though it was ten years ago.

Story and story-telling are the enablers of reflection and learning, of reconnection with purpose. Story too can be the enabler of believing in the possible, especially the possibility of compassion and fulfilment. The stories you tell are also a way of shifting your local culture.

A ward matron was invited to share a story of what she felt most proud of. She recalled:

There was a gentleman who had been with us on the ward for a while. He had suffered a stroke but had recovered well. Some of the staff got to know him quite well – I noticed that they used to take time to stop by his bed and have a chat when they could. They quickly realised that he didn't have close family and lived by himself. The time came for him to return home. Unbeknown to me, a group of them managed to get access to his flat one weekend – I have no idea how they did it – and they decorated it for him from top to bottom. No one asked them. No one paid them. They just did it, and I think they did it because they had formed a relationship with him and it probably made them feel good too. To be able to really care for someone makes you feel good. We don't always have time for that, you know, but it's great when we can.

A Fellow asked the nurses where he worked to share moments where they felt proud of what they had done for a patient. One senior nurse said:

I was a sister on ITU, and a child was admitted to the unit having suffered a cardiac arrest, after a long standing cardiac problem. Although he was resuscitated by his aunty, he needed ventilating and he was going to die. The child was moved to a side room and we got to know the family. We asked his parents how we could make his last few days comfortable. We remade the side room to look exactly like his bedroom. His father said his son loved making daisy chains. I went out and bought daisy chains and picked a load more and came back and together we made daisy chains for his son. He died shortly afterwards. I chose this story because we didn't do what the system wanted, but we did what the patient wanted and his family needed. It was a simple quality initiative, with direct impact on a patient with no processes involved and no restrictions. We need to do more to design systems around patients, whether that is at the end of someone's life or when they are admitted into hospital.

We hope that your mood lifts as you read these two stories or as you think about what you are most proud of where you work. This is a reminder of the way that as a leader you can shift the mood by what you pay attention to, by the questions you ask. Do you tend to ask what the problems are? Or do you ask what is going well round here? Do you ask what individuals and teams are proud of or ask about mistakes and missed targets? Do you take a deficit approach or an appreciative one? These are just some of the choices you have as a leader which can make a huge difference to the local culture as we explore in subsequent chapters.

Coming home to yourself

If you experience challenges as a leader and the idea of choice appeals to you, you might be asking what leadership guides there are, what might you aspire to do, or to be, as a leader? These are questions leaders applying to GenerationQ are often asking.

You might turn to what has been written about leadership. You would find that there are more references to leadership on Google than anything other than tax. The wide range of leadership models or "brands" on offer is extensive, with the majority offering idealised pictures of how you *should* be as a successful leader.

The same sense of "should" is also present in the notion of leadership competences, which are common in many organisations, including the NHS. In purporting to describe the underlying characteristics of individuals who are effective or even star performers, there is a suggestion, at least implicitly, that there is a right way of leading. "Perfection" is desirable, achievable and described; there is an identikit model of leadership to which all must aspire. Even when reframed as supporting leaders to "find their learning edge", such an idealisation sets up what we believe is an unhelpful comparison between current reality and the idealised state described. This can easily lead to individuals believing that they can "never be good enough". This problem can be exacerbated in organisational cultures, like some in the NHS, that tend to privilege deficit thinking.

John Scherer (2009) talks of leadership and development as "coming home to yourself". We encourage leaders on GenerationQ to understand their own assumptions about leadership and learn to be themselves as leaders, but with "greater skill and more self-awareness", a phrase coined by Goffee and Jones (2015). In putting together this book, we invite you, the reader, to do the same. Rather than setting up ourselves or the Fellows as having the answer, the silver bullet, we offer instead a light touch framing to help you to develop yourself as a leader. We also offer the hope and inspiration of the Fellows' stories.

In summary

In this chapter, our intention was to set the scene for the rest of the book and for the Fellows' stories. We acknowledge that the context is currently tough in terms of leading and working in health and social care, but we do not believe that it is hopeless. Keeping perspective, re-connecting with a sense of purpose and knowing that change and improvement are possible are essential to keeping hope alive.

A very senior official in the Department of Health was retiring. She felt depressed and demoralised that the NHS, an institution she cared deeply about, was in such a state. A contact of hers sent her, with permission, a story written by a GenerationQ Fellow as part of the work for his Masters. She read it and was moved to tears, and sent a postcard to say "Thank you for sharing your story. It gives me hope and hope is such a precious gift. It is what others need too."

This book and the stories you will read are our gesture to help shift any current despondency about the NHS and social care. It is a gesture of hope.

CHAPTER 2

Shifting Local Culture(s)

In this chapter we explore the notion of culture, and examine why local cultures matter in health and social care.

What we understand by culture(s) and how they come about

Culture is often loosely referred to as "the dominant way of doing things around here". Leaders, policy-makers and politicians often talk about "the need to change culture" without going on to say much about either what they mean by culture or how to go about changing it. We want to be more explicit about the assumptions we hold.

Culture(s) as pattern

The important thing to say from the outset is that we do not understand culture to be a thing or an object, even though the way we use the word may sometimes lull us into thinking about culture as an "it". Culture is not something static that can be accurately measured, diagnosed, known and manipulated. We think of culture as a set of patterns of behaviour that can become established over time, particularly if enacted by the more powerful in organisations and often reinforced by visible symbols and artefacts. These patterns of behaviour may have their origin in what people really care about, but when organisation values are listed out on posters these are often aspirations which may not be congruent with how the culture is experienced, or even desired, by the majority.

Depending where you work in health and social care, your experience of your local culture may be of blame, deficit talk and overwhelming scrutiny and bureaucracy as people try to "fix" the problems, the targets, the A&E waits. Alternatively, you might describe your local culture as being deeply caring and supportive, both to staff and patients. This illustrates another key aspect of culture that makes it hard to define and work with – it is shaped by individuals' own sense-making and experience. There isn't one NHS culture, for example, just as there isn't one NHS organisation, even though there may be cultural features in common across multiple health and social care organisations. There are parallels here with national culture. Being British may mean shared sense of humour and good queuing behaviour, but other aspects of being British will differ in inner London and rural Scotland, hence the importance of the notion of local cultures.

Culture(s) develop over time

Thinking about culture as developing over time, helps to understand how the more toxic aspects of some NHS cultures may have evolved or become amplified. If the dominant and repeated leadership gestures are those of command and control – of telling – the likely response is one where staff learn to wait for instruction, to be "told what to do", rather than spontane-ously taking initiative or responsibility. Over time, an apparently "stuck" pattern of "compliance" can soon emerge, particularly if the behaviours are wide-spread, repeated and enacted by those who have significant power. As you read this, you might like to think about the dominant patterns of behaviour you experience in your own local context, and whether or not you experience them as being conducive to high-quality patient care.

There is good news in this way of thinking about culture. If you accept that culture is not a thing, that it is always emerging in patterns of behaviour between people, then there is always the possibility of movement even when the patterns appear strong, uniform, stable and even stuck. Every change in leadership behaviour, however small, is the opportunity to invite a different behavioural response, thereby starting to shift the pattern and consequently shifting the culture. For example, the gesture of being willing to challenge through making a single, well-intended, comment can shift a stuck pattern. As one Fellow describes:

> *Two clinical leads were refusing to discuss interface issues which impacted on patient care. There was real tension and I really avoid conflict if possible. This stand-off had lasted 30 minutes. "What would*

a patient think if they were sitting here listening to this?" I asked. There was silence and the leads agreed to talk. Later, someone else who had been at the meeting reported that this had been going on for six months and my comment had really helped move things forward.

Another Fellow describes the moves she made to challenge a pattern of a senior leader being overly demanding:

In a Clinical Commissioning Group meeting, I was challenged by the GP lead for acute contracting to add detail, and milestones, relating to service redesign and cost reductions to the Borough's Strategic Plan for the next two years and beyond. This member of the CCG frequently criticises us, in public and quite aggressively, for failing to achieve the scale of change he thinks is required to avoid financial disaster. Normally I do not challenge his assumption that we need to both improve the scale of our service redesign ambitions and develop more detailed plans for delivering change over the five- year strategic planning period. However, on this occasion I felt able to point out that our experience of redesign projects was that often we ended up with a different result from the one we planned, and that this was not a failure to stick to the plan, but follows from the emerging way in which commissioning programmes deliver change. I argued that we should outline our overall objectives rather than the precise expected impact in each period, and be able to manage deviations from the plan with contingencies and "Plan B's".

This felt risky for me to say, as I was concerned that influential members of the management team would think that I lacked drive and confidence in delivering on our strategic plan. However, my view was accepted by the group and the next day the Head of Planning thanked me for articulating a different perspective on forward planning. I am glad that I found the courage to voice the level of uncertainty that there is in our planning, without losing the ability to predict a degree of change. I am less anxious now about needing to collude with defining the future in precise terms.

The leadership gesture might be to attempt to create a culture of better exchange through inviting a different conversation and connection, as recounted by a Fellow who works in Mental Health:

There was a great deal of animosity between clinicians and nurses when I arrived as the new lead on what was labelled a troubled service. There had been a very serious incident on the ward some time previously. I'd tried various things but it just seemed to evoke the same old patterns of blame, and indeed 15 percent of the staff were on some form of disciplinary. In the spirit of progress and hopefully reconciliation, I decided to invite some of the senior consultants to participate in a meeting about the effects of violence on nursing staff.

I was deliberately non-committal about the agenda, and let them work on their own assumptions about how they might be of use in the meeting. I simply said that it would be helpful for them to attend, as there might be some technicalities or clinical issues that they could help with. I worked hard to steer the meeting into a state where the experiences of all staff had some common ground – "we all get scared", being the most fruitful topic – and what emerged was something I could not have foreseen. Instead of the usual patterns of rationalising violence in terms of blame, lack of assertion, poor treatment and the underlying issues of class, race, poverty, trauma and abuse, the conversation had a deeply personal and moving quality. People spoke of how they cried, or seized up in fear, how they shouted at their kids and felt bad, and gave many more examples of how their experience of violence at work radiated into all aspects of their life. Importantly, they all felt it was "some kind of secret" they could not share outside of work. It was, and is, a real burden. I now realise that I was trying to encourage everyone to suspend judgement; to have a "conversation with a centre, not sides" (Isaacs 1999, p. 17) where thinking the thoughts, saying the words and being truly heard brought people to new understandings of one another. It was a good start and we have continued to meet, not always as successfully, but have moved a long way from where we were. I do not know what the long-term effects of this might be in improving the quality of our service, but I do know that better engagement with teams is a first and crucial step in thinking about how improvements might develop from within. It also makes subsequent efforts to address the issue much more credible as the shared understandings change the way the intentions, or gestures, are perceived.

The potential significance of shifting cultural patterns rings out loud and clear in the three vignettes just described. Each one of them resulted in changed behaviours that directly or indirectly benefited patients.

Culture(s) reinforced through artefacts

As already mentioned, patterns of interaction and behaviour can be reinforced through concrete aspects of the work environment which some writers on culture call artefacts (Schein 2010). One of the Fellows was a member of a professional royal college and decided to visit the head office and pay attention to the artefacts. This is his account of what he saw and how he interpreted this in terms of the culture:

There are plenty of busts watching over you, including two who guard the entrance to the President's office. For me this gives a sense of pride about the past – and a feeling of being tightly bound to it. There is a room that used to be called the council chamber, decorated with grand oil paintings of past presidents. It has been "modernized" now and renamed the parliament room. This and other artefacts speak of an organisation that places great importance on its formal meetings. There is very little in the pictures, and indeed in the building, that suggests the importance of patient care or safety. I looked at the straplines on the websites of different professional bodies and whilst others overtly mention patients, ours focuses on the members.

This illustrates the way that artefacts in the physical environment do not have any fixed relationship with the local culture. They are open to different interpretations. Yet if many people take the same meaning from different artefacts, they can certainly reinforce and contribute to the creation and maintenance of cultural patterns. When leaders change an artefact they cannot guarantee how others will interpret their gesture, but it can still be a signal of an intent to shift what happens and what is valued. For instance, when Clare Marx became the first female president of the Royal College of Surgeons, she commissioned eight large professional photos of female surgeons she admired and hung those in her new office. Instead of having the oil paintings of her illustrious male predecessors, Nicola Sturgeon, as the first female Scottish minister, did something similar. On their own, such gestures will not change gendered patterns of who has power and who does not but they can contribute to shifting the way things happen in a particular culture.

Artefacts can also be a potential guide and stimulus to working out or wondering how things actually happen in a particular place, especially if there is some dissonance or incongruence between what is said and what you see and experience. For instance, we heard of an example where an executive team exhorted the need for everyone to embrace quality improvement. However, at the same time the two Quality Improvement leads were are asked to vacate their office and move to the basement to make way for a new Strategy Director to be on the same floor as the executive team. This gesture was interpreted by some as suggesting that despite the rhetoric, quality improvement was not really valued. The executive team may not have intended that their gestures were interpreted as such, but meaning is made by those on the receiving end.

Why culture(s) matter

From working with leaders, we have come to realise that there are at least four good reasons why culture matters and why leaders need to take culture seriously.

Culture impacts performance

As culture is "the way things are done round here", it impacts how patients, and indeed staff, are treated. Another way of saying this is that culture impacts performance because culture shapes what are accepted and acceptable patterns of behaviour in any given context.

For individuals and groups, cultural norms and patterns provide answers to important questions such as:

- What can I and can't I do around here?
- What are the explicit rules? What do I have to do to stay out of trouble and/or get on?
- What are the implicit, unspoken rules which are often even more significant and which I might trip over?
- If I break the rules, what are the consequences? Will I be sanctioned or rejected? Might I be rewarded if breaking the rules is an accepted cultural pattern?

In deciding how to behave at any given moment we all, as individuals, tend to conform to what is the norm in the culture in which we find ourselves. There are many different "flavours" of local cultures in health and social care. What about where you work? Is it acceptable, for example, to show that you are upset when a patient dies and to take a private moment to recover? Is it acceptable to walk past an over-flowing rubbish bin or a patient struggling to open a sealed sandwich? Is it acceptable to try something out and for it not to work?

Culture impacts the degree of discretionary effort

Culture also influences the degree of discretionary effort staff, and indeed you yourself, are prepared to give. Many might say the NHS and social care system is only kept going by staff going the extra mile, beyond the job description. When people believe that they are evaluated but not valued, when changes are imposed that don't make sense or over which they feel powerless, they make a mental and behavioural adjustment. This may be done very consciously and may be encouraged and fuelled by conversation with colleagues. It may be barely perceptible to others, but there is a subtle and significant shift in how far they are willing to go beyond the basics of the job.

An important question for all leaders is therefore how you create the conditions in a local culture where people are willing, and want, to give that discretionary effort, to contribute their ideas and their energy to improve patient care. Small yet significant leadership gestures can make a big difference: offering genuine appreciation, helping staff get back in touch with the purpose of the job in an authentic way, giving constructive feedback, being seen to not duck difficult issues, acknowledging others' contribution and sharing success, to name just a few, can all play a part.

Culture impacts well-being

Local culture also impacts people's sense of well-being and belonging. A clinician shared his recent experience of working in two prestigious teaching hospitals, where the local cultures couldn't be more different:

> *I have spent two years of my life working in that hospital and at times I wondered whether I might be losing the plot; I certainly felt less of myself, de-skilled, and even considered leaving the profession, even after so many years of study and still loving the job. The hours and workload were relentless, but it wasn't really that. I'm strong and resilient and I know how to look after myself. It was just so competitive: clinicians jockeying with each other to show who could be the cleverest, shooting each other down in public, even resulting in patients' wishes sometimes being ignored. Students didn't get a good deal either and it makes me really worried about what sort of clinicians they are going to become. At times, it felt as if getting the data for the next paper to be published was all that mattered.*

> *I can't quite allow myself to trust that the culture of where I am now is so different. There is less criticism and blame, people look after themselves and each other more, and I don't feel the same level of hierarchy. Senior clinicians actively participate in student seminars and are interested in the student experience. I have a mentor, and my boss scheduled in 90 minutes of his time within the first eight weeks of my arrival for a proper feedback session. I feel more relaxed, more capable, and fundamentally I no longer feel judged. I feel supported and able to learn again.*

Cultures both define and divide us

Different health and social care organisations can have very different local cultures but, as no doubt you are already aware, so can different professional groups.

In Chapter 1, we described an exercise in which we invite Fellows to experience standing in the shoes of their patients. In another exercise, we invite the group to stand up and self-organise into their natural "tribes". We ask them to define their tribe as the one they most identify with, where they feel most at home and how they might choose to describe themselves.

This can evoke a lot of emotion and discomfort as the professional tribes quickly begin to emerge in the room: physicians, surgeons, nurses, professional managers, people who "feel on the fringe of health care" soon form various clusters.

We invite the group to physically move in the room to discover different connections and clusters, to explore different ways of belonging. New groupings such as being a parent, from the North of England, being second generation immigrants, begin to emerge, always creating energy and curiosity as Fellows get to see and know each other more. And yet, the memory of that first experience, of seeing the health care tribes, the professional sub-cultures so evident in the room, always stays with the group. Our sense is that the memory stays because the tribes, as sub-cultures, both define the Fellows and at the same time divide them, which is deeply uncomfortable. It brings into sharp relief the personal significance of belonging to one tribe, which can make working and collaborating with other tribes sometimes fraught, as we see across the NHS and health and social care more widely. Here a Fellow reflects on what it means to be part of a tribe:

> The term "siege mentality" has been used for many years in the team I belong to – a sense of being in battle, a relentless onslaught from all sides and having to hunker down, look inwards and look after our own. Newcomers to the team describe feeling intimidated by the apparent cohesiveness of the team, wondering if they will fit and what they will have to do to fit in. Outsiders, I think, feel a sense of otherness. I can now see that there is a risk that both groups of people may feel that they are looked down upon and not trusted. They may feel we see ourselves as superior and apart.

As this account illuminates, cultures and sub-cultures matter because they can create a great sense of belonging, shaping people's sense of identity, of who they are, and thereby their self-esteem. However, the shadow side, particularly of very strong or uniform sub-cultures, is that they can evoke exclusion, exacerbating a sense of them and us. This is where conversation and inquiry become vital as a means of helping people find commonality behind, and beyond, the labels and stereotypes. The power of this is illustrated in the story earlier in this chapter where clinicians and nurses, despite having been at loggerheads, found a shared experience and connection in their fear of violence on the wards.

The belonging and identity fostered through strong sub-cultures also explains why people often react so strongly to imposed changes. Efforts to merge, restructure or make changes which threaten groups' or individuals' senses of identity are likely to evoke strong and often negative emotions.

Others may in turn perceive and label such groups as being difficult or resistant. Mergers can be particularly challenging, and even years after the formal merger different sub-cultures live on.

Why we talk about shifting local culture(s)

It is a deliberate choice on our part to talk about *shifting local culture(s)*, rather than the more mainstream language of changing culture.

Change suggests to us, and to the leaders we have worked with, something big and concrete. It tends to evoke the need for leaders to feel certain and be deliberate in their actions; to know what they are changing and the steps required. The notion of managing change often seems to invite grip and, all too often, the shadow side of the heroic or grandiose leadership stance that we touched on in Chapter 1 and will go on to say more about in the next chapter. Our belief, and indeed hope, is that "shift" invites a more measured and human approach, smaller in scale and with less risk of grandiosity, yet still with the possibility of something different emerging.

Shifting suggests small moves, edging something, rather like moving the furniture around to see how it looks in a different place, to discover whether such a simple change can bring about a completely different feel, a new delight in our surroundings. Shifting suggests having a go, trying something out, having good intentions rather than becoming hostage to a fixed plan with set outcomes or definitive direction in mind. It allows leaders to acknowledge uncertainty and ambiguity when working with culture, and brings the possibility of movement and creativity. And shifting *local* culture(s) removes the constraint of having to transform the whole organisation culture, or even having to believe that there is only *one* culture to transform. Rather, it can mean working at a local level, appreciating the differences that exist between cultures on different wards or between different departments, or choosing to notice just one aspect of the local culture that needs to shift if patient care is to improve.

A concept that Fellows find helpful here, that resonates with the idea of shifting, is that of being a Trojan Mouse (Brown 1998). These are small, fast and under the radar experiments or moves that can generate great learning and confidence in what might work. They can create energy and the desire to behave differently in others too, and because they are not badged as some big change effort, there is no need to attract the attention of the Powers That Be. It is lighter touch, within reach and so less anxiety provoking.

Leadership and culture – toeing the line and walking the line

We hope that the close relationship between leadership and culture has become evident in this chapter. We go on to explore that relationship in more depth in the next two chapters. The Fellows' stories too offer further vivid illustration of how they, as local leaders and with the support of the programme, have made different moves and gestures to impact their local cultures to improve patient care.

In the stories, you will read an example of shifting from a pattern of clinical disengagement to one where doctors are engaged and taking responsibility to lead improvements. Other examples include moving from a pattern of competition to one of collaboration and, in another case, from a pattern of "doing-to" patients to "doing-with" patients. There are setbacks, and moments of doubt and anxiety, as well as times when things go much better than expected. In some stories, the leaders were clear about their intentions. In others, it was a much vaguer "gut feel" and it is only in hindsight that what they were doing becomes clearer.

A common theme throughout all the stories, however, is the notion of choice. Choice is not just about which gesture or move to make. It is also about timing. In some cases, Fellows have told us they made a move after reflecting beforehand, so the move was quite deliberate. In other cases, it was more emergent and in response to something happening in the moment that triggered a desire to act. Challenging dominant cultural patterns is not without risk, potentially evoking ridicule, retribution or even rejection. Whilst it is therefore important to be brave and take a calculated risk, it is also important to do so without being fool-hardy or politically naive (more on that in Chapter 4). Easier said than done and only you can judge what is safe enough for you personally in your own context.

A phrase that the Fellows have found helpful in this respect is to pay attention to the difference between walking the line and toeing the line. Challenging the existing norms too much can invite rejection, or even ejection, whilst overly colluding with the status quo risks no shift at all. This is not about acting at any cost and often about acting with others. Sometimes it is better to keep one's powder-dry, to choose not to act, particularly in the heat of the moment. Political naivety can be dangerous and judgement is required about when, where and how to act.

The Fellows talk about experiencing a desire to be "ten percent braver", and behind the individual acts of bravery sit many qualities, typically high degrees of integrity and humility, often altruism, often a good dose of moral courage, and always deep care for and commitment to patients. Being brave also means that you need to take your own safety seriously, paying attention to power and politics, to building relationships, to having back stage conversations, and to seeking to understand others' perspectives and motivations. Choosing to act wisely and well, with confidence even if not certainty, and with good intentions to improve patient care can be hugely rewarding and a benefit to all who care about making things better for patients, carers and staff in health and social care.

In summary

In this chapter, we have turned our attention to culture, and shared some of the insights and considerations the GenerationQ Fellows hold as they work to shift their local cultures to be more conducive to improved patient care. We have introduced the idea of shifting rather than changing cultures, seeing opportunity and possibility for leaders to improve their local cultures through their own gestures and shifts in behaviour.

In the next chapter we explore, in more depth, the subject of leadership, and how thinking differently about both leadership and organisations can be a great enabler to shifting cultures well.

CHAPTER 3

Thinking Differently About Organisations and Leadership

Why thinking differently matters

Participants on GenerationQ say they really appreciate the opportunity to pause, to breathe, to think differently, away from the pressures of everyday working. If you are feeling intrigued by what you have read so far, you might rightly be asking what you could be doing now to shift your local culture.

Our invitation and encouragement is to hold off leaping into action, and to first give yourself the time to think differently about leadership and organisations. That may sound unusual advice but we have found that in re-examining their assumptions and mental models about what it means to lead, Fellows saw new possibilities for action. The specific moves required for shifting their local culture then became more apparent and made much more sense. These are explored in Chapter 4.

In this chapter, we draw on different metaphors that have been used by thinkers and researchers on organisations. Metaphors are like a lens, a way of seeing something in a particular way. At the same time, a metaphor draws attention away from other aspects so by definition they offer a partial or limited view. We have found that many leaders' mental models remain rooted in an old way of seeing organisations, as types of machine. This metaphor so dominates mainstream thinking in the NHS it can seduce you into believing that this is the only way of organising and leading. In this chapter, we examine some of the unintended consequences of this for both leaders and the culture of their organisations. We then introduce an alternative way of looking at organisations which sees them as communities comprising multiple people interacting and connecting. This view looks at organisations through the lens of complexity thinking which, whilst sometimes challenging initially, has significant practical implications. It is a view that is gaining widespread interest, as it speaks to much of the unpredictability of leading in the current context (Kings Fund 2011).

Our hope and intention is that in rethinking organisations and leadership, you will be able to become both more "choiceful" and more confident about how you personally want to lead in practice to shift local cultures. (We know that the word "choiceful" doesn't exist but believe it should. We use it regularly in our work with leaders, who seem to find it useful too!).

Organisations as machines – the dominant metaphor

In our work with the Fellows, the metaphor that resonates closely with their experience of leading and working is the idea of an organisation as a *machine*. It is a metaphor that has its origins in early production lines, industrialisation and a belief in causal linear relationships. The division of organisations into departments with job specifications and protocols describing, and indeed prescribing, what people should do; the importance of standardisation and efficiency, with clear lines of control through hierarchy, are all examples of machine thinking. Phrases such as drives for efficiency, finding the levers to pull, diagnosis, quick fixes, roll-out, scale-up and re-design are examples of the way the machine metaphor influences the way people talk and think. If something isn't working, a restructure is essentially taking apart the machine and then putting the pieces back in a different configuration. Extending the machine metaphor to include cybernetics, (feedback and control systems, such as those that set the temperature in central heating systems), allows us to understand the prevalence of targets and target setting in NHS organisational life.

In using this metaphor, we are not suggesting that organisations *are* machines, but rather that we often make assumptions and act as if they were. Here one Fellow describes the relevance of the machine metaphor to her organisation:

> Processes are all designed within rigid boundaries and with management structures along hierarchical lines. Everyone has a "line manager", we have "theatre production control" meetings and have to meet monthly "productivity targets" whilst producing "performance and efficiency" savings. It is ironic as our business is the care and treatment of patients and their families, yet we try to fit them into boxes and give "standard care" according to "protocols". Although

patients and staff are all human beings, with infinite variations, we try to squash them in to a production line, which is linear.

This machine lens is also useful to consider staff behaviours when it comes to quality improvement. There often seems to be a lot of apathy, "jobs worth", and abrogation of responsibility once anything extends beyond individuals' immediate sphere, but this is in keeping with the dehumanisation of individuals when considered as a machine part, and encouraged by the mentality that orders come from above and they are just there to do what they are told. And it is vital to remember that the idea of an organisation as a machine is a metaphor. At times I think I forget this and regard my organisation as an actual machine, at which point it is very easy to get disillusioned and reinforce the unconstructive behaviours.

Leader in control

Thinking about organisations as machines tends to foster a view of leadership as command and control. The leadership required with this way of thinking is highly directive as the task of leadership is to ensure that people do as they are told and reliably perform their function, which in turn makes planning, measurement and control important. There are a number of interlinked assumptions that can be identified here: that control of the organisation as a whole is possible and lies with those at the top; that there will be a right answer to any problem; that leaders have ultimate power and authority and will know what is best for the organisation; that deficiencies can be identified and understood through diagnosis, problem solving and linear cause and effect; that the organisation can be steered towards desired and predictable outcomes – again from the top. Indeed, the more a leader knows about a situation the more tightly she can manage what happens and the better the outcome achieved. Hence the value often placed on technical expertise, and on having "grip", a phrase being used more frequently in the NHS to describe control of the detail.

Here another Fellow reflects on medical training and machine thinking:

It seems to me that the machine way of thinking is ingrained into clinicians during their training...and clinical leaders may therefore transfer this mode of thinking and acting into their leading. I was trained as a diagnostician: I would gather the evidence (symptoms), decide what was the cause (diagnose) and implement a change as a remedy (prescribe). Therefore, as the medical leader, I assumed that I could identify mechanistically the fault with the system and put in a fix.

There are, however, some significant shadow sides associated with this way of thinking. Essentially this mode of leading casts leaders in the role of super heroes, as transformational leaders. Many of the leaders we work with talk of the burden of responsibility that can sometimes feel overwhelming. They talk of the pressures to "know" or have the answer, even when there is no clear solution. For those as leaders who feel this but dare not admit to it, it is a short step to experiencing imposter syndrome (Clance and Imes 1978) and feeling lonely and isolated. All too often leaders can assume others are coping and therefore feel too ashamed to reach out and connect, or ask for help...or to find that other leaders feel the same as they do.

And there is a further vicious cycle enacted because the heroic model of leadership doesn't just set unreal expectations for the leader. It encourages followers to be passive onlookers, which can have a profound effect on culture. This is expressed eloquently in 'Living Leadership' (Binney et al 2012), one of the books we ask the Fellows to read. The authors write,

> The pressure of short term results, the sense of overload – too much to do and expectations that are confused or impossible to achieve ... have led to two damaging and self-reinforcing patterns ... The first is the leader staying distant from his people ... the second is followers leaning back and refusing to take responsibility ...Followers are left off the hook at the same time as leaders are impaled on it.

For the rest of the organisation, the shadow side of this way of seeing leadership is that it encourages dependency, with little opportunity for staff to contribute or show initiative. Instead they are likely to feel evaluated rather valued and, depending upon how power is used, to be subject to what may be experienced as coercion, or even bullying, even if that wasn't the leader's intent.

Here, one clinical leader who sought to emulate a heroic stance prior to GenerationQ writes of his experience:

> I was appointed to a leadership role at a time when our department faced significant difficulties: government reports criticised our approach to emergency care; the GMC (General Medical Council) rated the quality of training we provided as poor; and local perception was of a difficult group of consultants unwilling to contemplate change. We were failing in our core purpose, and we were stuck.
>
> I had an ambitious vision for the future of our department – and I was not just aiming to raise it to the average. My underpinning metaphor of the leader, at the time, was as a warrior taking his people to enlightenment through great personal effort and at considerable personal risk.

After taking up the leadership post, I offered colleagues two possible futures: continue the status quo and decline – or change and excel. I was good at being analytical and felt confident that I had divined "the" path forward, and now I expected my colleagues to embrace that path.

Unknown to me at the time, I was holding in my head the image of leadership as the transformational hero. I thought a leader should know where we are going, help everyone see the true path to the future, face down conflict and do so with enormous strength, bravery and resilience. I do not know where my belief in the heroic model of leadership originated, but my childhood heroes were the great heroes of history, particularly those who strove against great odds – better to struggle and fail than not to act. The consequences of this transformational visionary approach were predictable and painful.

As I "knew" the answers to our department's problems, I started from a position of telling. I relentlessly assumed the role of setting direction, and evoked relentless opposition. I cast any opposition as the enemy. By outlining two simplistic futures, I clearly stated that the opposition were wrong, thus closing-down involvement or any other possibilities. Those who might have agreed with me and acted as followers, or critical friends, withdrew, or took up a stance of opposition. We became stranded, focused on my needs and not the whole, and using blame not reflection in our exchanges.

A colleague commented: "Even when you try to involve us, you bring several options to solve the problem. You should bring the problem to us". My analytical approach and decisiveness had found its shadow – he perceived that I already had the answer (and indeed, I thought I had), felt excluded from decision-making, and knew he would have to work hard to convince me of an alternate path. Because of this, all problems became my problems and I carried all the responsibility, alone.

I felt ten miles ahead of my colleagues, pulling them over the horizon with an elastic band stretched to near breaking point. But they were pulling in the opposite direction – and the elastic did break. A group of my consultant colleagues asked the Medical Director to remove me. In response to this crisis, I had to learn to see a different way...

This account, with searing honesty, describes the seductive power and pitfalls of the heroic leader.

Another Fellow recounts a similar experience:

When I was appointed to my consultant post, I joined what had been described by the Care Quality Commission (CQC) as a failing department. When I introduced myself to people, they would reply with phrases such as "Ah! You're here to sort us out!" I took on – and relished – the role of transformational leader, but this only led to the people I was working with passing more and more of the important decisions that needed to be made on to me. This then resulted in me seeing staff as being incapable of making decisions about not only the big crises, but increasingly menial matters. This resulted in me having a lot of work to do!

Without realising it I was in the "command and control" model of leadership. As I took more and more control, this elicited a vicious circle where colleagues took less responsibility and placed more dependence on my decision-making. I decided what was best, made decisions, and then got frustrated when people didn't follow through. For example, when the CQC criticised the ward team hand-overs between shifts, I created an entirely new system to address their concerns. I did not liaise with the staff who would be using the system because I assumed they wanted me to fix it for them. I broke the connection between me and my team. Binney et al (2012, p. 37) say:

> *"If you treat others as the audience for your performance, then they will applaud from time to time – or throw rotten eggs – but they are unlikely to get up on stage and help you."*

My team threw rotten eggs at my ideas!

Complexity thinking – an alternative perspective on organisations

A very different way of looking at organisations is based on insights from complexity thinking. This sees organisations as inherently unpredictable communities of people in constant interaction and relationship. The insights this perspective offers can be provocative, particularly because they fly contrary to mainstream assumptions about control and hierarchy, yet they often resonate with people's lived experience of the sometimes bizarre and unexpected things that happen in organisations.

This alternative way of looking at organisations is informed by a broad range of more recent scientific thinking and discovery, spanning quantum physics, biology and meteorology, that are loosely held together by the term complexity science. They all embrace unpredictability and unknowability and offer the insight that novelty (what we might call creativity or innovation) can emerge "for free" in self-organising and complex systems. At the core of this way of thinking is a deep appreciation of the complexity and unpredictability of multiple non-linear relationships playing out simultaneously. In complex systems, "if we do x and y then z will happen" no longer holds true, at least not with certainty. To give some examples from the complexity sciences, mathematicians know that even tiny shifts in the accuracy of measurement of the starting point can result in very different outcomes if working with complex, non-linear equations. In quantum physics, light has the possibility of being both wave-like and particle-like at the same time. In chaos theory, a small change in one state may lead to a much bigger effect elsewhere in unpredictable ways: so, a butterfly flaps its wings in South America, and on the other side of the world there is a hurricane.

In applying complexity thinking to our ideas of organisations and organising, one of the main writers in this area, Ralph Stacey (2012) takes the everyday interactions between people as the key unit of interest – the gestures we make and responses others make in return, as we communicate together in relationship and conversation. He points out that we sometimes think about organisations as *spatial* entities which have an existence separate from the people who populate them. We talk about organisations or departments as if they are living things and ascribe motives and behaviours – "the organisation decided to pull out of community health care provision", "the department reacted badly to the news of layoffs". Although this may be a handy way of talking, it can blind us to the fact that organisations are *temporal* ongoing processes of interaction and relationship, not entities. It can also, of course, be used to justify abrogation of responsibility as pointed out in the earlier vignette.

When we interact with each other through gesture and response, we make meaning together. I speak to you. I have some intention behind what I say. You listen and interpret what I say based on your own context and experience. I can influence, but not control, what meaning you make from my gesture. You respond and together we make some kind of meaning. To use a philosophical term, meaning is socially constructed (Weick 1995). This is an ongoing process, in relationships and in conversation. Your gestures may or may not be picked up by the other person, or interpreted in the way intended – hence the inherent unpredictability of relationships. (And of course, these ideas apply to all interactions outside work as well as within!)

In the complex system of people relating and interacting, patterns of behaviour emerge that can appear stable and become what we know as the local culture. A particular location or department, for example, may always feel heavy; a group of junior nurses always seem keen and ready to learn. However, while patterns may often *appear* stable and predictable, this way of viewing organisations suggests there is always the possibility for a different response and a new pattern, albeit unpredictable, particularly to new and novel gestures. This is what we were suggesting in Chapter 2 when we described how cultures can emerge, and shift, over time.

GenerationQ Fellows, when first exposed to this way of thinking about leadership, sometimes throw their hands up in horror as this idea touches their own sense of identity as a leader. You might feel the same. In the words of one Fellow:

> At the forum [GenerationQ workshops are known as forums] *I felt disturbed by the idea of complexity thinking. It seemed to beg the question "Why bother?". If everything is ultimately chaotic, if diversity and difference are key to progress and whatever happens comes about by unregulated and uncontrolled processes, if the organisation only exists within the personal interactions of individuals, what is the role of the leader and what is the purpose of leadership? What had I been doing with my life so far?*

However, over time, as Fellows begin to experiment with this way of thinking about leading, they discover that it can be surprisingly liberating to realise that it isn't all about them as leaders, that responsibility can be shared. A sense of burden is often lifted. Complexity thinking takes the spotlight away from them. In fact, leading can sometimes be about getting out of the way. Leadership becomes less about the person in charge and more about how the collective is jointly engaged in conversation and action.

Relational leadership

Seeing organisations as inherently unpredictable, complex social processes has some fundamental consequence for leadership, not least the challenge to "be in charge but not in control" (Streatfield 2001, p. 9). This does not mean that as a leader you are impotent or irrelevant. Instead, the invitation is to see yourself as an active and powerful participant in the process of organising, giving enough sense of direction, and holding for others the anxiety evoked by uncertainty.

As a leader, much of what you say and do is highly visible, so your gestures will carry more weight, as will your potential to shift the local culture. What you choose to amplify, what you say, what you do, what you choose not to do – it all counts.

However, because the responses of others cannot be predicted, from a complexity thinking perspective, as a leader you are freed of the burden of feeling that everything falls to you to sort out, to decide, to control. Other people's response will inevitably shape and influence your response to them, and they will be shaped by you. What is required of you is to act with a sense of ethical intention and direction, to guide without being enslaved by a desire for certainty and a belief that you know best about everything. Leading instead becomes about creating an ongoing story or narrative, with others, that helps people make sense of what it is they have been and are experiencing, and where they might be going. The stories you as a leader tell are important, creating some stability and sense of direction and shifting as new possibilities emerge.

This way of thinking invites a re-framing and shift in some organisation rituals:

- Vision becomes less about scoping out a defined future and more about an intended direction of travel
- Strategy becomes less about defining how we are going to get from where we are to where we want to be, and more about having options and offering a useful defence against the human response to uncertainty and anxiety
- Strategic processes becomes less about data collection, analysis and reporting and more about collective processes of shared meaning making
- Processes of assurance become less about just control but also more about learning
- Planning becomes an exercise for thinking about what might happen rather than a fixed commitment to what must happen
- Conversation and talking with, rather than talking at, through email and presentation, becomes the default way to communicate
- The leader is a powerful participant and in charge rather than in control.

For leaders, the focus of attention also shifts to more of a balance between formal processes and the informal processes of engaging with people in one-on-one conversations, small and large group process. The informal is often referred to as the "soft stuff" which has the rather pejorative suggestion of being "easier". In our experience, soft relational skills are often the more tricky to develop and use well. This is explored in Chapter 4.

This approach is loosely termed relational leadership. The fundamental tenet is that leadership is not the property of an individual but resides in the relationship *between* the leader and those he/she is inviting to follow. As this Fellow describes, re-thinking leadership this way can be a great relief:

> *The ideas presented were like a revelation, a soothing balm for a*
> *struggling leader's soul – I did not have to be perfect; maybe I was*
> *good enough already, I just needed to authentically come alive. I could*
> *do that. The notion that leadership happens between people, and that*

*the vital ingredient is the quality of the relationship between leaders
and those who depend on them made so much sense to me. Another
idea that resonated was the notion that "Leadership is not about
knowing the answer and inspiring others to follow. It is the capacity to
release the collective intelligence and insight of groups and
organisations" (Binney et al 2012, p. 8). I realised that I was putting
myself under huge pressure and I was expecting others to just get on
with it without me paying any attention to their feelings or thoughts
or perspectives. I was not connected to these colleagues; if anything I
had become more detached. It was also helpful to know that from
Binney et al's (2012) research, it took the leaders they had studied
between 18 and 24 months for new leaders to become fully effective.
Maybe I wasn't failing as a leader after all; maybe I was right where I
was supposed to be.*

Implications for shifting culture

From the machine-perspective, change is plannable. You can diagnose
where you are, decide what needs to be done to fix problems or improve
how "the machine" runs, and prepare project plans about how to go about it
with clear goals and milestones. The potential for the unexpected, the
unpredictable and others having different ideas and making different
meanings tend to get ignored, even disappeared.

From the perspective of complexity thinking, change is something much
more emergent which arises from the ongoing interplay of gesture and
response, as you and others interact. As the leader, you have an intention
about what needs to happen but not a fixed view as to exactly how or when.
Change from a complexity perspective thus happens through changing
conversations and the dynamics of relationships. You can shift what seem
to have become stuck patterns. You do not need to be in each of those
conversations, indeed you cannot be. Your role is creating the conditions for
others to engage in different conversations.

In planned meetings and chance encounters, you may respond to and
amplify what you are noticing or start something in motion, engaging with
positive intent even if you do not know exactly how others will respond.
Your gestures are like the ripples on a pond. A core principle of complexity
thinking is that small differences can be amplified and become transform-
ative patterns, or what Malcolm Gladwell (2002) describes as tipping points.

*Complex systems display the capacity to change and produce new
forms only when they operate in a paradoxical dynamic of stability
and instability at the same time.....small differences can escalate into
major, completely unpredictable changes.*

If you feel comfortable with control you may feel alarmed at the idea of unpredictability. If you feel trapped and stuck, you may feel liberated by the new possibilities of instability that this way of seeing organisations encourages.

In summary

In this chapter we have suggested the machine metaphor is the dominant way of thinking about organisations in the NHS. Such a view sets leaders up to be heroes who are supposed to be in control. This explains why some health and social care leaders experience leadership as profoundly lonely and burdensome and why cultures can emerge that are not conducive to improving the quality of patient care.

Complexity thinking offers an alternative where leaders are "in charge but not in control", where the task of leadership is to focus more on the local and micro-gestures in the here and now, to create the conditions where others can contribute to shifting the culture to be more conducive to improved care.

In the next chapter, we offer more detail concerning some of the relational moves leaders can choose to make in order to shift and improve culture.

CHAPTER 4

Making Moves

If shifting cultures requires leaders to make different gestures, to be in charge but not in control, to encourage new patterns of being and working together, you may well be asking what this means in practice. How different is this to what you may have been doing already?

In the final chapter in this section, we turn our attention to the dynamics of relationships, productive conversation, and to power and politics. We share some of the frameworks and models on these topics that the Fellows find useful. These four elements rarely get explicitly explored in organisational life and yet they are key to the practice of relational leadership. As a leader, rethinking your approach to each of these can offer insight into specific moves you can make that might shift your local culture to be more human, relational and conducive to high-quality patient care. Many of the leadership moves or gestures that you will read about in the Fellows' stories arise from the approaches and insights shared in this chapter.

The dynamics of relationships

One of the tensions about relationships is that although you need them to achieve anything within an organisation, they are also a constraint. Relationships are not completely unbounded, elastic and changeable. We can't, or rather don't, just do or say anything. We are bound by our own beliefs about the nature of the current relationship we have with an individual or a group of people, which includes our expectations around the type of conversation we normally have with them and the power dynamics between us. We are also often constrained by our own preferences around control and how we deal with difference and conflict.

Relational leadership is an invitation to fine tune your understanding of some of the nuances involved in creating meaningful and productive relationships. We draw attention to two:
- When to push and when to pull in a relationship
- Acting from a place of Adult ego state rather than Parent or Child

When to push and when to pull?

There is a choice you will be making all the time, often unconsciously, when you are interacting with someone at work. You may be controlling or "pushing", in other words taking a directive stance, seeking what you want or need. Alternatively, you may be "pulling", letting the other person drive the agenda and pace of the interaction. In our experience it is helpful for leaders to consider such moves with greater thought and to sometimes make a different move to the one they normally do. The very act of making a different gesture in this way is to experiment with changing the pattern and the nature of the relationship.

We find it helpful to draw on research carried out by John Heron (2009) who was initially interested in how GPs interacted with their patients, but later looked at interactions between people in numerous work settings. He made the helpful distinction between a directive, "push" style, and a "pull" or more facilitative style. On the programme, to help Fellows experience what it feels like to be "pushing" or "pulling", or to be on the receiving end of such gestures, we ask them to do a simple exercise. They stand in pairs holding both hands up in front and lightly touching their partner's hands, palm to palm. Then, without talking, one person in each pair is asked to push their partner round the room. We reverse the exercise so that both people in each pair have a chance to experience pushing and being pushed. We then do two more iterations to experiment with how it feels to pull your partner, or be pulled, around the room, again without talking.

When pushing, some people enjoy being in the driving seat, being in control. Others notice how tiring it is to be always on the alert, feeling responsible for the other person, making sure they don't bump into any of the other pairs moving round the room. For those who are being pushed, some enjoy not having to do anything or to take any responsibility. Others hate the lack of control and find it hard to trust their partner. We see them desperately looking over their own shoulder to check that they are not about to hit another of the pairs moving round the room.

When pulling, people often talk about the way this feels much more collaborative; there is less sense of one person being totally responsible for the other. One person is pulling, but as they are moving backwards they are sharing responsibility with their partner who can see where they are going. Pairs generally move around the room much quicker when they are pulling.

This exercise illustrates very simply individuals' different responses and preferences to pushing or pulling. (It also begins to illuminate issues of trust.) Personality, job roles, professions, other people's expectations, our upbringing and family norms, all contribute to our personal preference for pushing or pulling. It demonstrates in a very physical way the different energies and dynamics created by whether your gesture as a leader is to pull or push.

For most leaders, the behaviours that go with a push, directive approach are familiar. They tend to fit with the dominant machine metaphor view of organisations and the idea of the leader as in control and in the know. However, if you would like to shift, moving away from a cultural pattern of command and control, with you doing everything and others being more passive, it requires you to break the old pattern by making a different move, pushing less and pulling more. If you want to create the conditions for novelty and innovation, especially in complex and uncertain situations where no one person has all the knowledge, information and ideas, this too requires more of a pull approach. Many of the Fellows describe being a little uncertain about shifting the dynamics between themselves and people they work with, but also recognise that if they don't make a move to shift things, who will? The biggest impact often comes from the smallest shifts: less telling and more questioning; less talking and more listening. One of the Fellows shared her story of doing just that:

> I tentatively broached the nursing team again. Previous encounters had not gone well. Initially I had tried to passionately offer them my vision for a new pathway. When this didn't work I tried to sell the benefits. And then, when this again didn't work I labelled the team as negative and was left sitting with my own frustration! This time I elected to try out a more relational leadership style, including more active listening. I spoke less and, rather than being defensive, I consciously demonstrated vulnerability by acknowledging uncertainties. Once I sensed some engagement I attempted to use "pull" rather than "push" questions. A pivotal point came when I named that I sensed there were mixed feelings which hadn't previously been acknowledged. The team begun to focus their comments on the positives and appeared to be more enthusiastic about the pathway, so I followed this up by asking how they saw it (the pathway) developing. By this point they were now offering their concerns, ideas and suggested changes. I became a surprisingly willing bystander as they

self-organised roles in development, implementation and audit of the new pathway. I was astounded at how much difference these seemingly small changes in my gestures had made. Perhaps unsurprisingly, although I had not predicted it, much of their true concern focused on having potentially difficult discussions over the telephone. What was interesting for me was that acknowledging this was enough for them, it did not need to be "solved", particularly not by me.

Acting from a place of Adult

Transactional Analysis (TA) is a theory that offers extremely rich insights into the micro gestures and moves we make when we are relating to others. The originator of the theory, Eric Berne (1968), locates the source of our gestures and responses in what he called three ego states: Adult, Parent and Child. According to this theory we are in an Adult ego state when we are thinking, feeling and behaving in the moment and are, therefore, really "present", alive to the here and now of what is going on. There is no interference from our past.

There are two "unconscious reservoirs" of past experience, known as the Child and Parent ego states. These are generalisations of past experiences, received messages and memories from our parents and carers that can become habitual in the gestures and responses we make, particularly if under stress or facing a significant power difference in a relationship.

The heroic model of leadership, which we explored in Chapter 3, encourages the leader to act from the Parent ego state, taking care of everything; and at the same time this encourages staff to be passive and dependent in the ego state of Child. All of us are vulnerable to being "hooked" by other people's gestures. For example, facing a powerful, demanding and dogmatic boss can often evoke the Child in us (Compliant Child for some, a more Rebellious Child for others). A colleague or staff member who says they don't know what to do can evoke the Parent in us (Critical Parent for some, Nurturing Parent for others).

Let's give a little more detail on the signs you might notice in yourself or others of being in particular ego states.
- Critical or Negative Controlling Parent – tells other people what to do; uses many "push" gestures; uses the words "should" and "ought" a great deal; may use quite extreme adverbs such as "you *always* mess up"; "you *never* do as you are told". Other signs of someone being in this ego state include pointing their finger while shouting

at another, having an angry or disparaging tone of voice, using belittling words such as "ridiculous" or "stupid" to describe their own or others' behaviour

- Nurturing or Positive Controlling Parent – shows concern for the other person's feelings and well-being; greets someone with open arms if they look distressed; has a gentle tone of voice; likes harmony; wants to make things better for the other person even if it fosters dependency
- Free or Natural Child – expresses feelings of joy, fear, sorrow, in a very uninhibited way; in this ego state the behaviour tends to be natural, spontaneous and creative. Often takes risks without seeing them as such, which is important to recognise in yourself if you are attempting to shift culture
- In the ego state of Adaptive Child, people's behaviours are adaptions to others' will. An individual may be *rebellious*, digging their heels in, questioning and challenging the authority of another. Alternatively, an individual may be *compliant*; their voice tone in this ego state is likely to be whingey or placatory
- When an individual is in the Adult ego state, we would describe them as being observant, practical, able to evaluate and make choices, clarifying, constructively questioning, and resourceful. You would see someone in this mode talking in an even voice with precise choice of vocabulary; hypothesising and processing information; sitting upright with open posture, alert and thoughtful about the problems they are facing

If you are aware of your own responses and can sense which ego state others are coming from, you can consciously choose to respond from a different ego state. Indeed, the very act of noticing and choosing is a mark of being in the Adult ego state. Staying in Adult is important for much of leaders' work, and if you can stay in Adult you can often help the other person to get back in touch with their Adult ego state too. For those times when you want innovation and creativity, however, being more playful and in touch with your Free Child for at least part of the time can be what is required.

Ego states can play a significant role in triggering both helpful and unhelpful patterns of behaviour. One of the most toxic patterns that can emerge, particularly in times of stress, is the drama triangle (Karpman 2011). In this pattern no one is in Adult, and Fellows tell us that this is a pattern they sadly very much recognise playing out in their local cultures.

To explain the drama triangle, we include Figure 4.1. There are three characteristic positions – victim, rescuer and persecutor. When hooked in this pattern, or game, all participants are likely to experience themselves in each of the positions for at least some of the time, each one evoking a strong emotional response and closing down the possibility of thoughtful Adult behaviour. In the *victim* role, people feel that it is not their fault, they are being blamed, they were only doing their best, it's not fair. They are in the Child ego state. In the *persecutor* role, people are looking to blame, to find fault, to punish, to tell off. They are in the ego state of Critical Parent. In the *rescuer* role, people self-righteously take on the role of sorting the situation, being the heroic leader, by telling others what they should be doing or feeling. They are in the ego state of Nurturing Parent.

The important aspect of this pattern is that, as mentioned, the positions are not static. For instance, being in the position of rescuer can easily trigger the rescuer themselves then adopting the victim position – "It's always me who has to sort things out", "Everyone else is useless", "Why does nobody do anything round here". Alternatively, the victim can be triggered into the persecutor – "How dare you tell me what to do"; or the victim may stay in victim – "I don't know what to do", "Why does nobody tell me anything", "It's always my fault". When the drama triangle takes hold, everyone becomes locked in a vicious and toxic dance. Nothing productive or useful can happen and local cultures can quickly feel toxic.

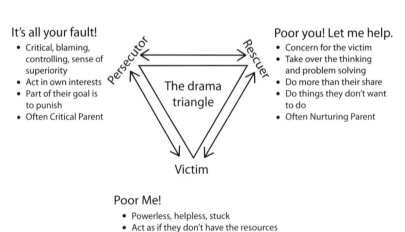

It's all your fault!
- Critical, blaming, controlling, sense of superiority
- Act in own interests
- Part of their goal is to punish
- Often Critical Parent

Persecutor

The drama triangle

Rescuer

Poor you! Let me help.
- Concern for the victim
- Take over the thinking and problem solving
- Do more than their share
- Do things they don't want to do
- Often Nurturing Parent

Victim

Poor Me!
- Powerless, helpless, stuck
- Act as if they don't have the resources to solve their problem

Figure 4.1

To get out of the toxic dance requires someone to make a move that is in Adult. This then allows everyone to create what is called the Winner's Triangle, a re-frame created by Choy (1990). This is a very powerful example of the way that making a different move, a different gesture both disrupts the old pattern and, equally important, allows a new pattern to emerge. In some cases, just one different move is all that is required. Sometimes several moves may be needed, repeated over time.

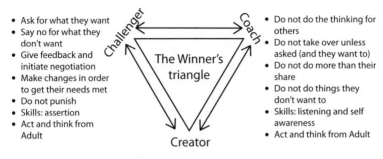

Figure 4.2

In the Fellows' stories several describe their attempts to "stay in Adult" or foster "Adult-Adult" relationships, as well as to avoid tripping into Parent or Child as they make moves to shift their local cultures to be more conducive to high-quality care.

Productive conversations

The type and nature of conversations that take place in your local context will very much shape the local culture so it is worth paying attention to the conversational, as well as relational, patterns playing out. Talking with leaders, we have found that good, productive conversations at work are rare, often because often people are too busy, agendas are too full or people don't have the skills required. In meetings, instead of there being a meaningful or useful exchange, we've observed one person after another putting forward their perspective with no one really listening to anyone else. Another pattern is for people to stay polite and formal with no one saying what needs to be said, and anything vaguely controversial being shut down, so important or tricky stuff is never dealt with. There is no sense of movement. Such conversations or meetings can feel like empty rhetoric and ritual, leaving you drained of energy and frustrated, and wasting time.

A key writer on this subject, Chris Argyris (1995), building upon the ideas of push and pull, distinguishes between advocacy – stating your own position, and inquiry – exploring and being curious about others' positions. Without inquiry we often fall into adversarial win-lose debate with each side assuming they are right and often failing to listen. Generally little movement or progress is made.

Research into productive conversations suggests what is needed is to approach others with an open mind and genuine curiosity. The benefits are that you learn from others' perspectives about what they think is important and why they hold such views. This can often lead to surprising insights for yourself that prompt fresh thinking and will give you a more rounded appreciation of the issues. People also respond well to being genuinely listened to, perhaps because in the general busyness this is rare. If you have listened first, people are much more likely to then listen to your perspective. This may not result in immediate agreement and a shared view, but is much more likely to lead at least to some mutual empathy and respect. This kind of inquiry happens best face to face. It is possible over the telephone or Skype, but almost never happens through an email exchange.

Another key researcher in this area, William Isaacs (1999), describes the patterns of conversation that contribute to dialogue, which he contrasts with debate. Isaacs talks of dialogue as allowing people to think together in relationship, avoiding both false harmony and the going over of well-rehearsed positions. Dialogue seeks to harness the collective intelligence of a group by creating conditions where people can safely and consciously reflect upon their differences through inquiry and listening to each other, creating something new and valuable together.

A powerful but simple way of beginning to create the conditions for dialogue with any group of people is to experiment by starting with chairs in a circle, no table, and a check-in. To ask, "How are you doing?" With no sides and no barrier created by a table, it is surprising how an atmosphere is created which enables a different quality of conversation. One Fellow, a surgeon, realised that within his directorate the senior leaders didn't really do dialogue. He decided to start meetings by pushing away the tables and sitting in a circle of chairs. He made a bit of a joke about it the first time, saying it was good to try something new. At the end of the meeting, everyone agreed that sitting in a different configuration had certainly shifted the atmosphere, more informal, freer, more like conversation. At the next meeting he initiated the same thing. For the third meeting he arrived late as he had to attend part of a board meeting, but imagine his delight to find that the group had re-arranged the chairs to form a circle without him being there. A new cultural pattern had emerged that everyone owned and cared about, not just him.

The leader who described clumsily implementing his handover checklist in the previous chapter now reflects on how he might have done this differently, using some of the ideas about dialogue:

What might I have done differently knowing what I know now? I might have brought the teams that hand over together into a room and explained the problem – "the CQC say we need a better handover system". Instead of imposing my ideas, I might have facilitated a dialogue. My views would not be more or less important than anybody else's – indeed, I might not contribute at all! This might allow a system of handover to emerge that could look very different to one I might envisage, but would make sense, and be useful to the group who would need to use it.

Another Fellow reflects on the way that asking a different question led to a very different conversation. In the first case, his question unwittingly encouraged people to rehearse all their annoyances, commenting on others "out there" and "over there". The second time, he reframed the question so that staff were far more present and personally engaged. There was dialogue with new insights and connections for all as people talked about themselves and told stories of their experiences.

When I started the GenerationQ program I asked a group of staff to describe what they felt about quality improvement within the Trust. The stories were depressing. Many were about how the Trust's quality improvement team was disconnected; they were seen as a group of people who told people what to do and how to do it. There was a lot of scepticism, especially from the consultants. The language was divisive; terminology was about "us and them", and antagonistic. A few lone voices tried to talk about their positive experiences around quality improvement but in general these were drowned out.

It seemed to me that through the continuous social interactions and conversations between people, a pattern of conversation had developed that reinforced people's beliefs surrounding how quality improvement was thought of and undertaken within the Trust. This disappointed me. I was annoyed that people did not recognise and acknowledge all the hard work that was taking place.

Later, I wondered whether the nature of the discussions came from me asking the wrong question, or asking in the wrong way. I subsequently tried a simple, story-telling process, asking people to share their own personal experiences of what had gone well. It was a pull gesture, inviting inquiry into their own experiences. I asked staff to describe when they felt they had improved the quality of patient care and what they felt they had needed in order to do so. The change in the quality of the conversation was surprising. The junior staff in the room contributed much more than they had done before. The language was more positive.

As the story telling progressed there was recognition that in the act of telling stories people were gaining much of the recognition and support they needed to continue. The conversation regularly turned to the sharing of ideas and discussing how others potentially had ideas how they could expand on the successes made so far.

Thinking differently about power

We turn our attention now to power. Power is important. It is the source of energy to get things done. If a change is to be sustainable power needs to shift in some way, for example from clinician to patient, or from the top to lower down the hierarchy. Perceptions of power and who has power also contribute significantly to the local culture: who gets to speak first, who gets listened to, who gets disappeared?

Given the importance of power and how it is used in organisational life, it is perhaps surprising that many Fellows reflect that before attending the programme they had not really considered their own power or using power well. This may be because of the negative connotations often associated with the abuse of power through coercion and oppression.

We also find that people often ascribe power to someone, as if it is a possession that you have or you don't have. On the programme we encourage Fellows to think about it in a more nuanced and fluid way, to think about power as a relational phenomenon between people. When we think of power in this way it enables it to ebb and flow. It also allows for a number of re-frames, to think differently and more positively about power:

- If power is something between people, then it's not a zero-sum game. It is not about "if I gain power you have to lose it". Rather we can grow power together, which is the intention behind engaging and empowering others. Power becomes infinite rather than finite
- Instead of power just residing in the individual, it resides in the individual *and* the relationship and will therefore be differently experienced in different relationships. It enables individuals and groups to reflect on what they need in relationship with others to be at their best, their most powerful
- From "power-over", often experienced as coercion, being the only expression of power to multiple expressions of power, including "power-to", "power-with" and "power-within"
- From position (in the hierarchy) as the only or most important source of power to multiple sources of personal power

Understanding your own potential sources of power, and being aware of the gestures you can make to moderate the power dynamic between yourself and others, are core relational skills as a leader. As a colleague says, the challenge for leaders is "radiate but not out-shine".

Turning to the idea of sources of power, you have probably already noticed that implicit in the heroic model of leaders is an assumption that the leader has a great deal of power and can therefore tell others what to do. Yet we have found that often one of the greatest disappointments for leaders new in post is the realisation that, despite their new title, everyone doesn't suddenly do what they ask, as has been illustrated in some of the Fellows' accounts which you have read so far.

Three sources of power – positional power, reward power and coercive power – may indeed go with the job title and place in the hierarchy. Positional power refers to power that is invested in the role, regardless of the person in that role. As the name suggest, reward power is a leader's ability to give others what they want, which might be promotion, investment in a project, choice around the rota, or a seat next to someone important at a retirement dinner. Coercive power is the power to withdraw things that others want; it may also involve threat and bullying. The use of such sources of power can significantly shape the patterns you and others experience in your local culture, and indeed will be influenced by the power dynamics that emanate from far up the hierarchy.

Yet other sources of power often have significant impact on how others respond to you and you to them. For instance, referent power is related to whether people like you, warm to you and admire you. Information power is the knowledge others perceive you have about what is going on, which may be because you sit on committees or have an office next to someone who is very much in the know. Expert power is the influence you have because of what others perceive to be your technical or professional knowledge, which might be as a clinician or an expert in QI or finance.

In the Fellows' stories you will see many of them coming to the realisation that they are more powerful than they perhaps believed. You might find it interesting to reflect for a moment about your sources of power: which you tend to use with whom, and to what effect.

Leading with political savviness

The idea of making moves that may be deemed political tends to evoke much conversation, and sometimes consternation, when we talk about this with the Fellows. Yet it seems that how different interests are explored or worked round is a key relational leadership skill. Again, as with power, this aspect of leadership is rarely explored explicitly, undoubtedly because there are moral overtones, even taint, associated with politics. Few people want to be thought of as political or Machiavellian. Such adjectives suggest managing upwards, manipulation, back stabbing and other self-serving behaviours to the detriment of others. They suggest something underhand and unfair, the antithesis of a level playing field.

Here is another example where rethinking our assumptions can be hugely helpful. The word politics comes from "polis" which refers to the way that differences were resolved through talking in the Greek city states. The word is neutral. In any organisation, department, team, even with two people, there will inevitably be different views about what should happen next, what should be the priority, or approaches to a problem. Politics is a way of influencing outcomes through conversation, by taking the time to find out who to talk to and how and when. This view of politics is about being politically savvy, being able to navigate the organisation, being adept at connecting. Most Fellows say they would be quite comfortable being thought to have these attributes and skills. Perhaps you may say likewise?

In thinking about politics in organisations, we introduce a theatrical metaphor (Buchanan and Boddy 1992). The front stage in an organisation is where formal, regular meetings take place. Focus on the front stage encourages you to identify and use existing processes and meeting structures to legitimise a change or gain agreement for the next stage. Here plans, milestones and project governance are discussed and remain vital because they are a form of communication, keeping others aware of what is going on and of progress. From a psychological perspective, such front stage meetings are also doing something equally, if not more, significant: they reduce anxiety for senior leaders, satisfying their need to know enough of what is going on, to have a sense of control. The front stage thus gives reassurance and confidence to allow change and improvement to continue. Given the anxieties, uncertainties and unpredictability of change and shifting culture, this is important and necessary, but it is not sufficient.

You have probably noticed that in large group settings it is also often hard to explore what people really think and feel. Group dynamics, power and ritualistic patterns often dominate rather than there being a culture of genuine dialogue. Front stage is therefore important, but decisions and outcomes are often the result of back stage activities.

Focus on the back stage encourages you to have different and often more honest conversations, to create a different pattern. Greater honesty is possible as it is psychologically safer for both you and the other person. You are both out of the public eye, away from the spotlight of others' expectations, which means you can explore where someone is really coming from, "off line". A back stage conversation also allows you to test out your own thinking, rehearsing the story of what you intend to do, hearing which of the benefits you've described really make sense to people and where further reflection is required. This may give you the opportunity to modify what you are thinking of doing as you learn from others and inquire into their knowledge, hopes and concerns. You may discover that others have more nuanced views than you may have assumed.

Through back stage conversation you may help others make sense of what you are wanting to do, so that differences are less likely to harden into resistance. People who feel listened to are less likely to be resistant. You might also use a back stage conversation to connect with senior people or influential colleagues to ensure that they are aware of important facts or ideas. Our encouragement to you and to the Fellows is to make greater use of back stage conversation. In our experience, the need to actively engage in back stage activity is often underestimated.

A framework for thinking about political behaviour that the Fellows find helpful was developed by Baddeley and James (1987). They explored political behaviour in local government and then rather colourfully described four different styles that emerged from their research by using animal characters. They plotted them on a matrix depending on whether or not they were politically aware and whether or not they acted in the interests of the organisation, or out of self-interest.

A framework for exploring political behaviour

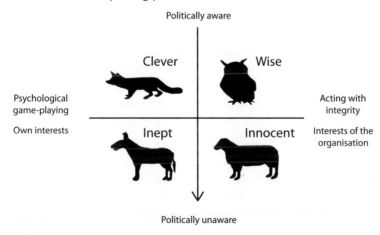

Figure 4.3

The fox is politically aware but tends to act in his or her own interest, often engaging in what is seen by others to be game playing. Machiavelli would have been a fox and it is fox behaviour that gives politics a bad name. Foxes like to be powerful. They enjoy manipulating others; tend to create winners and losers, and are superb at the subtle put down, cleverly tripping people up, wrong footing them, landing them in awkward places, but all done without it being obvious, especially to people further up the hierarchy. Whenever there is trouble, they aren't there. If there is a tricky piece of work, they will duck out of it by flattering someone else and suggesting they would be better suited to the task.

The owl is also politically aware and knows how to navigate the organisation or wider system. However, owls' intentions are perceived to be for the good of the organisation rather than personally self-serving. Their interest in power is seen to be because it allows them to influence organisational purpose rather than purely for reasons of status or power per se. They tend to be assertive, tactful and emotionally literate. They are excellent listeners, so are skilled at inquiry, interested in and aware of others' viewpoints. This means they tend not to be defensive, to be willing to learn from mistakes, reflect on events and be open with information and how they feel about things. Because of these interpersonal skills, they tend to be good at building coalitions around them to get support, and when they negotiate they attempt to create win-win situations, but can cope with being disliked.

In this schema, there are two groups of people (or animals, to keep to the metaphor), that are unaware of or blind to politics. **The donkey** is often characterised as inept or awkward, perhaps hired originally for their technical competence but lacking in interpersonal skills. As they are focused on themselves, they are poor at reading others, and tend not to pay attention to others' feelings or to cultural or organisational norms, nor do they consider what might be diplomatic in the moment. Their assumption is that it is acceptable to call a spade a spade – it's their right after all – and then they are often angry and surprised when people get upset by their behaviour and things don't go their way. This lack of self-awareness and failure to understand their personal impact makes a donkey tricky to performance manage if you have one in your team, as they rarely get the message from feedback!

The fourth animal is **the sheep** who in the model is labelled as "innocent", or perhaps more unkindly as naïve. Sheep tend to rely a great deal on authority, assuming that those who are further up the hierarchy will be right and that decisions are based on rationality alone. They are therefore very compliant, good workers who put their trust in organisational procedures so would not even consider that building a network or finding support might be necessary. They share information openly with anyone who asks, wanting to be helpful and do the right thing for the organisation, especially as described by those with expert or positional power. The sheep would not really consider that others were acting with ulterior motives so, while the sheep listens, he or she misses double messages or nuance and sees things as "either-or".

Rather than seeing politics and political activity as good or bad, as something to engage in or avoid, we see political activity as neutral and a reality of organisational life. Rather than dismissing politics and political activity, we believe that engaging with it is both helpful and important, especially when done with good intent.

In summary

Our encouragement when shifting cultures to be more conducive to high-quality care is to use more pull than push gestures, to create dialogue at every opportunity rather than debate, and to be in an Adult ego state when you can, whilst being aware of by whom and when you might get triggered into Child or Parent ego states. We encourage you to see power as a dynamic, relational property between individuals, and to learn to use your own power well. In terms of politics, try and be an owl, but pay attention to the foxes and give attention to back stage activity. Identify those with an interest in the improvement and actively engage them in conversation. In doing so, you will be being politically competent and organisationally agile.

Tempered Tenacity

A theme emerging from each of the stories in this section is a quality of persistence and resilience; a holding on to and staying true to a belief that something in the local culture, whether department, organisation or the wider system, needs to shift in order to improve the quality of care. There is a sense from all those sharing their stories of a profound dissatisfaction with an aspect of the status quo, and an energy to create something different, and hope – motivated by strongly held beliefs – that better is possible. We are calling this quality of persistence and resilience, tempered tenacity.

Some of the stories take place over a considerable period, and for a few Fellows the stories they tell have become part of their life's work, with beliefs shaped by early experiences at work, or even as children. Knowing *why* you hold dearly to certain beliefs helps sustain you during the inevitable moments when it feels tough going. This can act as a personal moral compass, your true north. In each of the stories, a sense of purpose and endeavour shines through.

These are stories about making moves that shape and influence, that offer an alternative, that create a new way of doing things and do so repeatedly over time. These are not stories of quick fixes but of holding to a direction of travel, even if the exact route is unclear and winding. They are stories of being willing to take advantage of what emerges and to work with what is, as well as keeping sight of what is needed in the future. Hence the need for tenacity and persistence.

The term "tempered" we borrow from Meyerson and Scully (1995, p585) who write,

> *Temperedness reflects the way (individuals) have been toughened by challenges, angered by what they see as injustices or ineffectiveness and inclined to seek moderation in their interactions with members closer to the centre of organizational values and orientations.*

Tempered in the language of physics describes a metal being made tougher by alternately heating it up and then cooling it down. In these stories, there are certainly accounts of both challenges and setbacks as well as significant progress. Tempered also refers to having a temper. Here too, some of the Fellows talk of their frustration and anger at what they see as injustices or inadequacies. Yet being even-tempered also means having composure and being thoughtful about how and when to act, so the frustration and anger needs to be tempered, controlled, channelled wisely. Herein lie some of the subtleties and relational skills required when challenging and shifting the dominant culture.

Tempered tenacity means leaders need to balance how and when they challenge the dominant culture and offer an alternative view, or act in a different way. There is need to speak up and ability to do so in a way that others can hear without rejecting the idea or the leader. Understanding and navigating organisational politics is key. Leaders need to be wise owls rather than dismissed as donkeys who keep braying without connecting with what is going on for others in the context. Judgement is required too about timing in the moment, balancing considerations of risk and safety so that neither the leader nor the idea is rejected or even ejected from the system. Leaders who show tempered tenacity also tend to see power more broadly than as a possession gained through position or expertise. Growing others' power as well as their own is one of the ways they influence and shift the culture.

The energy and tenacity required to keep going can be draining, especially if the impact of your gestures seems elusive. Personal resilience is therefore vital and aided by having other, like-minded leaders to talk to, whether that be good colleagues, a coach, or an action learning set.

In this section there are five stories which illustrate these themes:
- The first, *Blocking the Door*, tells the story of a clinician persistently making moves to improve patient safety and service provision, taking risks
- The second, *It's the Little Things that Make the Biggest Difference*, is a personal account of a surgeon re-connecting with his compassion for his patients

- The third, *The Cycle Helmet and the Fire-Starter*, tells the story of a clinician challenging unacceptable behaviour and accepting that happy endings can sometimes only be achieved in part
- The fourth, *They'll All Die Anyway*, is a story of challenging assumptions about mortality rates and the role of paramedics
- The fifth, *Leading from the Heart*, tells the story of a Fellow's work to foster and enable cultures where humanity and Quality Improvement are the norm and are an endeavour shared by staff and patients

CHAPTER 5

Blocking the Door

Setting the scene

The way our local hospital services are configured has frustrated me for a long time, although I am pleased to say that we are now making progress and improvements. We have multiple sites with services often duplicated in each. All the evidence suggests this is bad news for quality in terms of patient outcomes, and is in addition a real challenge for us to staff appropriately. I understand how services have been developed piecemeal, over many years, without always reflecting the changing needs of our populations, yet the current state of play seems to me subject to the vagaries of local politics, and often who shouts the loudest. This makes me worried for our patients and hot under the proverbial collar.

This is my story of persistently trying, with others, to do something about this. It's a story of trying to shift the culture of our organisation to one that puts safety and quality of care at the top of the agenda, even if this means taking big and risky decisions. It's not going to be a story of plain sailing. At times it has felt more like being on a roller coaster. It does have a reasonably happy ending although, be warned, there are cliff-hanger moments!

I am now a divisional medical director. The story begins though when I was newly appointed as a consultant. My job-plan included sessions on multiple acute sites, and I was supposed to be harmonising working practices and building relationships between them. I soon became concerned about how emergency surgery was being delivered. Everyone seemed to be doing things their own way, so there was as much harmony as a primary school orchestra tuning-up before a performance. In one hospital, the consultants seemed to have a rather hands-off approach to surgical emergencies, largely leaving their junior medical staff to look after patients. The juniors on this site frequently turned to me, as a willing new-comer, for advice before "their" consultant had even seen the patient. It felt as if I was doing their job as well as my own. Another hospital seemed to be receiving more than its fair share of complex emergency surgery, and staff, including me, were having to work incredibly hard, long hours to cope. The mortality statistics on Dr Foster were stark too. There were significantly more deaths than would be expected on one site, but somehow this had gone unnoticed. Perhaps the regulators only got to see the overall Trust mortality figures, which were average. There were patient safety incidents too, some related to inadequate supervision of surgery, others to significant delays in operating. Initially I tried to bring these issues up with the relevant teams in real time, as they happened. Also at our joint audit meetings we discussed patients who had had poor outcomes, yet despite this, nothing seemed to change.

We made other moves too. Colleagues and I wrote a letter to the Clinical Director for Surgery, detailing our concerns. We were told he had passed the letter on to the Medical Director, but nothing was done, despite our continued protestations. We decided to be braver and wrote directly to the Medical Director with our concerns. We eventually forced him to meet us face to face so we could explain our concerns, and even got him to write a letter summarising the meeting. Still nothing happened! At the time I was furious: "How dare he ignore our concerns about patients". It felt that he had closed the door in our faces.

Looking back, I can see that I had quite a simple, machine view of how things happened in organisations, assuming that those up the hierarchy had the power to sort things on behalf of the rest of us. I can see now that colleagues and I were in a completely stuck pattern. The crosser we all were, the more we banged on about our concerns, the more those further up the hierarchy seemed to us to have shut their ears. It felt like throwing paper aeroplanes at a dart board – absolutely no impact!

I was in "tell" mode, push, push, push, quoting more and more data, as the longer this had been going on the more important it felt to tell and explain again. I wasn't asking many questions and I certainly didn't fully appreciate the strain and impact of an annual deficit of £30 million on the behaviour of the Medical Director and the rest of the executive team. The deficit was completely preoccupying, perhaps even paralysing, the Trust board at the time who were trying to deal with this and constant financial scrutiny. I still don't think this completely absolves the Medical Director – he should have been the voice for patient safety on the board. However, there is much learning here for me about the importance of empathy and the willingness to stand in the shoes of the other, to be able to reach out and understand what is going on. Now that I find myself in the role of divisional Medical Director, I can see that repeated and belligerent demands from others to sort things can be overwhelming. Demanding attention and action can sometimes shut down the ability of others to respond.

At about this time, a new Chief Executive, Deborah, started.

She made a number of changes in the board and the management structure of the Trust. Andrew, the same Director of Surgery we had initially written to, took a dossier with detailed evidence of all the problems we were having in surgery to her. Maybe something would now happen.... Eventually, after what felt like an inordinate amount of time, there was a public consultation about the configuration of acute hospital services, with the preferred option being to centralise three services on one site: in-patient general surgery, paediatrics and cancer services.

I argued at the time that we should also discuss centralising A&E and critical care on one site, but I didn't win that argument. Perhaps that would have been politically speaking in the "too hard" box at that moment. There is a learning here for me that timing, paying attention to the context, choosing your moment, is important, particularly if a "big bet move" is required. I guess I also wasn't very sophisticated in my own political approach. I hadn't heard about front stage and back stage at this point: having conversations to influence thinking behind the scenes. I also continued to do lots of pushing and not much pull (more on that later).

The public consultation was predictably acrimonious, with members of the public marching in the streets and vicious letters in the local press, especially about moving children's services. Strangely, and surprisingly to me, no one really seemed too fussed about what happened to surgery, and so we were given the green light to begin to plan and design for a reconfiguration in surgical services.

However, sometimes life gets in the way of plans and planning horizons. I found myself becoming Acting Clinical Director of Surgery, as the incumbent was off with long-term sickness. The situation in one of the surgery departments began to rapidly deteriorate to an alarming extent. One surgeon resigned after we began to scrutinise his surgical outcomes in detail; another surgeon stopped emergency on-call because of ill health. By now, the emergency surgery service on this site was being run by just six surgeons, four of whom did not do any planned abdominal surgery and were becoming deskilled, and two of whom were near retirement. It felt woefully inadequate. When I thought it couldn't get any worse, one of the breast surgeons approached me to say that she wanted to stop doing on-call work because of her age and ill health.

I knew that we could not wait another two years to plan for reconfiguration. We needed to reconfigure now, as there was a significant risk of complete collapse and harm to patient safety. It was December. I put this issue on the agenda for the Hospital Management Committee (HMC) meeting in January. In the meeting the CEO, Deborah, said that the board needed to consider the situation and a decision would be made by the next HMC meeting. In February, there was again no decision but a promise to have a decision at the next meeting in March. "Procrastination again," I screamed silently inside. "Why don't they get the extreme risks to patient safety? How can I get my voice and concerns heard? How can I get through to the decision-makers and be taken seriously?" I remembered as a young child my grandfather trying to teach me how to box. I'd pummel my fists into this wonderful gentle giant and, despite all my best efforts, he remained immovable. This was the same, but it felt like punching a duvet. The duvet was then shaken out and the dent I briefly made disappeared without a trace.

The March Hospital Management Committee (HMC)

I approached the HMC meeting in March full of trepidation. The decision to reconfigure surgical services now felt more and more urgent, as we also needed to move surgery to one site before the next cohort of junior doctors arrived in August. The night before the committee meeting I sat down at home and began to read the papers for the meeting. I read them through ...I read the agenda again ....surely not....but no, to my absolute horror, and despite all the promises to the contrary, there was no item on the agenda about accelerating the plans to reconfigure surgery. I felt sick. I texted Cassie, who was the business manager for surgery. She texted back, "Meet me 08.30 tomorrow for coffee – we need to talk."

We met in the hospital restaurant the following morning. We sat together in the red plastic chairs by the far window, out of ear-shot of patients and colleagues. Cassie blew at her coffee, creating tiny ripples across its black surface, wanting to cool it down so she could get on and drink it. Cassie and I worked well together, and I totally trusted her judgement and good intentions. It was a relief to feel that we were in this together and to have someone to talk over the points we needed to make. We were in agreement that the decision had to be made today if we were to have enough time to reconfigure surgery before the arrival of the junior doctors in August. We also agreed that I would ensure that the need for a decision would be brought up under any other business.

"You're agreed? We absolutely have to get the yes today!" she said.

I nodded. She was right, but all the same I felt a little sick in my stomach. The stakes felt very high. I drained my coffee and picked up the large pile of papers and we both went to the committee room.

It was a long U-shaped table with the executive directors at the head, the screen ready behind them for the PowerPoint presentations. The CEO's chair was in the middle, an ancient thing with an elaborately carved back and arm rests so it looked a little like a throne. I had often thought how uncomfortable it looked. Cassie and I sat down at one corner, so we were in easy sight of Deborah. The meeting started with a review of the minutes of the last meeting and the Trust's performance, the normal ritual, the same pattern that I was well used to, but it passed in a bit of blur for me. I was finding it difficult to concentrate. Slide after slide of RAG ratings (too many in red!) flashed up on the screen. Finally, we got to the end of the agenda, a little over time. Deborah was tapping her sheaf of papers into a tidy pile and asked, without really looking up, if there was any other business to discuss. She didn't look like she was expecting to discuss anything else. The chair scraped on the floor, as she pushed it back and stood up. Cassie nudged me: "Now". Instinctively, I also stood up. I could feel my heart thumping.

"Umm yes. There is actually one thing we need to agree – reconfiguring surgery right now. We promised that a decision would be made today."

The heads all swivelled round, pens that were about to be put away were set back on the table, glasses were taken back out of pockets, papers were left where they were. All eyes were on me, shocked at the breach of the normal routine.

Deborah was still moving, walking towards the door, holding her papers in front of her. I was still standing, so I moved again, towards her, mirroring her movements like some bizarre dance. I was now standing in front of the door, physically blocking her exit. This was the CEO and here I was literally eye-balling her, in public.

However, I found my voice. From where I don't know. I didn't shout and scream. I was in Adult, I hope, so firm, clear, reasonable.

"Deborah, I'm sorry, I know it is difficult, but we have no choice. The situation in surgery has got worse. We need to act now to be able to complete the reconfiguration before August, or the new doctors will have to move as soon as they have started."

We were both still standing up. What move would she make? Shout at me? Shame me? She briefly chewed her lip. No one spoke. I couldn't read her....in that moment anything seemed possible.

"Sit down. We obviously need to talk," she said, turning back towards her chair. I almost collapsed into mine, weak after the adrenaline rush, fearing momentarily for my career as well as my service. Cassie explained (once again!) the situation and the risks. Deborah asked others around the table what they thought and to my utter relief, finally, we had a proper discussion. The surgery reconfiguration was brought forward.

Looking back at this episode there is much to notice and much to learn. I acted instinctively and spontaneously and in so doing broke the social norms and patterns of how people are expected to behave in a formal meeting. In the moment, I challenged the dominant culture. I worry, now, about what would have happened if I had not stood up and confronted the CEO in this way. I fear we would have continued in our unsafe configuration for another two years and I would have had to live with the knowledge of my own collusion. I worry too, about the personal risk I took in acting in this way, but to her credit Deborah never reprimanded me for this. In fact, my respect for her grew enormously as a result of how she handled what could have been an explosive situation.

I'm sure that my relationship with Cassie was vital in helping me to be brave. We were in this together, manager and clinician, and we both cared. I think we sometimes under-estimate how important the manager-clinician relationship is. I think emotions and tension played a part too. On GenerationQ, I read about Heifetz's idea of "controlling the temperature of conflict" (Heifetz 2002, p107) which seems relevant here. He describes how a leader needs to sense the emotions of a group and pace his or her actions accordingly. Importantly some tension is needed to create change, yet too much tension can be destructive. When I stood up, the tension in the room was palpable, all eyes on me: "What is he doing? What is he going to say? What will happen?"

I also acted in the moment. I felt acutely aware of everything that was going on in the room. I could feel this was my moment to lead, to shift the pattern. And the small gesture I made, the gesture of simply standing up, made a huge difference. It increased my power and physical presence in that moment. And I guess this was also an example of leadership according to complexity thinking – making a gesture without knowing what the response would be, stepping into the uncertainty, guided by good intent; assuming equal power and staying in Adult despite the stakes being high. There's a quote I like that seems relevant:

Courage is a noun that shows up as a verb. We recognise it by what people say and do. We do what frightens us even in the face of perceived or real personal risk. (Scott 2002)

Meeting the surgeons

Once the decision to reconfigure had been made, there was so much work to do in such a short time. I set up a meeting with the lead surgeon, Mary, in our out-of-town hospital to decide how we would handle the transition, and specifically how we would look after children who needed surgery. I have always got on with Mary. I arranged to meet her with Cassie over coffee.

On the day set up for the meeting, Cassie and I drove over to the hospital together and went into the meeting room. I was rather surprised to see all the surgeons sitting in a row, not just Mary. Their faces were like thunder. In hindsight a bit of noticing the mood and some inquiry into it would have been good, but I was still on a high from getting the reconfigure decision and I was a man on a mission, with no time to lose. I explained that the purpose of the meeting was to plan the transition of moving in-patient surgery to another hospital, and that I would value their help and advice. Gunther spoke first. He's a big Danish man and there is a touch of the Viking about him. He slammed a large fist on the table as he spoke,

"I am against."

"Against what?" I asked.

"I am against moving to the other site."

"OK, Gunther. As you know we've been discussing this for over two years, and we have been out to a public consultation to centralise in-patient surgery."

"No one told me," he replied.

"For $%*@'s sake," I thought. How could he not know, how many meetings have we had? It had been in the local press almost constantly for ages. I bit my lip.

"OK, Gunther, I am sorry if you weren't asked about this. We are going to move all in-patient surgery to our other site by July. I wanted to talk about how we do it and about how we look after children who need surgery in this area."

I turned to Mary.

"As you know the plan is for…"

"I don't know anything about that and we are not going to do it," said Mary. This meeting was really getting out of hand.

"Mary, this has all been discussed in public meetings and ratified by the Trust board."

"Well, we are not doing it. What is your plan B?"

"There is no plan B," I said, feeling a hot flush of anger rising. I then added, "I think we sometimes forget that we are all employees of this organisation – that we work for the organisation, not the other way round". I'm sure I sounded pompous or sarcastic but I was absolutely furious.

"What if we refuse to do this?" said Mary, clearly enjoying her moment as I dug myself deeper into a hole.

"Well if necessary we can give you three months formal notice of change, and then if you refuse you would be in breach of contract."

I had really lost it now, abandoning reason or persuasion and going right for coercion, using my positional power.

We left. Cassie and I walked back to the car, the positivity about improving services lost for now. Cassie opened her mouth and began to speak.

"You shouldn't have…"

I cut her off.

"I know."

We drove back in dejected silence. So much for applauding myself for using my emotions effectively in the HMC meeting. Here, I had really let them get the better of me. My Adult voice used to good effect in the HMC meeting had been taken over by an angry, punishing Critical Parent tirade. I'd spent so much energy focusing on those up the hierarchy, I hadn't been sufficiently tuned into colleagues who were perhaps feeling done to and were therefore exerting their own power by saying no, we won't do this. I'd also been talking about this reconfiguration for so long I assumed that all the other surgeons understood it too. I hadn't paid any attention to their potential need to express their sense of loss of the services moving from their hospital. I was reminded of a metaphor introduced at one of the GenerationQ workshops – a leader who has been thinking about a change for a long time is like a man in the front carriage of a train. He has passed through the dark and gloom of the tunnel and is already out into the sunshine. However, his followers who haven't had the same amount of time to think about the change may still be in the dark of the tunnel. The enthusiastic leader can easily forget that others are in a different place. I'd been that leader and, in hindsight, I could have explored this first with a "pull" gesture, rather than going straight in with a heavy-handed "push" gesture.

Over the next few months we recruited two new consultant surgeons, completed a £1million refurbishment of two wards, and moved an entire service by the end of July. From my perspective, this was a great success, as well as a great relief. It has allowed us to provide a safe, sustainable consultant-led service for emergency general surgery. We have been able to establish new services for our local population and we seem to be able to recruit good people. Oh, and Mary and her team? Well, in that one, awful meeting, I had done untold damage. The surgeons wouldn't move so we had to find a sub-optimal work-around to look after patients on that site.

The board meeting – telling tales

In the current context of the NHS, CEOs don't seem to stay around for long. Deborah left the Trust before we completed the move of emergency surgery and was replaced by Jack, an experienced CEO who was keen to further reconfigure hospital services, going well beyond the three services we had managed to reconfigure so far.

Whilst I am delighted with the emerging outcomes, the process has been unbelievably time-consuming and has taken a lot of back stage conversations to get to a point of agreement. At times, I have felt that trying to help the CCGs and GPs understand the pressures we face in the acute hospitals has been an impossible task; they probably feel the same about us. We've also had delays in the work for financial reasons and because of purdah during various local and national elections. In the meantime the recruitment problems in our organisation, particularly in emergency medicine, acute medicine and critical care have worsened, as is being experienced nationally. The uncertainty of how and where services will be in the future has made people particularly reluctant to commit to working for us. Complexity thinking, with all the emphasis on unpredictability, seems more and more to describe my work world.

At a recent reconfiguration meeting, I said to Adrian, our Strategy Director, "I don't know why we are planning for a new configuration in five to six years. I can't even guarantee the critical care unit will be staffed in six months' time!"

He looked at me rather quizzically and I elaborated on the current staffing problems. At the time, I thought little more about this interaction. I had not planned to say what I did. A couple of days later, Cassie said that Adrian had asked her if I was crying wolf about the problems with critical care staffing. He'd been doing his own bit of back staging. Cassie told him how precarious the situation was, even though we were doing what we could to maintain the critical care service. Later that same day, I received an "invitation" to speak to the next Trust board, in private session, about the critical care staffing issues.

Before the board meeting, I made sure that I spoke to both the Director of Workforce (Jessica) and Jack (the CEO) face to face. I am getting better, I hope, at being a political wise owl rather than the rather naïve sheep. Jessica and I talked through a shared approach to the meeting – she would give the board a flavour of the problems across all specialities and I would talk about the specific details of issues facing critical care. In private, Jack confided that he too was fed up with the lack of pace on reconfiguration and what seemed to be stalling tactics by some. He said that he wanted the board to feel the immediate risks we were facing, so that they would agree to take action, and he thought that they would be likely to listen to a clinician. His style has certainly started shifting the culture of the board at least. We have a new MD too – Gerald. It was good feeling that I had allies. I was also beginning to become more aware of my own power and influence in the many conversations. Unlike earlier, where I diminished my own power and influence through my actions, I was now becoming much more astute in noticing what it takes to get really listened to, as well as what is needed to stimulate robust discussion and to get difficult decisions made.

On the day of the board meeting I had a clinic first thing, so my anxiety about attending the board meeting was heightened by the risk of running late. Rather than offer a PowerPoint presentation I decided instead to tell a story. Several years earlier I had been deeply moved by Martin Bromiley's film, "Just a Routine Operation" (Bromiley 2011) which tells the story of how his wife died following a series of preventable errors during elective surgery. That story, and my emotional reaction to it, is what motivated me to improve safety in a way that numerical data hadn't done previously. On GenerationQ, we've been introduced to Brené Brown's work (2011). She talks about the power of story to create an emotional connection with others to stimulate action. I also got feedback from other GenerationQ Fellows that I was good at telling stories.

As I went into the board meeting, I knew Jessica would have already given them plenty of facts. Jack's words were echoing in my head, "...I want them to feel it...they will listen to a clinician". The stage was set. I didn't have to rack my brain for a story. I just told them what happened the last time I was on call. I only spoke for about five minutes.

> I was on call a few weekends ago and someone died unnecessarily as a
> result of our current staff shortages. It was busy, but not exceptionally
> so. The on-call consultant anaesthetist asked me to come and see a
> patient in ITU who was clearly very sick and needed an emergency
> operation immediately. At the same time, there were other ill patients
> in ITU who needed reviewing and a very sick medical patient in Resus.
> I had no choice but to take the ITU patient straight to theatre for a
> re-operation. The consultant anaesthetist was stuck in Resus so
> delegated my operation to a junior staff grade doctor to give the
> anaesthetic. The operation was difficult but, I thought, went according
> to plan. The next day the patient didn't wake up and had signs of a
> stroke. The central line had inadvertently been put in her carotid
> artery during the anaesthetic. Overnight she had an infusion of
> noradrenaline into her brain which caused the stroke from which she
> later died.

As I told the story, I recalled sitting in a rather Spartan interview room to tell the patient's husband that there had been a mistake and that his wife was going to die. He thanked me for all we had done which somehow compounded the pain of the error. I also recalled sitting in the root cause analysis meeting, when Alison, the junior anaesthetist, tearfully told the story of how she put in the difficult central line on her own. I looked up at the board as I spoke. I could see the faces around the table looking visibly shocked at the fragility of this crucial service, together with a rather uncomfortable realisation that they were accountable for this. After I had spoken, the Chair asked me to sit down with the board and join in what became an intense discussion, where both the Medical Director and Nursing Director spoke out for the need for action. It felt like a defining moment for the organisation, a culture of waiting was shifting to a bias for action. It was almost like watching a film as the events unfolded before my eyes.

I felt listened to, that my views were helpful. The Chair told me that of course the board would want to see the business case, but that we needed to implement critical care cover immediately. I was given the go-ahead to spend an additional £500,000 a year. I knew that I would likely have to find that money from elsewhere but even so, the board's willingness to act felt wonderful.

Within months of the board meeting, the new critical care rota was up and running. The influx of new consultants brought ideas and energy into the department, morale improved, it felt different, a new local culture. The money we have spent to bolster the critical care rota is still a cost pressure on us and I need to find another way of improving efficiency to pay for it. Yet, telling that story has had a huge impact on improving the quality of our critical care service. As Brené Brown says, "stories are data with a soul" (2011).

I talked over the board meeting with the Medical Director and Jack, the CEO. The Medical Director said, "I could see what you were doing telling that story and I sat back to watch the rest of board as the story unfolded...It worked because you were there. It was about you, your patients and the anaesthetist. It was you saying we are not going to do this anymore."

Jack the CEO agreed. "You're right," he said, "In a complex world, it's the narrative or storytelling which helps us to build a shared meaning. Storytelling is a bridge between the world of numbers and relationships."

We then went on to have a fascinating philosophical conversation about how those of us schooled in the scientific method of linear cause and effect have difficulty coping with uncertainty and paradox; how we want to look for the right answer and how we can become paralysed into indecision if there is no data to guide us. Who would have thought such a conversation was possible in an NHS trust!

As I read back over the story I have written I see myself rather like a dog with a bone, not willing to give up on patient safety and the quality of care. Writing the story has also caused me to reflect more deeply on two important themes; personal safety and personal power.

I feel a strong sense of moral purpose in trying to improve our local health services. In some ways, this is helpful in sustaining me through the inevitable delays and glitches in the process, yet I recognise it has also put me at risk. In refusing to allow the CEO to leave a meeting room, for example, I was breaking social norms that could easily have resulted in disciplinary action. I don't remember consciously deciding to take a risk at the time; the issues at stake felt bigger and more important than my fear. Yet in looking back and writing about these events, I do feel a little worried for myself and, somewhat belatedly, have begun to think about what I need to do to keep safe-enough in an organisation and context where change is constant.

I certainly don't have all the answers as to how to stay safe-enough, yet there are things that I think have helped me and that I need to hang on to. Most significant is paying great attention to relationships. I have no doubt that we wouldn't have achieved what we have, safely, if it were not for my relationship with Carrie and now Jack, Jessica and the Medical Director on the board, to name just a few. I have really come to understand what John Donne meant when he wrote "No man is an island". I also now recognise the need for soul-mates, trusted friends with whom I can talk through ideas for change and be well challenged. In this regard, I have found having a coach and working with peers in an action learning set invaluable. I have also learned that generosity is well rewarded, whether that be sharing the credit or the blame in change; and lastly not everyone might feel as strongly as I do about some of my ideas. Sometimes, being evangelical can be experienced by others as a real pain in the neck.

And finally, a few reflections on power. I had not really thought about my own power before GenerationQ and I probably need to acknowledge that I have more power than I feel comfortable with. I suspect that I am not alone in this regard and that I, along with fellow clinicians, sometimes choose to forget that I have significant personal power which, when harnessed effectively and ethically, can have great impact. As I look back to my early attempts to shift the culture and get things done, I notice that I almost exclusively used data and front stage, formal approaches. Reading this now, I can see that I have become more adept at using a range of approaches including engaging with politics and using my own power. I think a few years ago, I would have dismissed the idea of me having any power, and I would have thought that using power was almost an abuse. Adam Kahane's work on *Power and Love* (Kahane 2010) has helped me come to terms with the more positive aspects of power. He makes the distinction, for example, between "power to", the ability to get things done and "power over", the ability to control or coerce:

> Power has two sides one generative and one degenerative. Our power is generative and amplifying when we realise ourselves while loving and uniting with others. Our power is degenerative and constraining – reckless and abusive, or worse – when we overlook or deny or cut off our love and unity. (Kahane 2010)

And, I am only now noticing, why did Cassie and I agree that it would be me and not her who would intervene in that meeting?

CHAPTER 6

It's the Little Things That Make the Biggest Difference

"Hello doctor...you don't remember me, do you?"

It's the one sentence I dread hearing when I'm out in public. When you meet as many people as I do during a working day, every face starts to look familiar but impossible to place. Even if I do recognise them, it is rare to recall even the most basic medical detail about them. It's like those social conversations with someone who knows you, but you haven't a clue who they are. Are you going to be honest or pretend in the hope that a snippet of information jogs your memory?

The situation in the local supermarket is particularly difficult. I feel very comfortable listening to my patients' medical problems in the privacy of a consulting room, but not in the vegetable aisle. I become acutely aware of anyone else listening in, just in case something confidential is said. Are they better? Did I do a good job for them? What if they have a problem? Despite all these years of practice, I've reached the conclusion that the best strategy is just to avoid the local supermarket entirely. I've even done the statistics to support my conclusion: 12 years of practice, seeing 2,000 patients per year equals 24,000 people. In a town with a population of 300,000, that equals one in every 15 people. During peak hours, there will be approximately 200 people in the shop. It's therefore a statistical certainty that I will bump into someone I "should" know.

When I was training as an orthopaedic surgeon and sitting my final exams,

I was told that "you never stop learning throughout your whole career". That's completely true, but what was not explained to me at the time was who I would be learning from. Of the 24,000 patients I have treated, and who I am probably unlikely to recognise in the supermarket, there are some who I will never forget. What they all have in common is that they taught me something important about the meaning of medicine. The greatest lessons I have learnt are from them and from the families of those patients. In this chapter I will share some of these stories and what I have learned from them over time about the meaning of health care. Some of this learning I wish I had experienced much earlier in my career.

"Doctor... you don't remember me, do you?" said an elderly lady to me at the end of a long day of consultations. She had waited six months to see me with arthritis of her ankle, and I hadn't noticed until she made this comment that she had specifically requested to see me. She said it as if it were an after-thought just as she was leaving the consultation room.

"No, I'm sorry." I thought it best to take the honest approach and prepared myself for a complaint about the waiting time or something else.

She took my response as an invitation and sat down again.

"I'm going to tell you something and I don't want you to say anything until I'm finished." Now I was certain that I was going to have a bad day.

"OK," I said. What choice did I have?

"I'm going to tell you a story. Several years ago, I broke my wrist and I attended fracture clinic and I came by hospital transport. I had to have my wrist set and the plaster changed a couple of times. By the time it was all done, I had missed my arranged transport home and so wouldn't be picked up until late that afternoon. At the end of the clinic I was sat in the waiting room on my own, everyone had disappeared for lunch, when a young doctor passed me and stopped. He asked me if I was OK and what had happened.

He proceeded to make me a cup of tea and some sandwiches and called the transport office. He stayed and chatted a while.

"I will NEVER forget what you did for me that day. That doctor was you."

When I was a medical student, I really believed that my purpose in medicine was helping people. Ninety percent of all medical students say that during their interviews, and I'm sure most mean it. I had assumed that helping people is simply a product of my work as a surgeon, that if I did my job technically well, people got better. What I realised at that moment, sitting listening to this lady sharing her story with me, was that empathy and compassion were just as much of medicine as any of the technical skills I had accumulated after years in training. Had I forgotten this, or had I never learnt it?

She explained that it wasn't the cup of tea or my call to the transport office (which didn't make a difference) that meant so much to her. It was simply because I stopped. I noticed her. There is so much fear and isolation within our hospitals, particularly for those without family members to look after them. As I sat and listened, I began to wonder what it would take to build a compassionate health care system, where we weren't just doctors, nurses, surgeons and porters but where we were free to see our patients' world through their eyes, as if we were their sons and daughters.

Fortunately, both my parents are in amazing health both physically and mentally. Neither of them are medically trained and yet they are obsessive about their diet and taking regular exercise. The same can't be said for my lifestyle. It's my general observation that doctors are on the whole less likely to look after their own health than the health of the people that they treat. Returning to my parents, maybe it's just their Japanese genes, in which case I hope I can pass good health on to my children.

Christmas in our family is usually a small gathering with a great deal of attention placed on the food to be served on the day. It comes from having a professional chef as a little brother and a mother who has spent her whole life cooking for her family. Watching them argue about the best method of cooking roast potatoes is my entertainment for the holiday season. Will it be gourmet style with a pound of lard or the no fat healthy option?

My mother prides herself on never getting sick, and it's true that growing up I very rarely saw her take to bed with a cold. This wasn't so when my parents arrived on Christmas Eve one year.

"You don't look well mum, you should go to bed. Leave the lunch to us." I meant, leave the lunch to my brother.

"I'm fine, it's just a cold. I'll take hot lemon." She was a great believer in hot lemon and honey.

She stayed up that evening preparing the Christmas lunch and took to bed just a little earlier than usual. I wasn't worried about her because she clearly had the energy to display the annual mother/son potato spectacle, which she won.

I'm used to being woken in the middle of the night from the countless on-calls I'd done as a training surgeon, and after a while you develop a sixth sense of when something serious has happened and needs urgent attention. It was four in the morning when my dad came in and woke me up with a whisper.

"Mum's collapsed, she's really pale." Pale means cardiovascular shutdown; causes are cardiogenic, septic, neurogenic, traumatic and anaphylaxis; the list went through my head as I rushed to their room. When something medical happens at four in the morning, it's almost always very serious.

I saw her lying next to the bathroom door and for a moment, in the darkness, I couldn't see her breathing. I felt myself default to doctor mode: see if she speaks, check breathing, check pulse.

"I feel like I'm going to be sick." My mother was conscious, pale, sweaty with a pulse rate of 180. This was fast atrial fibrillation, probably brought on by flu or other infection. I had no doubt she had to get to my hospital straight away, otherwise her heart would not be pumping enough blood around her body and she could die of cardiac failure.

We only live minutes away from my hospital, so my car would be the quickest way to get there. I thought that an ambulance might take too long, especially on Christmas Eve. When I say *my* hospital, this is the hospital where I work. My good friend was the emergency consultant on duty and she immediately started to assess my mother in the resuscitation room. A full cardiac workup including ECG, bloods, chest X-ray and IV line had been completed within 20 minutes, and medication given to rapidly lower her heart rate back to normal rhythm. I was right, she was in fast rhythm precipitated by a chest infection.

The emergency care my mother received was amazing. Courteous, expeditious, thorough, safe and very professional. I couldn't have asked for more and I was proud that my mother could see what a fantastic hospital I worked at.

Over the next few days she stayed in hospital on intravenous antibiotics, and I visited her several times a day to check that her charts were being reviewed and the medications given at the right time. Although she was exhausted, I could see that she was getting better, and by the third day she was desperate to leave hospital.

"You have to have the flu jab from now onwards, OK?" I said to her as she got into the car to go home.

Several weeks later, I visited her at home. She still hadn't recovered fully, partly because she had been so scared by having to be admitted into hospital, and because she was still so weak.

"So, what did you think of my hospital?"

"Oh, everyone there was amazing, I really want to thank them so much." That was the answer I was expecting, but didn't get.

She proceeded to tell me that the three days in hospital were the worst three days of her life. She was constantly scared because she didn't know what was happening. Was she getting better or worse? What were those pills she was told to take? Was the pain she was feeling in her chest normal or had the doctors missed something? She didn't even know she could go home until an hour before she left.

I listened with a deep sense of guilt and betrayal. How can a mother's son, who is a doctor at the very hospital she was staying at, not have recognised how scared she was? What was it that I had or hadn't said to her while I visited her in hospital? I realised that what she had needed wasn't yet another doctor making her better with drugs, but a son who would just listen to her.

Compassion isn't easy, even with the very people we love the most in the world. So many things can prevent us from seeing the world through another person's eyes. With my mother's experience, I failed her by just being another doctor. Maybe it was hubris on my part? I realised that if I could be this way with my mother then what chance do any of my patients have, when I don't really know them at all?

From a patient's perspective, I have come to understand that their illness is a journey with short interactions with nurses, doctors or other members of health care. In their journey through our health care system there are big gaps where there is no one looking after them, and even though we may do everything right for the patient at the right time, it does not mean they will have a positive experience. Health care is not just about the things we do for patients but also about the things we don't do, in the eyes of the patient.

I have learned that compassion comes from that sense that someone else is looking out for you, and is most needed when we are at our weakest and most vulnerable. Without compassion, life is just a series of events, and for many of my patients in hospital, is death too just an event?

I met Minnie for the first time in the accident and emergency department after she had fallen at home resulting in a broken hip. A broken hip is not just a simple broken bone, it is often a sign of a gradual deterioration of health that has resulted in frequent falls. If a 90-year-old person falls enough times, it is an eventual certainty that they will break their hip.

Minnie was 92 years old, a spritely and determined lady, still living on her own in a one-bedroom bungalow. She was one of those people who I might have feared had she been my mother-in-law, because she had a talent for saying things as they are.

"Just give me some painkillers and a cup of tea, in that order," was her first response as I introduced myself to her as her treating surgeon.

"I'll get you painkillers, but I'm afraid we'll have to keep you 'nil by mouth' because you are going to need an operation to fix your hip."

The recommended treatment for almost all patients with a broken hip is an operation to either replace the broken joint or to fix the bones back together. It's risky surgery, with a one in ten chance that the patient will die in hospital. The consequence of not operating, however, is nursing home care in the best-case scenario; most will not survive that long.

Although Minnie's mind (cognitive function) was working with absolute clarity, unfortunately her physical condition wasn't quite the same. She had the severest form of aortic stenosis, which is where the valves of the heart are so narrowed that the heart is barely pumping enough blood around the body to keep you alive. An assessment by a senior anaesthetist gave her a 90 percent chance of dying from the stress of the surgery.

She had a right to know the risks involved so I told her straight.

"The surgery you need is very risky, because of the condition of your heart; the anaesthetist says you only have a one in ten chance of surviving the operation." In my mind, I hoped that she would agree to let nature take its own course. I could make the pain better, but she would never walk again.

This is one of the most difficult paradoxes a surgeon faces. Perform surgery with the knowledge that there is near certainty that it will cause a patient's death, or else leave a patient to gradually deteriorate in pain with an equal chance of death. That night, I went to sleep hoping to wake up with a eureka solution because I didn't want to do her operation. The first tenet of the Hippocratic Oath is "Do no harm". Does performing an operation with virtually no chance of success or survival break my oath?

By the next morning, I was just as uncertain as the previous day and, having given Minnie the same time to reflect upon her decision, I asked her in the presence of her family.

"I don't want to be left like this in pain. I'll take my chances. I want the operation. You'll see, I'm a fighter," she said. She looked to her grand-daughter sitting next to her, who nodded her head in agreement with a "good for you" look. I was now certain that she was making the right choice because this was what she wanted. I would do everything in my power to carry out her wishes in the safest way possible.

The challenge, however, was that I could not find a surgeon or anaesthetist to perform the procedure, as they felt the same conflict as I had initially.

"She won't even make it onto the operating table," said my wife, who is also an anaesthetist and my go-to source of second opinions.

"I don't think she really understands the risks; you need to speak to her again," said my orthopaedic colleague.

I started wondering what I would want if I was in Minnie's situation; what I would say to her if she were my grandmother. Whilst we may not be in control of everything that may happen to us in health, surely we all have a right to determine the dignity by which we live the last moments of life? I began to understand and agree with Minnie's wishes. Lying in a hospital bed in pain, unable to walk and unable to return home, diminishes the wonderful life that she had lived for over 90 years.

That afternoon I went through the list of contacts on my phone, calling every senior doctor I trusted to ask for their help, to help Minnie fulfil her wish. Four orthopaedic surgeons, three anaesthetists, a cardiologist, a care of the elderly physician and an intensive care physician all came to speak with her that day. I saw them speaking with each other and slowly the story they were telling themselves changed. Their conversations mattered.

"She knows what she wants and it's her choice isn't it?"

"It's a miracle she's alive anyway with that severe aortic stenosis, so I guess she's tougher than we think."

At three that afternoon, word had spread to the theatre complex that the most senior anaesthetists and surgeons were to carry out the risky surgery for Minnie. Staff in other areas started talking about Minnie and came over to wish her well. Every safety precaution that could have been taken was carried out for her and, amazingly and against all the odds, she survived.

We had achieved a brilliant feat of medicine together, and what I felt going home that day was more than a sense of achievement. These are fleeting moments which pass every time a patient thanks me for making them better. What Minnie showed me and reminded me of is the difference between achievement and fulfilment.

For days afterwards, I received calls from the theatre staff asking how Minnie was. She was doing well and recovering slowly. Several weeks later, during my ward round, I was asked by the ward physiotherapist to speak with Minnie about her lack of cooperation with trying to get out of bed. I saw her neatly tucked up in bed with a cup of tea beside her as I had done so many times before. It hadn't dawned on me until then that I had never seen her out of bed.

"You would feel much better if you listened to the physiotherapist and at least tried to get out of bed, Minnie," I said to her in my most "I am your consultant" voice, treating her as if she were a Child in Transactional Analysis terms and I was the one with some form of power over her. I should have known better. She turned and looked me straight in the eyes with her "I told you" look.

"I'm 92 years old, why do I need to walk? If I wanted to walk, then I would tell you." Now it was my turn to be treated like a Child. I felt like a school-boy, but I chuckled as I walked away.

Two months later, she passed away peacefully surrounded by her family. I understood that she had lived her life as she wanted, and she had left it how she wanted as well.

As I reflect on these stories again now, it feels to me as if health care in modern society is increasingly turning into another form of consumerism. Have a cold, take this pill. Have a bad hip, we'll give you a new one. Have some inexplicable symptoms, I'm sure there's a test to find out what it is. Whilst the progress of medicine based upon scientific knowledge has been a positive force in humanity, I have come to know through my own experience that not all health care can necessarily be quantified, nor is one human being the same as another. I feel strongly that we mustn't allow health care to become blinded by science and probabilities. The best form of health care is a partnership between the patient, the system and the people that work within it. What would it take to create a culture, maybe many cultures, in our health care system that respects and adapts to the individual needs of a patient and that regards compassion as being at the centre of quality?

I now live with this question every day in my work and take every opportunity to learn more, to ask questions, to try and find out for myself what it takes. As part of a local quality improvement (QI) project, I asked all the patients on our hip fracture ward who they felt delivered the highest quality of care during their stay, and why. Astonishingly, but perhaps not surprisingly, seven out of ten patients picked the ward cleaner, Sian, as that person. She was the happiest person at work and would chat with patients and staff alike, with a genuine sense of interest. She knew the personal stories of all the patients and was a constant daily face during their stay. If they had a problem, they went to her because they had a relationship with her and trusted her.

Sian became an integral member of our quality improvement team and helped us to see things that our patients see, and to feel what our patients feel. With her help, we learned that much of our patients' experience had become invisible to us, faced as we were with the need to ensure correct dosages, follow checklists, complete charting and documentation, and so forth. In privileging the science, we were at risk of losing sight of our humanity.

As the appointed leader of the QI project team, I wanted to understand the meaning of compassion in health care. What does it look like? How is it delivered? What effect does it have upon patients and their families? Why are some people more compassionate than others? I spent several evenings dressed deliberately in jeans and a t-shirt sitting with and chatting to patients coming in through the A&E department with hip fractures. I wanted to feel and see what they felt and saw. Despite good intentions to try and stand in their shoes, I couldn't help myself: my mind focused almost immediately upon the technical details of care. When had they been offered painkillers? Was their clinical examination satisfactory? Was the X-ray requested appropriately? Overall, I felt that the standard of care was very satisfactory. No glaring omissions. This was the first of many occasions when I was reminded that shifting the patterns of thought and behaviour is not easy, and that the trap of hubris is ever present.

One evening, I was with a lady in her 80s who had been brought to A&E, by herself and with no family or carers, with a suspected broken hip. She was in significant pain and clearly very dehydrated. I asked her if there was anything I could do for her, trying to be compassionate.

"I'm so scared," she said.

"No need to be worried, they'll take some X-rays and find out if you've broken your hip and......" I was promptly interrupted.

"No, no, you don't understand. I've left my cat at home you see, and I need someone to check in on her."

Why had I again defaulted to surgeon mode? When someone says they are scared the last thing they want to hear is "don't be". A more empathic approach would have been to ask why. I felt like a beginner. I decided from that moment on that the best approach to understand what my patients were experiencing was not to talk at all, but to listen and see.

It's amazing what happened when I just let myself forget why I was there, what I began to see for the first time. I had not realised just how bright the lights are in the A&E department; you can see them even with your eyes closed. A couple of nurses chatting with each other, laughing, maybe telling each other a joke, broke the seriousness of the harsh clinical environment and it helped me feel that they were part of a great team. One of the nurses came over and offered both of us a cup of tea with a smile. She held my lady's hand for just a moment. I wasn't the one with the broken hip but even I felt cared for. It was all the little things, the small gestures, which seemed to be making the biggest difference.

I had always held the belief that the job of the clinical leader, my job, is to find solutions to problems. Sitting in A&E my thinking was beginning to shift as I began to contemplate that no one individual can fully know what a patient needs, or what constitutes a patient's experience. This depth of understanding comes from multiple, spontaneous moments of compassion between staff and patients, and between staff members themselves. I had misunderstood my purpose as a leader. My real purpose was not to find the solutions, to be the hero, but rather to create the culture where all the staff felt valued, able and supported to offer compassionate care and to find their own solutions.

I thought again about Sian. What is it that enables her to be spontaneously compassionate? The answer seemed evident as I reflected upon it. Sian *enjoys* her work deeply, because she is free to talk to whoever she wants as long as her work is done well, which it always is. It is the people around her and her relationship with them that makes the job so enjoyable. I realised that the way to build a compassionate culture is not to mandate compassion as part of a measurement system, but to build an environment that allows compassion to flourish; an environment where staff feel trusted and trust others to care for them. An environment where staff, like Sian, are supported to enjoy their job and build relationships with others around them.

I am certain – my experience tells me so – that 99.9 percent of all people who work in health care have more than average compassion for those in need; they wouldn't be able to do what they do otherwise. If we create cultures of health care that support and nurture our staff, then compassion will become a natural product of that environment. This, as well as being a good surgeon, is becoming my work.

Remembering back to my medical student interview, I did say that the reason why I wanted to study medicine was because I wanted to help people. I don't recall whether I meant it at the time but now, after practising for many years, I have come to realise that the reason why I do what I do is because the patients I treat, and the people I work with, are the ones *helping me* become a better human being.

CHAPTER 7

The Cycle Helmet and the Fire-Starter

"S***, I forgot my helmet." I was already late for work when I realised that I'd forgotten to put on my cycle helmet. I carried on feeling a bit guilty but strangely free. Further along my 20-kilometre journey is a really steep hill. It is a narrow lane, winding and climbing for approximately a kilometre through a national park. I've never managed to cycle all the way up and usually push the bike up the last third. That day I made it! The view over the countryside below seemed even more beautiful. It was a good day. The view was the same but I had achieved something new, and so the view was framed in a different context. On the rest of the ride I felt energised; I wasn't wearing a helmet and felt freer than normal. It felt risky, but the roads were dry and the weather good so the risk was acceptable.

Was it the absence of the helmet that allowed me to ride up the hill? It certainly felt so. In my leadership role, metaphorically speaking, what is the cycle helmet that keeps me safe but can sometimes also constrain me? Can I safely take it off once in a while to achieve that bit more? Perhaps taking the helmet off occasionally is less risky than I imagine, and may enable me to achieve more, and just because, at another time, I choose to put the helmet back on it does not mean that I lose the gains I've made.

As a clinical leader, attempting to improve quality to the benefit of patients and their carers, I now see leadership as involving multiple small, but potentially significant, choices on a daily basis: How much to challenge the current culture? How much to go with the dominant way of doing things, for now, in a particular moment? In what situations, and with whom, is it helpful to offer an alternative perspective? When would doing so invite attack? When to keep my safety helmet on? When to take it off? This is my story of some of these choices.

INADEQUATE: Action is being taken against this provider

Sitting at home, in front of my computer, I read these words describing my organisation on the regulator's website. I feel ashamed. "Against" makes me feel vulnerable and open to attack; after all, who is the "provider" if not the staff who work here? "Inadequate" makes me feel powerless. Who is going to listen to me if I want to influence the actions of the new leaders who have been implanted to turn around the organisation? How can I hope to nurture a culture of improvement in this environment of deficit and blame?

I read the headlines about other failing organisations – Mid Staffordshire, Southern Health – and the personal criticism of their leaders. The relentless attacks on individuals in senior positions with little explanation about what they did wrong make me afraid for my reputation, my position, my livelihood.

I have been a senior physician and patient safety lead in an acute hospital trust for ten years. During this time, the Trust has grown considerably. Its buildings are confused; from the super-modern PFI building, through 1970s concrete, to the dilapidated "nightingale" wards of the early 20th century. The culture is as confused as the estate: the espoused organisational values are to deliver excellent care, but my observation has been a managerial focus on financial control and operational performance. I observe an increasingly disengaged workforce that, in spite of the relentless operational pressures and negative reviews, continues to deliver excellent care.

I notice that people are leaving the organisation. After a difficult winter our interim CEO went on leave. He didn't return. His services were no longer required. The regulators had found someone more suitable. I liked him; he lived locally and seemed to care about the staff and the people who use our services, but he's gone. We have had many CEOs in the ten years I have worked here; for each one I've invested time, energy and emotion in making connections. Other senior leaders have also disappeared; Chairman, Chief Operating Officer and Medical Director – no fanfare, just a few platitudes. Leading in this environment is difficult. I know I am more powerful and influential when I am connected with others, but political winds of change blow away these connections. With others, I have been initiating improvement activities, but to sustain them we often need senior support, and it requires considerable skill and effort to keep connecting to keep the flames alight. Even finding out who are now the right people to connect with can be challenging!

Making connection isn't easy for me. I'm quiet and introspective. I don't say much but, from feedback, I've been told that when I do speak others listen, as what I say is considered and thoughtful. I place great value on integrity and connection. I feel more confident and powerful when connected. From being on GenerationQ, I've learned that making connection and building relationships often requires us to expose our vulnerabilities, to show that we are human, yet this can also feel risky and make me want to hold back. Is this the "cycle helmet" that whilst keeping me safe also prevents me making it to the top of the hill? Brené Brown (2010) in a wonderful TED talk discusses how being able to share feelings of shame in a positive way allows us to connect as human beings, to bring about joy and belonging. I find this is a powerful concept as well as a potentially circular argument: connecting well with people enables me to show vulnerability, and in order to connect well with people I need to show vulnerability without risking my integrity or feeling over-exposed. A tricky but essential skill to be learnt.

In early spring a new interim CEO was appointed by NHS England; she wasn't from our area but had come from another Trust elsewhere in the country which was also in difficulty. I first met Liz when she visited the Trust before her official start date. I was interested to understand how she would approach leading such a troubled organisation. The fact she was female felt significant to me. I'd read Joyce Fletcher's *Disappearing Acts* (1999). She describes the relational activities of reflection and open conversation as being typically feminine attributes. She describes how more masculine attributes such as control, measurement and logic predominate in organisational life, and relational attributes are often "disappeared". Perhaps Liz could bring some of the typically female attributes to leadership that had been missing in our organisation, some reflection and dialogue to balance the grip and control that seemed to predominate.

Liz was in her early 60s with silver grey hair. She was wearing a smart business suit and high heels. There was hint of a West-country accent. She told me of her successes in other organisations and her initial assessment of the failings in our organisation. I noticed that she spoke for most of our encounter. I asked a few questions but she didn't enquire about me or my role. Prior to our meeting I had discovered that Liz had an interest in quality improvement methods, and in particular the Toyota Production System. I inquired about this and her enthusiasm for Lean methodology was very apparent. My initial impression was of extreme confidence, bordering on arrogance, but we shared a common enthusiasm for QI. I couldn't work out if this apparent confidence was in fact covering her own anxieties about the magnitude of the task ahead of her. I felt uncomfortable and uncertain but could see an opportunity.

When Liz joined the organisation I quickly began lobbying for investment to build a quality improvement capability in the organisation. I didn't particularly warm to Liz or her leadership style. She often used the mechanical metaphor of grip and control to describe how we could change the organisation's performance. I found that this was different from my understanding of creating a culture of continuous improvement. The importance of developing a "profound knowledge", as described by W. Edwards Deming (2000), requires an understanding of the people who work in an organisation and how they interact. This level of knowledge can only be achieved through dialogue and inquiry and seeing an organisation not as a machine but as a complex network of individuals, whose daily interactions lead to the complexity we see in modern health care. Despite this apparent difference of perspective, Liz agreed that we needed to develop an approach to QI in our organisation that empowered staff to identify and deliver improvement work using a recognised method. So it seemed that the QI work I had been doing could stay alight.

It was a Wednesday morning, and as I walked down the corridor I passed Emma, a nurse colleague who had been working closely with my team on a project to improve hand hygiene rates. Emma looked distracted; I said, "Hi". Emma looked up a little startled and asked me if I had heard the news. Tracey had been suspended.

Tracey was a senior nurse working with the Patient Safety Team. She was a bubbly, enthusiastic person who cared deeply for the staff she managed and the patients they looked after. She had reluctantly moved into a nursing management role, as her heart was in caring for patients. She wanted to be able to make a difference. Those around her saw that her commitment to improving patient care and the respect she had from colleagues made her a good candidate to take a leadership role. Tracey disliked meetings and the burden of producing data to provide assurance to senior leaders and regulators. Her strength was in dialogue, building teams and repairing relationships.

The suspension occurred with no warning and without obvious reason. It was widely suspected that the suspension was linked to the CQC report and poor reported hand hygiene compliance. It felt like Tracey had been disappeared: no warning, no explanation, one day she was at work and the next day she was not. When I enquired about the suspension from Tracey's manager I was advised not to contact Tracey for fear of jeopardising the investigation. It made me feel sick in my stomach, a sense of anxiety. Attempts to discover more information were met with the response that either they did not know the details or no information could be divulged to protect confidentiality. Two days later another senior nurse, whom I knew less well, suddenly went "on leave" and no one could say when she would return. There were whispered corridor conversations, but no official news on what was going on. She never returned from leave and was seconded to another part of the NHS.

I was deeply troubled by the suspension of the two nurses. Both were known to be trustworthy and caring professionals, supportive of efforts to improve the quality of care we deliver to patients. I was dismayed at the message this sent to me and other leaders in the organisation who were trying to support improvement. The interpretation I took from this was: keep your head down; don't do anything innovative or different; keep to the rules; don't challenge; be very careful, as those at the top have coercive power to remove you; it is unsafe round here if even good people are disappeared. It felt that a strong political wind was threatening to extinguish the flames of improvement, as who would dare to try anything new in such a context?

I didn't know how to act. Should I resign in protest? I felt a moral need to do something to support Tracey, but organisational politics were also in play.

Baddeley and James (1987) provide a simple model of political behaviour . They divide political behaviours into clever, wise, inept or innocent. These behaviours are then given the descriptive symbols fox, owl, donkey and sheep. The clever fox and the wise owl both understand the context in which they are operating. Both are skilled in dialogue and inquiry; able to gain knowledge about the political environment to inform their actions. The difference is in what actions are taken because of that knowledge. The owl acts with integrity and aims to get the best out of the situation (for all involved) using creativity and imagination, whilst the fox is likely to play games to achieve self-serving aims. This notion of integrity is important to me. What would the wise owl do in this situation?

A consultant colleague, Mark, called me unexpectedly. Mark is from the East End of London, he's full of energy. His hobby is stand-up comedy, performing in local pubs and comedy clubs. Today he was serious; the usual gags were notably absent from our conversation. He told me that his colleagues were writing to the CEO in support of Tracey and implored me to get my colleagues to do the same. We discussed the current state of the organisation; he expressed support for me in my leadership role and we talked about our fears for the organisation.

My initial reaction was to keep my head down, put my "helmet" on and wait for things to settle down. Maybe I could just sign a letter from all of my consultant colleagues and thereby find some anonymity?

By now I had been negotiating with Liz for some months to develop QI capability in the organisation. We were close to signing a deal to bring in some external expertise to help us deliver a Lean training programme. I had been uncharacteristically vocal in senior meetings about the importance of QI and why I wanted to lead it. If I spoke out, would it damage my connection with Liz? If I didn't speak out, would it damage my connection with Tracey and my reputation for honesty and integrity? What move should I make to keep the fuel in the flame and protect it from the wind that threatened to extinguish it?

I decided that I should write to Liz, not as one of a collection of consultants but from me, as an individual in a respected leadership position; an individual with a reputation for honesty and integrity. Leave the helmet behind, take a risk and do what felt to be the right thing.

The letter I wrote was powerful and emotional. It referred to the recent suicide of a colleague who had endured a suspension, and how the exercise of power without care is abusive and cannot create a culture conducive to quality improvement, as it breeds fear. I tried to articulate my respect for Tracey and the work she was trying to accomplish. I sent the letter by email but did not copy in Tracey. I was concerned at how she might receive the email and did not want my intervention to unknowingly harm her case.

The reply from Liz was bland and corporate.

A few days after Liz's reply, I was contacted by the Royal College of Nursing (RCN). They were seeking evidence to support Tracey's reinstatement. Without hesitation, I forwarded them the letter I had sent the CEO.

As spring moved into summer my plans to increase QI capability began to gain momentum. Liz signed off the funding for an external consultant and I worked with a team to organise a programme to train staff in improvement science. As part of this initiative, I organised an engagement event for the Trust board and senior leaders. A PowerPoint presentation would have been in my comfort zone, but I wanted to do something different. I knew some of the attendees had already completed our training course and I needed to keep them engaged and use their experience.

I had primed these audience members that I would ask for some specific feedback about the course, so a bit of back stage activity. I moved around tables with a microphone and was affectionately described as "Jeremy Kyle" (uncharacteristically extrovert!). They all gave resoundingly positive reviews of their experience and articulated what support they needed to make the improvements happen. Liz enthusiastically supported the session and expressed her wish to bring continuous QI to our organisation. To end the event, I shared a story about what I believed was needed from us as senior leaders to keep the QI flame alight. This is that story.

I was on a camping trip with my family. It was an adventure holiday with other families there too and a qualified woodsman. I was given the task of lighting a campfire with only a fire steel, a ball of cotton wool and one sheet of newspaper. Which team could keep the fire alight the longest? I went off into the forest and gathered kindling and dry wood. I assembled a pyramid of kindling around the paper and cotton wool, struck the fire steel and ignited the tinder. The cotton wool and the paper burned but the wood never caught; a breath of wind and the flame was extinguished. So the woodsman showed us what was needed. He gathered two bunches of very fine, dry twigs (imagine the end of a witch's broom) and some larger wood. He made a base for the fire out of small branches and placed the cotton wool on top. He shaped the newspaper into a loose dome and positioned himself facing the prevailing breeze then set light to the cotton wool and placed the newspaper over. As the paper caught alight he held the twigs in the flame and moved the twigs as the wind shifted to ensure that the twigs were always in the flame. When the wind was too strong he would shield the flame and if it was too light he would gently blow. Sure enough the twigs caught and soon there was a roaring fire.

If the twigs are the people who work in the organisation and the flame is a culture of continuous improvement then the wind is the unpredictable combination of factors that influence success or failure: culture, politics, external regulatory pressure, organisational priorities, financial concerns and the like. As leaders, it is our role to provide the spark and keep the kindling in the flame; to notice, predict and react to the winds that seek to extinguish or fan the flames of improvement.

Then I produced a fire steel from my pocket and struck it producing a shower of sparks.

As the summer progressed, my team worked with our external consultancy to train more senior leaders in improvement methods and I took part in the training myself. There had been no word from Tracey and we were still strongly advised not to contact her.

Part of the QI training was the requirement to lead a Rapid Process Improvement Workshop" (RPIW). This is a discrete improvement event based on the Lean process of Kaizen (the Japanese term for improvement that has become part of Lean terminology, to refer to a philosophy of continuous improvement). It is an eight-week period of observation and measurement followed by a one week period of plan, do, study, act (PDSA) cycles leading into a 30-, 60-, 90-day implementation phase.

We needed to identify improvement projects to prioritise. The participants on the training had many ideas for projects, but the executive were focused on CQC improvement priorities. We took the participants' projects and mapped them to CQC priorities. In this way we hoped to retain the enthusiasm of the participants and demonstrate to the organisation the power of improvement science. It felt like a balancing act, a political dance, trying to keep the different interest groups on side and aligned enough for us to maintain momentum, to keep kindling in the flames.

As part of this process I included a project that was of particular interest to me; the care of the acutely ill, deteriorating patient. I needed to choose an improvement event to lead, to complete my training, but the deteriorating patient project was not a specific concern of the CQC. Should I argue my point of view or get behind a different project that met organisational objectives? Another choice point.

Our organisation has a particularly poor record on elective waiting lists with a considerable number of patients waiting more than one year. Chris, the new Medical Director, had identified that this waiting list could be reduced considerably if our day surgery theatres were more efficient. He had a major interest in Lean improvement methods. Chris was a straight-talking, sharply dressed cardiologist from London. He had led the introduction of a Lean organisational programme at a previous organisation, and was keen to tell me what a success this had been. At our first meeting I entered his sparsely decorated office with enthusiasm that he would share my passion for quality improvement methods. However, as the meeting progressed I became increasingly disillusioned. He informed me of his success in applying Lean principles to other health care systems and showed me the 300-page manual on Lean improvement that he had written, but told me that our board were not ready. He asked me if I had produced a "value stream map". When I said no, he suggested I go away and produce one and then we would talk again. I was confused. In my mind we should be team mates fanning the flames, but he seemed to be willing to let the fire go out that I and others had started. In hindsight, I realise that he had a different approach to QI compared to what I had learned on GenerationQ. His focus was on the technical rather than engaging others, more expert rather than relational.

Around the same time the new organisational structures were beginning to take shape. Liz, the CEO, had appointed a new Interim Director of Strategy called Deepak and identified him as the executive sponsor for the organisation's quality improvement function. Deepak had worked in strategy development for a number of trusts, but had little experience of Lean or other QI methods. Deepak was another character with strong opinions. He too had made a career of multiple temporary appointments where he helped turn around organisations and then left. Deepak was very vocal in his opinion that focusing on day surgery was not going to solve the Trust's problem with waiting lists. Chris was not happy with this situation. He was clearly used to running the QI elements of an organisation and was not familiar with having his views challenged. How could I resolve this conflict? Did I need to?

I took some time to reflect on my next move. I needed to keep close to powerful stakeholders to keep the improvement work going. While Deepak had managerial responsibility for the programme, he was in an interim position and his assertions about the future of day surgery seemed uncertain. Chris understood improvement and he was in a substantive post. He seemed to have data to back up his position on day surgery. Therefore, despite the challenges I decided to champion and lead the day surgery Rapid Process Improvement Workshop (RPIW), as I decided it was more important to keep close to Chris since he was the Medical Director. Here again I found myself trying to make the right choice that would keep the improvement work going whilst also keeping myself safe. It felt like walking on a tightrope.

As the pros and cons whirled round in my head, I reminded myself that there was the potential of major organisational benefits from a well-run RPIW in day surgery; patients would benefit from shorter waiting lists; the potential success of this project could highlight the benefits of our approach. Then there were personal advantages – if I personally led this project then I could demonstrate my skills as a leader and increase my ability to negotiate for more improvement capacity. But I still had some internal conflict. In my heart of hearts I believed that the deteriorating patient project would deliver greater benefit to patients: preventing potentially fatal deterioration versus shortening elective waiting lists. However, I had to make a choice and chose to prioritise the day surgery project for now with the hope that it would give me the negotiating power to later focus on the deteriorating patient project.

The day surgery RPIW progressed throughout the autumn. Deepak and Chris became distracted by the need to develop region-wide sustainability and transformation plans; so we were left to get on with the improvement work. There were many challenges along the way, not least getting staff released to take part. Without any form of improvement office, space was difficult and our meetings took place at people's houses or at a nearby leisure centre that rented meeting rooms. Strangely, these unusual and informal settings brought the group together.

The RPIW team consisted of staff from all parts of the day surgery process: surgeons, anaesthetists, nursing staff, receptionists and booking clerks.

Soon we were uncovering where the delays were occurring, but the real power came when very different staff understood how their work impacted on each other. Mr Cheetham , the cynical and bullish surgeon, bemoaned the fact that his lists were often underutilised because of late cancellations. He couldn't understand why patients couldn't be asked to attend at short notice. Shirley, the booking clerk, had never met Mr Cheetham. She talked him through the process. He began to understand that despite all the clinical information on the booking forms there was nowhere to indicate if the patient was willing to attend at short notice. Shirley also talked about a new project being trialled in the ophthalmology theatres using text messaging to reduce last minute cancellations. Shirley phoned a colleague, and before long Mr Cheetham had managed to extend the trial of text messaging to include day surgery.

At the end of the RPIW week we held a "report out". The team set out the current state as described by their observations and the results of their PDSA cycles. The board room was packed; Liz was there but no Deepak or Chris. Although I was the RPIW Lead I chose not to present the work, but rather gave a brief introduction and left it to the team to deliver the message. The power of working outside the usual professional silos was obvious to all. The pride with which the staff presented their own work on improving their own service was humbling. The audience was buzzing and there was excitement in the air; maybe we could make things better round here!

It was a cool but sunny winter afternoon; I was running back to my car. I was late to pick up the kids from school. My phone pinged. It's not unusual for one of the safety team to text me for advice so I had a quick look at the phone. I could call them on the way home. But I didn't recognise the number. It was Tracey:

> Hi, I've been exonerated. I am totally relieved! You will never
> understand how beyond amazing it was for me to receive a copy of
> your email from the RCN! Kept me going! Can't wait to come back and
> crack on with everything. Thank you.

And at an organisational level there are rumours of more changes. Better to keep my safety helmet on for now.

CHAPTER 8

They'll All Die Anyway

Hard to say when it all started because there was no grand plan, but back in 2009, when I was working as a paramedic, loving my job but wanting to do something more, I met a young doctor who changed everything. Ewan Mackie was working in a research group in the local hospital. His research question: When a patient collapses with a cardiac arrest, what difference might change in their core body temperature make to survival rates? What happened if they got too warm? Were they more likely to survive if they were cooled down? I became the ambulance person on the team, collecting the data. I wasn't expecting any great personal benefit from being involved in this. I was just genuinely curious and enthusiastic about the topic. Having been on GenerationQ, I can see now that this is a powerful example of what can happen when you stay connected with what you're really passionate about, without worrying about where it might lead, without having an exact plan. It is what I would now refer to as being willing to be emergent and go with the flow, rather than trying to predict and plan the future.

There's a widely accepted belief amongst the Scottish population that we are an unhealthy nation. We may blame the cold, wet weather, the collective DNA or the diet of chip butties and beer but we've long recognised that we tend to loiter at the bottom of the third division of western countries when it comes to health statistics. Twenty years ago, a clinician called Allan Crowther gave a presentation in Glasgow about Scotland's out of hospital cardiac arrest (OHCA) survival. Only one in twenty people who have a cardiac arrest in Scotland were likely to leave hospital alive. A senior medic in the audience shrugged his shoulders. "They'll all die anyway," he said. His reaction made me want to scream – surely it didn't have to be that way? It's certainly very different in other parts of the world. In the US in Seattle & King County, Washington State, go-home survival rates were 22% in 2013. This is one of the best places in the world to have your OHCA! The European average is around 9% survival. That's almost twice that of Scotland. In Sweden, work has been done across the whole country to get survival rates up from 4.8% in 1992 to 10.7% in 2011.

This is the story of the part I played in helping to shift the culture in Scotland away from accepting the status quo of our poor OHCA survival statistics. It's also a story about how I was able to eventually make some changes to something else that had niggled away at me for ages – the way others, and often paramedics ourselves too, dismiss us as "just" ambulance drivers. To make these shifts, I've had to change my style. Instead of shouting to be heard with no one listening, I've become someone who others are inviting to come and talk.

Back to when I first met Ewan and became involved in his research. I had been working in the Ambulance Service for a good number of years and was aware of the very rigid hierarchy. It's visible in the green uniform that aligns us in some people's eyes with the military rather than the medics. Things are very much dependent on what rank badges and markings you wear. In terms of relationships, the service is quite top down, which is appropriate when the context is a crisis situation. Ewan, though, was refreshingly different from other people I'd worked with. I guess you could say counter-cultural. When he came and talked with me and local ambulance crews about the data we were collecting, he didn't talk down to us. He wasn't setting himself up as someone with expert power. It was much more Adult-Adult, taking us and our experiences seriously. That different stance made a real impact on me. He led in a different way than I was used to. Having him treat me as an equal made me start to see myself differently.

Ewan wrote up the research findings which were published in the *Emergency Medicine Journal*. He had added my name as a co-author, a really generous and unexpected gesture. One day soon after, the phone went. It was Ewan.

"We've been invited to speak to a conference in Birmingham. Do you want to come and co-present with me?" he said.

I was petrified at the thought. I'd never done anything similar before. I didn't have a research background. I hadn't been to university. I wasn't confident in my writing due to the fact that I have dyslexia. I'm at ease leaping out the back of an ambulance or a helicopter in an emergency but hopping up on stage in front of loads of clever people? The thought was horrifying.

"You've got to be kidding!"

But he wasn't. He was serious. Here was an opportunity to develop who I was and what I could do, for me to be 10 percent braver. Ewan coached me on how to present on stage and then after the Birmingham conference, which went well, we became a bit of a double act. More joint publications came out of the partnership and we were even invited to present at international cardiac arrest conferences in Melbourne and Seattle, enabling me to build a bit of a name for myself and build key relationships. These would be crucial a few years later when I was organising a similar conference in Edinburgh. More on that later. Speaking at conferences was, culturally speaking, the sort of stuff paramedics don't normally do. Again, there wasn't a grand plan but through small, incremental steps I was starting to see myself as someone who was able to do more and to have more influence.

I was also trying to gain some traction around building the case for having a Royal College of Paramedics, something else I cared passionately about. It really angered me that Paramedics weren't recognised as Allied Health Professionals. Physiotherapists, occupational therapists, speech therapists all had this recognition. Why not us? I had believed for a long time that a Royal College would help professionalise our service. It would help shift the culture to be more similar to that of other Allied Health Professionals. It would be a powerful signal to others and ourselves that we were taking our skills and experience more seriously. I had a few meetings with officials at the Scottish Government but got nowhere. They didn't seem to get it, or perhaps I didn't get them.

A director's job came up on the executive team of the Ambulance Service locally. I applied. I was confident. Now that I had all that extra stuff like the research and presentations, I felt I could really make a difference...

I didn't get the job. I was utterly gutted.

The fact they had given it to a nurse really bothered me. I didn't understand how they could hire a nurse to professionalise an ambulance service. In terms of trying to shift the culture, what sort of message was that?

I met Jenny, the nurse they'd appointed as Director, about a week after she'd started in the job.

"I'm not going to like you but I'll be professional," I said frostily.

"Well, let's wait and see," she said.

I am pretty sure I didn't give any encouraging body language at this point.

She continued, "Look, I know nothing about the Ambulance Service and I know you didn't get the job. Give me six months."

Later, when I was on GenerationQ, I was introduced to the "drama triangle", which I've found really useful in making sense of my own emotional reactions. The drama triangle describes three characteristic "positions" of victim, rescuer and persecutor. Looking back, I can see that when I applied for the director job, I was viewing myself in the rescuer position – as a paramedic I could be the hero, sort out all the problems in the service and show just how great paramedics were, thus also elevating the status of the profession. When I didn't get the job, I fell straight into the victim role, the voice in my head shouting, "It's not fair", "How could they do this to me, especially after all this extra stuff I've been doing", "And they've given it to a nurse not a paramedic!" And of course, when I met Jenny that first time, I was in full on persecutor mode, angry with her because she had been given the job I thought was mine and punishing her by being rude and stand-offish. Fortunately Jenny, being the mature person she is, didn't get hooked in the drama triangle. She could so easily have gone into victim mode and screamed at me "You aren't being fair. This is your problem, not mine." She could have been angry and gone into persecutor mode, "How dare you talk to me like that. I am your new boss." However, she stayed calm and Adult. I was too emotional at the time to notice that she was role modelling, which was something I had yet to learn. Being "shouty" isn't the only way to respond to situations I now know!

Jenny offered to help me get in to see the right person at the Scottish Government to have another go at getting agreement for paramedics to be recognised as Allied Health Professionals rather than ambulance drivers. She had worked in the Civil Service and knew her way around. She understood the culture and had relationships there. She also had a very different style to me. A couple of days later she said, "We are having a meeting next Thursday at three o'clock." At the meeting there was listening: both sides asked questions and listened without interrupting or getting shouty. By the end, she had negotiated agreement that paramedics could be Allied Health Professionals. I was amazed and delighted at the result but, if I'm honest, I still hadn't really understood that my whole approach, including getting angry, had been part of the stumbling block.

That only started to become apparent when I got into a proper shouting match with one of the full-time officials from the Union. We even offered to "go outside" to sort it out. Afterwards, Jenny reflected with me on what was going on. Basically I was playing the game the same way they were, and so I'd lost any moral high ground by getting into a scrap. I'd also lost any chance of having productive dialogue to find some common ground. The thing is, my frustration used to just boil over and I didn't know how to channel it. With the benefit of hindsight and some fantastic mentors along the way, I can now see that a major factor in my not getting the director job was that I simply didn't have the leadership skills needed.

Two things then happened that have enabled me to develop myself as a leader and shift the culture in Scotland around cardiac arrest. Jenny spotted the advertisement for the GenerationQ leadership programme and encouraged me to apply. She also encouraged me to put myself forward for a secondment at the Scottish Government. To my great surprise I got both.

Now, I love being the hero. Perhaps most paramedics do. I feel it is not that paramedics become certain types of people, it is that certain types of people become paramedics, and that shapes the action culture. I love a crisis and being the go-to guy for the solution. However, being on the leadership programme made me realise that being good at dealing with dramas is what got me here, as a senior paramedic, but it wasn't what was going to get me any further; it wasn't going to help me work with others to deal with deeply complex issues, the kind that are sometimes called "wicked problems".

I have now learned from Jenny, and from being on the GenerationQ programme, that although I cannot control how I feel, or how others make me feel, I can be selective about how I react and respond. This was especially vital when I started the secondment to the Government. Absolute and total culture shock. I'd been leading ambulance crews, on call, highly active, well known to lots of colleagues, wearing uniform, speaking at conferences. When I joined the Government I was just another bloke sitting at a desk in the corner, and after nine or ten months was feeling disillusioned. I felt I had lost sight of my professional identity. I pride myself on being authentic, yet I was feeling that I was becoming less authentic with myself in this position.

I was fortunate that during this time we had a GenerationQ workshop. We were asked to work in pairs, identifying what we were passionate about at a really deep level. We discussed what we wanted to have as the focus of our "Ambition into Practice", and write about in our Masters. After the exercise, my GenerationQ partner gave me written feedback.

> *Intentions*
> *Save More Lives*
> *Want to do it better*
> *Want to be as good as the best*
> *Wants everyone to work TOGETHER*
> *Wants to be the enabler*
>
> (GenerationQ, Cohort 4 2014)

There weren't many words, but it helped me reconnect with my true passion and what really matters to me, my true north. The piece of paper sits in my briefcase today, in case I ever get lost again. It is a reminder to me of how important it is to reach out to someone you can trust when you are feeling low, to share your feelings of vulnerability and get back in touch with what really motivates you.

After the workshop, when I got back to the office (talking about the office rather than the station is another mark of those cultural differences!), I felt a renewed sense of purpose: I would do something to improve Out of Hospital Cardiac Arrest (OHCA). I called up my old mate Dr Allan Crowther and persuaded him to help me put together a document about what could be done to improve the situation. I had now learned that writing papers is the cultural norm in government and the way to start influencing. The document landed at the same time as people were asking questions about investing large amounts of money to provide dentists with defibrillators – was this the best way to improve OHCA survival? Our paper was seen by a senior civil servant called Andrew who asked to meet Allan and me. I wasn't expecting much from the meeting – he was a civil servant after all!

"We can make this into a government strategy," said Andrew enthusiastically.

"Yeah, right," we said.

He said, "No, seriously, we can. Just listen to me." And he ushered us along to meet the then Health Minister.

"How long would it take to pull together a strategy on OHCA for Scotland?" asked the Minister.

I said, "Northern Ireland have been working on one for a couple of years and aren't there yet."

"Could you have something for when we are back from summer recess?" he asked. It was May. I just said "Yes". I knew Allan could do the writing, as he is both a medic and an academic and he had been wanting to hold a big conference to raise the profile of OHCA in Scotland. We realised we could launch the strategy by having a conference and inviting speakers from around the world. In Scotland, senior civil servants can nominate two events a year to be held in Edinburgh Castle. Andrew suggested having the launch event for the strategy at the Castle and inviting the Minister to come along the evening before the conference. And that's what we did...

I know I've said people make assumptions about paramedics, well I had made assumptions about civil servants and their culture. I had thought of them as just administrators rather than as key influencers who could act with speed. I discovered that civil servants are not faceless bureaucrats, but highly skilled at distilling and summarising information. Working with them has also helped me learn how to balance speed with the need to sometimes be measured in response, and to have robust paper trails to provide assurance and to aid communication. I have a far greater appreciation now of the constraints under which Government operates. As a result, I have greater willingness to listen and allow necessary time to involve people, whilst retaining my ability to bring fresh thinking and an action-orientated approach to reach workable solutions.

I've always believed that to be the best, you learn from the best. I'd been to Seattle, I'd been to Copenhagen, and I'd been to Melbourne and seen and heard what was happening there to improve cardiac arrest survival rates. I had built up good rapport with key folk, so I phoned them up and said, "Will you come to our OHCA conference? We're going to launch our Scottish strategy. The Minister's going to be there and I want you to come and help." And everybody came. Their presence built a sense of confidence that it really was possible to improve things.

My role was really being the connector, getting the right people to the right place at the right time, having different conversations and pulling it together to make something happen. Seattle is the best place in the world at resuscitating OHCA. At the conference they didn't say "We know better than you; we are the experts." It was much more like "This is what has worked for us in our context. Your context will be different but we hope this stimulates your thinking." It was a very mature approach to helping us, and they were keen to learn from us too. In fact, they even asked for a copy of our strategy so they could use it!

It wasn't without challenges along the way. After the summer recess the First Minister changed her cabinet, so there was a new Health Minister. I was concerned that our support might vanish but fortunately the new Minister was equally keen. On the night we launched the strategy, she came to the dinner for sponsors and speakers at the Castle and did the opening of the conference the following day. To have real evidence of political support behind the OHCA Strategy was so important for symbolic and practical reasons.

The audience at the conference the next day was probably 30 percent medics and 70 percent paramedics, reflecting a key message that resuscitation needs to take place first outside the hospital. If you keep taking dead people to hospital, then they stay dead. As there is hardly any funding for continuing professional development in the Ambulance Service (another example of cultural differences between health professions), right from the beginning we knew the conference had to be free. We funded it partly from government money that Andrew helped secure and partly from industry sponsors. We were helped by the timing as the Ambulance Services was looking at re-procuring all the defibrillators that year, so suppliers were falling all over themselves and were keen to sponsor the event. The aims

and objectives of the day's conference were:
- To announce Scotland's plan to revolutionise the way we deal with OHCA
- An opportunity to hear some of the best practitioners around the world describe how they have built systems of care to save lives after OHCA
- A chance to join the conversation about saving lives after OHCA in Scotland
- To network with colleagues from across Scotland and elsewhere in the UK
- To inspire and motivate further enhancements in the delivery of care to patients after OHCA.

It was a big next step on the journey to improving OHCA and a clear indication that the culture of tolerating shockingly low figures had ended.

The 300 or so paramedics who came to the conference did so on their own time; we couldn't get them off their rotas. One paramedic drove down from Aberdeen – that's a three-hundred-mile round trip and he had to pay for his own petrol. They came because people join the Ambulance Service to save lives. If there was an opportunity to get better at saving lives, everybody wanted a piece of it. That aspect of the culture needs preserving not shifting. Eventually I'd like to make sure that paramedics on the road get time off or funding to go to conferences the way nurses and doctors do. That's what I'm striving for, but we aren't there yet.

Even though I am learning that leaders don't always have to be out in front, my natural hero tendencies meant I was really keen to play an up-front role on the day and chair one of the sessions, but when I found myself on the stage with two professors I was totally overawed. I felt a bit like a school boy playing football with Pelé and David Beckham. I had given presentations in bigger rooms with bigger audiences, but as a speaker not as the Chair. As the Chair, with no slides as props and not speaking specifically in my area of expertise, I felt uncomfortable and too intimidated by the speakers to challenge them when they went over time – so we were all rather late to lunch.

One of the speakers had to leave early, so I facilitated a workshop session. This felt more comfortable. I could get participation from the group right from the start, asking "Hands up who's from the Ambulance Service? Who's a nurse? Who's a clinician? Who's from the charity sector?" This is a tactic I use often. I asked other questions related to the content as we went along, and if no one answered I would pick on someone with a light-hearted expla-nation – "I'm going to pick you Brenda because I know you...." I tried to give enough silence for folk to offer a response, but then kept up the pace. I always tried to give a reason for why I picked people, reassuring them, because I did not want to make people feel worried that they were going to be chosen next. As I reflect, using humour works well for me as long as I strike a balance and don't end up as the court jester. This is also an example of how I've learned that how I feel and behave as a leader is dependent on the immediate context.

That first Edinburgh conference was an important milestone in shifting the way we deal with out of hospital cardiac arrest in Scotland, but shifting cultures and shifting the recovery rate is going to take multiple different actions by a whole host of people. The following year we ran another conference, but this time with simultaneous satellites in Glasgow, Dundee and Aberdeen so more paramedics could attend. There has been a programme of teaching school children CPR, called "Save a Life for Scotland", and in 2015/2016 over 60,000 people were trained in CPR. The target is half a million by 2020. There have also been changes to resuscitation procedures in ambulances, and to what happens in hospital when patients arrive. It is really satisfying to know that, for instance, the survival rate after OHCA in Edinburgh was around 3% in 2011 and is now consistently over 17 %. For Paramedics, there are even more encouraging figures about their role across the whole of Scotland. In 2011, 288 patients were successfully resuscitated after a cardiac arrest and alive on arrival at hospital. In 2017, the number had more than doubled to 667 patients (Gowens, P. and Sinclair, N. 2017) – wonderful affirmation that they don't "always die anyway". Multiple gestures have thus shifted the culture, if we were going to describe this in complexity terms.

As part of shifting the culture in the Ambulance Service, I and a few others have been introducing some Quality Improvement language. Where we used to talk about just trying stuff, and trial and error, we're now helping people see that this can also be described using the IHI Model for Improvement. Using the right language is important because if staff are speaking to people outside the organisation, or people at the very top of the tree – our exec team – that's the language they understand. It also validates what we are doing as paramedics. The culture is also shifting because now half a dozen paramedics have been on quality leadership programmes and the Patient Safety programme in Scotland, so there are more people talking about quality improvement.

And where does this all leave me personally? Well I used to feel that I was always having to justify the profession or justify myself, so that I had the legitimacy to be in the room even though I didn't have a degree, hadn't gone to university and wasn't a doctor. I always thought I was starting on the back foot, whereas now I feel far more confident. I've found my voice and I'm comfortable. I used to think I had to turn the volume up to be heard, but I now know that's not the case. And you can't turn it off either: you can't sit there and be a shrinking violet. Right tone; right time; know what you're talking about, and ask questions when you don't. I think I was trying too hard, as if I wanted to say "Look, I am really good and I know what I'm talking about, so you need to listen to me." Now I understand that when somebody shouts at you and you put your fingers in your ears it is because it hurts. But when somebody speaks really softly you lean in so you can hear.

I now have a far better understanding of others' perspectives, which makes me more patient with people and less frustrated. I think far more about how I am making people feel rather than just achieving the task, and am more thoughtful in how I react to my own feelings. I know in the past I would just jump into a Parent-Child relationship, giving direct instruction or doing things myself if it was easier or quicker, risking getting into the drama triangle too.

The skill of being a paramedic is getting in fast and doing what needs to be done with calmness and decisiveness under pressure. In this context excessive pondering costs lives. On the street, it does not matter much if you cut off someone's best shirt. In the office, that level of direct action can damage relationships for a long time. No need to shout either. Shifting cultural patterns, challenging stereotypes and assumptions, doing strategic leadership work is a different matter, and requires time to have dialogue and to take others with you.

CHAPTER 9

Leading From the Heart

Leadership is full of surprises, not least discovering, evolving and finally accepting and valuing the kind of leader you eventually become. These next few pages share my story about how I discovered that leading with compassion was the only way for me, and how I have come to appreciate over the course of my career that empathy, kindness and gratitude are powerful but often neglected quality improvement (QI) skills.

I made my first tentative experiment to lead quality improvement in a child and adolescent mental health service many years ago. I felt valued by my colleagues and had a strong sense of belonging to the team. I mention this because I think the secure base provided by the team and the collaborative culture we had at the time was critically important to what happened next.

I remember having a light-bulb moment. A little girl of three or four had been referred into our service. She had witnessed her father murder her mother and was extremely distressed. The referral letter spelt out how traumatised she was, how her remaining family had been affected and how people weren't sure, given her very young age, what to say or do. Hearing about devastating life-changing events like this never fails to motivate NHS staff to want to reach out and help. However we faced a huge dilemma.

We were a very small team with an incredibly long waiting list, one of years not weeks (not uncommon in the UK at that time, where most child and adolescent mental health services were, and still are, underfunded). As we discussed this referral at the team meeting, I looked around at my colleagues and realised we all wanted to do the right thing and offer this girl immediate help, but we had lots of other needy families waiting and our diaries were full. It's hard to describe how this makes you feel as a clinician; you feel very responsible, guilty and impotent. It also makes you feel angry because you want things to be better.

Our system for referral processes stated we could only prioritise her if she met the criteria for an urgent assessment. The trouble was, the prioritisation criteria which would help to make this a fair decision had been written to meet the need of the majority of young people who needed urgent help (typically self-harm, psychosis or risk to others). Nowhere in the criteria did it describe the kind of distress and extreme behaviour this little girl was experiencing, because the criteria were not written with the needs of under-fives in mind. This meant that to do the right thing and see her quickly we had to break the rules of the system, ignore the prioritisation criteria and act as if she was top, rather than at the bottom, of a very long list.

As I looked around the room, every clinician turned their eyes down to their diaries, as if searching for a new appointment space to magically appear. None of us had a free space, but equally we all knew that one of us would offer to see her within a few days. It would mean either personal sacrifice (no lunch or being late home to our own families for example) or by not doing other clinically important, but non-urgent work (record keeping, communication, statutory or mandatory training, audit, for example). Every week we found ourselves with these kind of difficult dilemmas, in a system that we felt we could never get on top of and that was slowly defeating us all.

My light-bulb moment was a simple one. I realised it was simply not enough to strive to be the best therapist I could be, because no matter how hard I worked, if the system was fundamentally flawed it was never going to improve, or as W. Edwards Deming says "A bad system will beat a good person every time" (Deming 2000). As I followed these thoughts through, the penny slowly dropped, that unless we tried to improve the system we worked in we would never be able to provide the kind of child and adolescent mental health service we all aspired to deliver. Once this paradigm shift had happened, I started to see system issues everywhere. It was if someone had lifted the scales from my eyes. I started to pay attention to how many times I had to break the rules to do the right thing, how many times I spotted waste and how often we/I used "rules" to justify "what we do around here", when even 15 miles away I knew that another team did it differently to the same or better effect. I started to notice unwarranted variation and ask myself why this was happening, and what impact it was having on the families we served. I noticed just how many temporary work-arounds we made to accommodate urgent work, whilst also noticing how often we neglected the important but non-urgent tasks of making things better at the root cause.

My next step was to take a one-day introductory course, on how to improve child and adolescent mental health services, where I met two inspiring psychiatrists who worked for the Department of Health. They changed my life. They shared the QI resources they had created and slightly tucked me under their wing, offering me occasional coaching conversations and exposure to their expertise. Without this support, my story might have been quite different, so I am incredibly grateful for their generous leadership.

In the next few weeks I sought out the original texts that their work was based on and began to read about quality improvement, systems and complexity. Joseph Juran (1999) and W. Edwards Deming (2000) became my nightly companions, as I realised they had written about my light-bulb moment, had tangible solutions to problems about flow, and had already figured out theories and solutions. I also discovered that their work was already being applied to health care in some parts of the world. I became curious about why systems-thinking and quality improvement methods had never been taught to me over the course of my eight-year clinical training as a health care professional, when they felt so relevant to my core purpose in the NHS.

Having always been a highly curious and creative person, I have a tendency to dive in deep and get carried away in the flow of learning. I notice that my energy levels increase and I become somewhat consumed with trying to figure out the answers to puzzles. This can happen just as easily at home or work and my family will lovingly recount tales of how they had to peel adolescent me away from a new Tony Hawk skateboard game at 4am on Christmas Day, or gently suggest to six-year-old me that I do a jigsaw in more than one sitting. Psychologists call this excited and preoccupied state "flow" and can see from MRIs when people's brains are active in this way. It is associated with high productivity and personal satisfaction. Being in this state gives me deep joy. I also notice that because I'm an extrovert, I can't contain my enthusiasm and I talk about my discoveries. Luckily for me, one of the many benefits of working in the NHS is that there are lots of fellow enthusiasts to interact with, and other people pick up and amplify my fledgling ideas, adding diversity to enrich and strengthen the approach.

After diving in to quality improvement theory, I told the team I'd had an idea about how we could improve the service and we agreed to all have dinner together to discuss it further (more evidence of how important the team dynamic was to this process). This led to several weeks of discussion about whether or not to act, a growing excitement about how there might be a different way of doing things, and then finally a decision to just give it a go. Ultimately, we felt taking this approach was unlikely to make things any worse, as the situation was already so dire, and maybe, just maybe, we might see an improvement. Our attitude was hopeful: "Why not go out on a limb? That's where all the fruit is." (Original quote attributed to Frank Scully 1950, p. 61.)

We took several months to get to know and improve our system, giving this important task as much vigour as the therapeutic work we did with our patients. We mapped and measured our system, discovering that what we thought we did (referral pathways, team practices, treatment and so on) did not match what we really did. This process of "un-peeling" the reality and revealing the truth was uncomfortable at times. We discovered things about our processes, our system and our own personal habits and patterns that we did not always want to see. Like Oedipus, we had a big shock when we realised what we were really up to! We had to radically accept that we had been doing some things poorly and focus on taking small steps, experimenting with different gestures, towards something better. Maya Angelou nails this when she says "I did then what I knew how to do. Now that I know better, I do better."

When we understood our current systems (as best we could in a pre-digital era), we came up with change ideas and started to do what I now know as plan, do, study, act cycles, making small incremental changes towards a common vision for improvement. We also had to embrace the fact that if we were to improve, we had to stop acting as a collection of individual clinicians and begin to work more effectively as a team.

One of the hardest things we had to do was to give up holding our own individual diaries and instead have a team one. This meant we had to trust each other to allocate work to each other in a fair way. As I write this, I'm aware that this will seem like such a small and simple shift to the external eye, but our team culture had been one where the waiting lists were so long, and the work was so hard, that each person had used their diary to protect their own health and wellbeing from harm. In order to manage their workload and to ensure that they survived another day, diaries had become personal defence mechanisms. Asking the team to give up even a portion of control of their diary was asking them to give away the very thing that had been protecting them and keeping them afloat for years.

I have since learnt that when a lot of emotional heat arises from relatively simple improvement proposals like this, there is no way the change can occur until you understand what is driving the heat. This is the human and psychological aspect of leading quality improvement and, whilst it's fully acknowledged in Deming's lens of profound knowledge, it's often the aspect of QI theory that I feel is most neglected in QI trainings. My experience has taught me that the human and psychological elements of change are the power-house of QI and if not managed well can lead to failure of improvement ideas. QI is not glossy; it's messy, it forces you to notice the world around you and accept some hard home truths. Psychologically it's easier to blame an anonymous system for failures than accept that you *are* the system and that your individual input matters. Often it's painful to realise how long you have been working in an unhelpful way, perpetuating unhelpful patterns of behaviour, whilst believing you were doing the right thing. Equally, it's hard to hold people to account when their performance or attitudes are problematic to the team.

When we were able to reflect and understand why giving up our diaries was worrying to us, we were able to make the change to a joint diary and agree ways in which we could measure to see if the change was OK. I have found that measurement is key to successful change in emotionally charged situations. Measurement helps you to know when a change is an improvement and when you should stop the change because it's not working. It's like a compass. It helps you to carry on prototyping and refining ideas and acts as a logical balance to the emotion of change..."So you fear X will happen? OK, how about we measure X to see if you are right? If you're right, we'll stop straight away." There is something really important about using transparent measurement to test fear, because often it is only fear, habit or lack of consensus that is holding us back from changing. It becomes a way of reinforcing the benefits of collective decision-making and growing group trust. Measurement also helps groups to mark and celebrate key moments of success, triggering a moment of reflection and joy because you know your change idea is working.

To my surprise and delight, after nine months of exceptionally hard work and dozens of small tests of change, I could see and *feel* a huge difference in our team. The waiting list had dropped from years to under 10 days. Not only that, I noticed that we were happier, patient satisfaction scores were higher, we all felt more effective and had cut out lots of waste. Thinking and attending to the system I worked in and contributed to helped me to feel better about my job. I was more hopeful and felt more in control. As a team we had released more time to care for patients, but also to better look after ourselves, and so our sickness rates decreased, adding yet another improvement to our productivity. We were doing less work-arounds and we had improved systems in place to deal with urgent clinical issues. As a consequence it felt much less stressful.

Why am I telling you this story? I'm telling it because it captures my approach to embedding quality improvement; for me it's always been a deeply human and personal process. Yes, it's about equipping people with helpful knowledge, tools and methods, but it's equally about putting your own heart into the work. This happens through investing in relationships with colleagues, owning your flaws, involving patients and staff in co-production, encouraging ideas, positive disruption and striving towards things that we discover matter to us all. It is also about taking a decision that you, (not someone else) will do this; you will step up to the plate. It is also a signal that you are resiliently prepared to try something new that might succeed or might fail. Leading QI in this committed and deeply personal way has taught me that grass roots direct action works when we have a common vision, a collective will and a way to track and celebrate our successes. I strongly believe that QI is a "team sport" and that in health care it often sits best in the clinical microsystems nearest to the patient, where it adds significant value to patient experience.

I have also realised, time and again, that many clinicians falsely believe that they have to ask permission to do QI, or falsely see the responsibility for system change being the weighty duty of managers rather than the collective responsibility of everyone who works, uses and pays for the NHS. I have learnt over the years that as a leader I am comfortable with speaking up and challenging illogical nonsensical rules, habits and norms that are out-dated and no longer represent best care. I believe in "responsible rule breaking" or "disruption with a purpose". This is not a process of hostile or destructive rebelliousness, but a healthy challenge or provocation in situations where active experimentation is required to find a new way of doing things. On several occasions I have gently questioned why a rule or habit exists only to discover that its origins are lost in time or, even worse, that the main reason for doing it has now gone. In one of my roles I noticed teams were being asked to deliver a report full of metrics every month to headquarters. Each report took the manager up to four hours to produce. My question was "Why are we collecting this and what use are we putting the data to?" It turned out that this report had evolved from a distant Department of Health request, was no longer needed and in fact hadn't been needed for the past five years! Interestingly, even in a situation like that, when it's barn-door obvious that something needs to stop, it's sometimes not easy convincing people they can do things differently and can stop following a rule or a norm they have been accustomed to. Change is not always a positive experience; it can sometimes make people anxious or angry. Yet change is essential when we work in very complex systems that require us to consistently re-check the relevance and purpose of our actions.

Continuously promoting the habits, norms and culture of improvement in an organisation is the toughest part of QI leadership. The challenge is to find ways to help people realise that everyone's smallest actions and gestures make a difference to whether you have an improvement culture or not. I recently walked into the staff toilet and saw that a colleague had placed a post-it note on the empty soap dispenser with a hand-drawn (and rather talented) picture of a person with a grumpy face and a message saying "Empty". The effort of creating and placing the post-it note was probably equal or greater to that of walking to the nearby cleaning cupboard and replacing the soap. This is a great example of what I think of as a cultural "micro-flag"; the tiny, but powerful, conscious or unconscious gestures that we all make every day in our workplace. These gestures are often emotion laden and collectively help to form and communicate the local culture. Micro-flags can be deeply subtle and hard to detect, or glaringly neon-yellow apparent.

Each of us has a choice about whether or not to work on the types of micro-flag we leave in our workplace for our colleagues or patients to find. We can do that consciously as a leader, by deliberately trying to plant positive micro-flags as a leadership gesture and seeing the response they generate. We can also try to work on how to discover and adjust our unconscious micro-flags, by seeking out feedback and constructive challenge from peers, coaches and mentors to increase our awareness of the impact that our non-verbal or unplanned micro-flags have on the teams/organisations we lead. With external support and internal reflection we can notice our own repeated behavioural patterns and try to improve ourselves. Equally each person discovering another person's micro-flag also has a choice, to ignore it, react badly to it, amplify its effect through agreement, or to compassion-ately challenge it. This process is massively affected by the culture of the organisation, because if an open and transparent or "just culture" prevails, the spirit in which this is done can be very different to the way it operates in a "blame culture".

I have learnt how hugely important it is, as an improver, to pay attention to micro-flags and the reactions they evoke, as they often act as a litmus paper to illustrate elements of the wider culture. I find that using quality improvement tools, like experience based co-design and emotion-mapping processes with staff and patients, helps to surface the emotional touch points in the health care journey. You can then use this feedback as an emotional Pareto chart to determine where and how you should start to do improvement work that will have the greatest psychological impact.

It's really important as a team to notice and then be curious about habitual behaviours and patterns. Asking "Why do we do it this way?" in a non-blaming and curious way helpfully reveals deep insights into the team culture, habits and norms. Stephen Covey quotes "Between stimulus and response, there is a space. In that space is our power to choose our response. In our response lies our growth and our happiness" (Pattakos 2007, p. vi). QI in the NHS is essentially a journey towards establishing an improvement team culture in the clinical microsystem, where we try hard to make positive responses and choices in a consistent way and are curious and open about what diverts us from our improvement aim.

When I reflect back on my first experience of QI, I realise that several factors helped to make it successful. Firstly, we were a small team, making small incremental changes to a system we knew really well and none of our initial changes required huge managerial input or financial resources. Secondly, because we were working in a "Cinderella" NHS service that received little attention, we had a high level of freedom to act and also had a strong sense that if we didn't act, no one else would.

What interests me now as a leader of quality improvement is why did we make the move to evolve in that way rather than stay as we were or, even worse, give up (easily done in those circumstances)? What motivated us to change?

I think it was all about hope. Despite how bad things were I still held onto a hope that things could get better. I wasn't so burnt out or depressed that I had given up. I wanted and believed we could make a difference and I had a very strong driver for change; I did not want any other child to have to wait as long for help. Hope was my micro-flag and I planted it in the team and asked others to plant theirs next to mine too. We became a team that invested in and farmed hope, turning hopeful ideas into tangible reductions in the waiting list through the use of a clear quality improvement methodology and measurement system. It was a combination of logic and passion; the improvement science helped to structure and organise our response, but it was our hearts that led us to want to do it in the first place.

I think my role in it all was to be an "enthuser", somebody who celebrates good ideas, enjoys encouraging people to join in with collective design and prototyping processes and then has the energy and determination to follow through and make it happen. I am deeply motivated by knowing that my work makes a difference to people's lives. I have therefore always been keen to collect data that highlights the view of patients, carers and key stakeholders. I realised early on that it was not enough to show that we had improved the system purely from our perspective as staff members, if we had failed to actively seek out what "good" looked like from a patient, carer or stakeholder perspective in the first place and had measured progress against this aim. I realised it was great to have improved waiting list times and patient access, but we couldn't assume that we had improved patient outcomes and experience too.

As this realisation dawned, I started to try and work in a very different way with patients and staff by blending co-production techniques with quality improvement methodologies. I hit the books again, but discovered that blending these two methodologies was an undeveloped area (something that is happily now changing). I decided to try to incorporate both theories and reached out for help from the mental health and patient leader communities where a lot of expertise in co-production existed.

I will leave academic definitions of co-production to one side, but say that for me co-production is about trying to re-balance power, autonomy and trust in the relationships between health care providers and those with lived experience of illness and the health system. It's about equally valuing people's experience and expertise in living with an illness or a condition as well as valuing evidence, treatment and clinical knowledge and it's about acknowledging that health care is only one tiny component of how a person lives well. It can deepen the effectiveness of the customer voice in quality improvement methods and ensure that health systems are better informed by patient and carer experience.

Co-production is a powerful quality improvement process for generating empathy, reminding staff working in the NHS that they, or those that they love, are also likely to experience being a patient at some point in their lives. When you are ill, it's likely that you feel more vulnerable than when you are well. You may feel less able to be assertive and will probably put up with things that you wouldn't do in better circumstances. Co-production helps remind staff what this experience is like. It illustrates the system from all sides and brings attention to areas for improvement.

Last week, when swapping hats and being a patient for 30 minutes, I had to take my clothes off. As I undressed a nurse barged through the door without knocking, saw me naked and temporarily exposed me to other patients in the corridor. It was somewhat embarrassing and I won't lose sleep over it, but I will remember it more than any other element of my care that day. I'm sharing it because it exemplifies that quality of care and patient experience metrics often lie in those tiny moments. They are the emotional touch-points of the patient journey, and if we ignore them then we fail to see their potential impact on the overall experience of care. They are also the moments when, as a health care professional, you have the choice about what kind of micro-flag you leave in that patient's hands. Will you leave them with something that enhances or depletes, is compassionate or unkind, treats them like an individual or a number? As it happens, that kind but busy nurse apologised to me, made me feel OK and helped me empathise with why she was in a rush. We recognised each other's humanity and had a laugh together. It left me feeling warm and valued, but if she hadn't recognised the impact of her actions on me, I'm sure I would have felt very differently.

Improvements can often occur when we understand where emotional touchpoints like this congregate or repeat frequently in an organisation; the unfriendly reception area, the MRI waiting area where there's no place to put the jug of water you are told to drink, the clinic where it is the norm to talk about you as if you were not there, the staff team that feels bullied... Leaders have to be able to understand and genuinely engage with these emotional elements of health care and affirm the pain of people's poor experience of care or employment in the NHS. Equally important is learning from what is going well and using appreciative inquiry to understand what behavioural micro-flags help to spread good practice.

I think my interest in helping to surface these voices of experience stems from working for so many years with children and with people with a learning disability, where often power dynamics and inequality prevent opinions, views or ideas from being sought or heard. Genuine active listening is a really hard skill to acquire, but is key to co-production, as you have to "dial down" your own internal view of the system in order to facilitate an open conversation with patients and carers about what they see, hear and feel.

> *The heart of dialogue is a simple but profound capacity to listen.*
> *Listening requires we not only hear the words, but also embrace,*
> *accept and gradually let go of our own inner clamouring. This means*
> *listening not only to others but also to ourselves and our own*
> *reactions.* (Isaacs 1999, p 84)

A wide range of pro-active co-production methods exists to help the system have a dialogue and listen to its customers and to gather in their experience of it. These techniques can illuminate the emotional touchpoints of care and generate improvement ideas. My first large scale attempt to combine co-production techniques with quality improvement theories started in 2011 when I helped to co-create a recovery college.

A recovery college is a peer-led educational approach to support people with mental health difficulties on their recovery journey, where recovery is a set of personally defined goals to improve wellbeing and live well in the presence or absence of one's mental distress (Meddings et al 2014a). Recovery colleges provide courses and educational workshops to teach people the skills to support recovery from mental illness and stay well. Through developing knowledge and life skills, students are able to learn more about their condition and treatments, and gain the power and resilience to get the most out of life. Recovery colleges aim to enable people to "... discover who they are, learn skills and tools to promote recovery, find out who they can be, and realise the unique contribution they have to offer" (Ashcraft as cited in Perkins et al 2012, p. 2).

A group of people with lived experience of mental illness helped to co-create the college alongside staff from the NHS, adult education and third sector charities (Burhouse et al 2015). The team developed the course using the latest academic evidence based on mental health treatments, in combination with personal testimony of what had helped and practical resources showing how to deal with difficult situations like panic attacks, suicidal thoughts, low self-esteem, poor self-care etc. The richness of the curriculum was staggering; a product so much more valuable than if it had been produced by health care professionals alone. After further refinements students define this approach as one where:

> We learn for ourselves how to rebuild, re-focus or enhance our lives. We change the relationships we have with health practitioners from them being in charge and 'on top' to them being 'on tap'. Where we are recognised as the experts in our condition, and use our shared experience to learn from each other through co-production and co-delivery. (Recovery College student body 2015)

The college employed two peer trainers to deliver the course. The peer trainers had lived experience of mental health difficulties alongside a wide range of teaching skills and techniques. When the course ran five months later I was struck by how personally invested I had become. I saw first-hand how the peer leaders demonstrated empathy and taught the evidence in a way that felt deeply personal. The course blended different learning styles, so that it was cerebral, pictorial and kinetic and invited people to practise changing their coping mechanisms and approaches to long-standing issues. It complemented traditional mental health treatment but also challenged some of the traditional power structures; patients became students and the peer leader's own personal testimony was valued alongside knowledge gained from academic research; wellbeing was discussed as much as illness.

Fifty students undertook the first cohort and 94 percent of them felt more hopeful about life at the end of the six-week course. Other outcomes were amazing too. Many people went back into education or employment, people needed less support from secondary mental health services and many described improvements in how they felt about themselves, how they managed their impulses to self-harm, how they cared for themselves when in distress, and how they accepted help from others more readily and generally felt more confident to offer help in return.

One student, Vida, (I'm changing all students' details and creating example vignettes to preserve anonymity) was in her fifties and had come to the college because she had been depressed and anxious for most of her life. She had struggled to hold down a job and felt that life was passing her by. Using the recovery approach, Vida started to think about what she really loved to do and where her strengths might lie (it's so easy to forget this when you are depressed). One day Vida came to the course with a poem she had written about her mental health. She read it to the student group. It was rich with imagery, powerful and emotive. It blew people away. Several students affirmed Vida's experience of mental health and provided an empathic response, but in addition, many people commented on how technically brilliant the poem was. Vida had a real way with words. When people asked about whether she had ever been published, she admitted she had and that her real dream was to run creative writing workshops to help other people express themselves. Vida explained that her low self-esteem and high levels of social anxiety meant that she'd never had the nerve to try it. Fellow students encouraged her to have a rethink and maybe experiment with having a go.

At the end of the Recovery College course we hold a Space Day that is co-created by the cohort of students to provide skill-sharing workshops to offer extended learning opportunities. Vida decided to volunteer to run a creative writing workshop. This sentence makes it sound so easy and yet had you been there you would have seen just how monumental this decision was and what effort it took. Despite her nerves, Vida delivered an excellent session. It was a deeply moving experience. A visiting senior NHS leader and I had to wipe a tear away from our eyes. Moments of intensity like this are precious, they teach us that what we do in health care really can have a profound impact. Afterwards Vida reflected that she had passed through a Rubicon, she had challenged her inner doubt and overcome a great fear. At the graduation ceremony several months later, I asked Vida what impact the Recovery College had had on her. Vida told me that she had already delivered other workshops and was beginning to feel that this was becoming a key part of her recovery. She hoped that one day it could become a livelihood too.

This way of working has a deep influence on the staff involved in it too. One student, Shilpa, was taking accountancy exams but couldn't finish her qualification because no one would offer her a work placement that made reasonable adjustments for her severe depression. A finance lead in the Trust, Sarah, heard about her plight and not only found an NHS placement for Shilpa, but also set up a system so that other students in a similar situation could have this opportunity too. No one had asked Sarah to do this, it was her intrinsic motivation to want to contribute that led the way. Sarah's actions demonstrate the huge potential the NHS could have if it chose to create opportunities for recovery as a large employer and volunteer centre.

The qualitative and quantitative results of the Recovery College were outstanding. The independent evaluation showed that people felt the course had changed their lives for the better. Never have I felt so proud and humble, knowing that none of my efforts equalled that of the students and peer trainers. For instance a student, Vicky, was initially too frightened to attend the college on her own, so came with her family. Vicky has autism and social anxiety and had never been to a community social group before. By week three Vicky was attending independently, spoke up in group situations and on the Space Day made her cohort of students the most delicious home-made cakes, alongside giving each person one along with a personalised message about how she felt about them. Her family were amazed and Vicky said it was the first time that she felt she had made some friends. There are no easy ways to measure the impact of these type of life-changing outcomes, but unless we try to get better at capturing these moments we run the risk of dismissing work like this because it has no evidence base.

Using QI to help support health, resilience and recovery has become a strong part of my improvement approach. I have a deep commitment to this way of working, but I know it doesn't suit everyone and appreciate that co-production and patient experience initiatives can appear too "touchy-feely" or distracting for some. Other people can find the process draining and exhausting, and some have no interest whatsoever in the emotional components of health care, arguing strongly for the benefits of dispassionate neutrality. I guess at this point we just have to agree to differ. Even if I require a health care worker to undertake a highly technical intervention that requires concentration and logic, I still want them to remember that I am a person and treat me with compassion.

Most resistance to this approach tends to come from people who feel scared about how to do this, or who are frightened that patients will "ask for the impossible" in times of resource scarcity. That has not been my experience at all. I find great joy in co-production; it has never been scary and I have never found that patients and carers are asking for unreasonable improvements. Just the opposite in fact! Critics often say co-production slows things down and that there isn't always time or money to explore multiple approaches. I love it when people used to focusing on processes and costs are surprised that co-production can also decrease waste and costs, or save time in the long run because a root cause has been unearthed.

Co-production often takes me in directions I would never have imagined. It also helps me to see the system through multiple lenses. As a result, I have learnt as a leader not to be afraid to comment on the emotional temperature of the meeting, have the difficult conversation, or be the one talking about feelings, even when I know that the NHS has traditionally valued processes and cost more than experience of care. Sometimes I see tangible relief in people when difficult emotions are named and unspoken atmospheres or barriers to change are explored.

I hope that we will go on to find ways to innovate in health, not just illness and promote healthy lifestyle choices using epi-genetics, bio-technology and digital wearables to radically reshape the way that patients structure and drive their own care. The reality is that most patients already have the power to tweet or post an instant picture of their care in real-time and this is already changing the traditional power dynamics between the patient and health care professionals. No longer will patients put up with being given little knowledge or involvement in their care, being treated as if they shouldn't know what's going on. The repeated emotional micro-flags each professional chooses to leave with the patient will become more obvious, as collective comments on social media about an individual health care professional's treatment of them continue to grow. Already, patients tell me they have Googled me before the first appointment and one mother said of a colleague, "I'm not letting my daughter go and see her; did you see the photos of her on Facebook on her friend's hen night?"

In my view, this means the social and emotional elements of care will become even more important drivers for health care improvement. I can see a time when patients will choose their provider of health care not just based on metrics about clinical success rates, but also on sophisticated triangulated patient experience measures and on how successfully a health care service helps them back on the path to wellness and recovery. My hope and belief is that all of us who work in the NHS and social care will respond positively to this new era and will embrace the greater transparency, the flatter hierarchies and the innovative co-production it could bring.

Recently I stood at the front of a room full of 250 NHS staff, opening a training day in QI. I do this regularly and the demand for training is growing all the time. The "hope behind the headlines" for me is that quality improvement methods are becoming much more mainstream in the NHS than when I started out on my own QI journey. Nowadays the chances of finding someone to support or coach you through your first improvement work are higher. It's less lonely too. You can connect with a wide network of improvers through social media, social networks and through leadership programmes. Even co-production and patient experience measures are becoming more familiar concepts in the QI world. We now have many more people who understand what quality improvement is; but we need many more who know how to apply these skills in practice and we need researchers interested in the messy world of complexity, who can help us learn how to keep improving our approach in the NHS. I worry that the way QI is often being taught focuses too much on QI tools and measurement techniques and misses out on the importance of the psychological elements of improvement. I hope that appreciation of this will grow as people's experience of implementing QI increases.

Health care is personal. It impacts on you and me and those we love. As leaders we can choose to ensure it remains personal by leading with our hearts as well as our minds. We can do this by planting as many compassionate micro-flags as possible throughout our organisations and by encouraging patients and staff to plant theirs too. Together we will make a difference.

Bridging the Divides

In this section, we highlight a further theme that emerges from the Fellows' stories, that of *reaching out*. The stories tell of leaders reaching out to foster connection, co-operation and collaboration across boundaries in order to bridge some of the divides that exist in our health and social care systems.

The divides highlighted in the stories include:
- The divide between professional "tribes", such as clinicians and managers
- The divide set up by hierarchies and power structures, for example between those at the top and the bottom of organisations
- The divide between different departments and diverse organisations who need to work together to deliver high-quality care

Bridging the divides is not straightforward or easy. It requires working across different cultures and sub-cultures which, as described in Chapter 2, both "define and divide us". For leaders it requires more than shifting their local culture to be more inclusive and tolerant of difference. It often challenges their own sense of identity, requiring them to step out from the comfort of their own tribe and see themselves as, for instance, not "just" a clinician but a clinician *and* corporate manager.

The following stories suggest that what is required from leaders to bridge the divides is rarely about making structural changes, even though that is often the dominant, "quick fix" solution. Instead, it is about individual leaders making small but significant moves to shift and build relationships; to reach out to understand others more; to learn to stand in others' shoes;

to demonstrate empathy and see the world from others' viewpoints. As they do so, you will read about leaders struggling to let go of control; finding it hard to admit their own vulnerability; acknowledging they cannot be a hero, and allowing themselves to challenge some of their own deeply held assumptions. Sometimes this requires leaders to really pay attention to their own personal patterns, which is not always easy and takes persistence and resilience.

There are four stories in this section:

- The first, *Seeing Through the Eyes of Another*, tells the story of a clinician choosing to improve, rather than fuel, difficult departmental relationships
- The second, *Now for Something Completely Different*, is the story of a consultant who steps into a corporate role and helps both doctors and managers see each other and the context differently
- The third, *Choosing Wedlock over Deadlock*, tells the story of co-leading a three-way merger
- And fourth, *Quietening the Wind* tells the story of shifting the culture of a network from one of competition to one of collaboration

CHAPTER 10

Seeing Through the Eyes of Another

*The only true voyage of discovery... would be not to visit strange lands
but to possess other eyes, to behold the universe through the eyes of
another, of a hundred others, to behold the hundred universes that
each of them beholds, that each of them is.*

Marcel Proust
Remembrance of Things Past
Vol 5, *The Prisoner* 1923

Not a good start

The very first time I met Julian, who was to become my boss, was during my
interview for the Clinical Director position in my department. Julian had
only arrived two weeks previously as the newly appointed Care Group
Manager, joining us from a similar role in Scotland. We were in the middle
of a restructure in which the care groups were each to be led by a group
manager and a group medical director. As part of this reorganisation, the
clinical lead position I already held was to have additional responsibilities
incorporated, and to be re-badged as Clinical Director.

When I turned up for the interview I was feeling quietly confident, perhaps
overly so with the benefit of hindsight. My colleagues and others in the
Trust seemed to feel I had done well in the Clinical Lead role for the previous
three years, and I was the only applicant. Colleagues told me they didn't

want the stress, responsibility and additional work the role brought. As the only applicant, I suppose I had assumed that the interview was a formality, and I approached it more as a contracting opportunity about what support I could expect from the new care group management team, as well as to discuss what they in return could realistically expect from me in the eight hours per week allocated to the role. I felt I answered the questions in the interview well, demonstrating a good understanding of where I thought we could improve in the future. I also explained the help I thought I needed to be able to manage such a large department of 40 consultants effectively as well as introduce new quality initiatives.

At the end of the interview, I was asked to stand outside the office while Julian and the Care Group Medical Director discussed what to do. In the subsequent feedback to me Julian said he wasn't happy. He said he felt I was "holding a gun to his head"– that if I didn't get the resources I had requested (including a deputy I had asked for) I would blame him for any of my failures to achieve care group objectives. He said he had considered three options: (i) not offering me the role, (ii) offering it to me with a probationary period, or (iii) offering it to me outright. He then said that after careful thought he was going for option three and would offer it to me outright.

I was confused, and I was also seething. I felt completely unappreciated for the work I had done for the last three years as Clinical Lead – essentially the same job as the one I had interviewed for. I was tempted to decline the offer of the new post and simply go back to be a regular clinician; work which I found frankly easier than leading the largest department in the hospital. However, I decided instead to accept the post, to try and stay calm and remain in an Adult frame of mind, using Transactional Analysis terms, as hard as that was at the time. Being frank again too, I was midway through GenerationQ, a leadership development programme and I needed the post to give me material to reflect upon and write about for my remaining assignments.

However, the episode left me wounded and feeling isolated from, and unsup-ported by, both my immediate line managers. It reminded me how small and yet significant gestures from others, particularly others who have power over me, can sometimes make me feel undermined and "less of myself".

Relationships in the care group

Perhaps unsurprisingly, after this bad start, my personal relationship with Julian remained difficult. Our leadership styles were very different too which didn't help things. Julian seemed to have a strong preference for a directive style, very much "push" rather than "pull". He was, in my view, at times both aggressive in his body language, using inappropriate hand signals, and disrespectful in his use of labels, calling more junior staff "blockers" in public meetings. He also seemed to find any challenge difficult and quickly appeared defensive. Several interim project managers were appointed, new to the organisation on temporary contracts and not well placed to directly challenge him. As one of my consultant colleagues observed, "He has appointed 'yes' people all around him."

In this context, talk began to emerge amongst my colleagues that we were not achieving our targets because of poor leadership from Julian and the Care Group Medical Director, Simon. There was a real divide emerging between the level above me, inhabited by Julian and Simon, and the rest of us and they began to become an easy target to blame. Some of my clinical director colleagues even spoke in private of a vote of no confidence in Julian's leadership, but took it no further. One senior clinician resigned from his leadership role as he said he was unable to work with Julian. I was clearly not the only person in the care group who was having a difficult interpersonal relationship with him.

My leadership journey

I had enjoyed my first three years in a leadership role. I was appointed at a time of significant financial pressure within the NHS in general as well as within my hospital Trust. At times it was hard work. I found the necessary difficult conversations emotionally taxing and sometimes I felt as if I were trying to push a heavy weight uphill. Quality improvement work, however, gave me a real sense of satisfaction and a sense of purpose in addition to my clinical work. Increasingly, I began to recognise that I was leading by trial and error, leaning heavily on intuition, and so decided the time was right to embark on some personal leadership development of my own. I applied for and was accepted on the GenerationQ programme.

Through the programme I began to examine myself in detail. My self-awareness and ability to choose my behaviour grew. I came to understand better my personal patterns and how these may at times serve me well and at other times be my Achilles heel, reducing my effectiveness as a leader. How, for example, I sometimes doubt myself and look for affirmation from those around me, and in so doing may neglect their needs. The seeds of the early difficult pattern in my relationship with Julian!

Yet, despite all this personal development, still I found myself often in the same situations, with the same pressures as before. At times it felt as if the context and the culture were stuck. For many of the changes happening in the care group, I felt at times torn, pressured or squeezed between the competing demands of my line managers (Julian and Simon) and those who reported to me (my consultants, nurses and other team members). This was a recurring pattern and theme throughout my efforts to lead, and will probably be familiar to you in your leadership role. I found myself in the middle, seemingly trading off one set of agendas against another, trying to satisfy both parties, never able to square the circle: trying to represent the views of my colleagues *to* the Care Group Management Team about change, and reciprocally trying to drive through change *from* the Care Group Management Team. I began to feel more isolated at work, and I was worried I was taking this pressure into my family life. No one else I asked seemed to know how to deal with this. Previous clinical directors said my role was to represent the views of my consultant colleagues upwards (the notion of a union representative came to mind). Conversely, senior leaders in the organisation told me my role was a corporate appointment and I should use my influence to ensure the department was aligned with corporate objectives (this sounded like coercion). How to bridge this divide in the hierarchy? Sometimes it felt like trying to mediate two warring tribes; hard work and with no meaningful exchange or dialogue apparent between the two.

I asked myself why these habitual patterns of behaviour were so difficult to break free of, despite my growing self-awareness and developing leadership skills. I wondered if it was perhaps not me, but the culture and relationships at work which were inviting me to make similar gestures again and again, resulting in the same old stuck pattern. I asked myself how I might work better with others whom I may not particularly like or admire, or those whom I had judged to be inadequate in some way and had mentally dismissed. How could I break free of my mindset, set my prejudices to one side, and liberate *our* relationships in the service of patients? If I could see the patterns of behaviour in me and in the way I relate to others anew, then I wondered whether this might invite a different response, and increase both my effectiveness at work, and that of my team.

For Julian and me, our combined power to lead change had been diminished because of our poor relationship. I had personalised much of my view of Julian. Wounded by that first encounter, I had judged him, evaluated him, and questioned his competence. I had also been part of perpetuating a negative narrative about his leadership within the care group. Was it fair of me and other clinical leaders in the care group to blame all our failures to meet targets on the senior leadership team? Was it fair to cast him as Persecutor and us as Victims? Slowly, and it did take some time, I began to ask myself to what degree we were all responsible for the relationships between us. Perhaps, I thought, if I could change my relationship with Julian, could I help us both to lead more effectively? One of the many things that I had learned on the programme is that we cannot change the other, we can only change ourselves. The time had come for me to really look closely at myself and ask what I might do differently.

At about this time, fortuitously (or maybe it was synchronicity), one of the books we were given to read on GenerationQ was by Barry Oshry. His book, *Seeing Systems* (2008), became important in helping me to understand some of these relational dynamics.

Oshry's basic premise is that organisations are composed of "tops", "middles" and "bottoms". Individuals experience and behave in organisations because of *where* they are in the system rather than *who* they are. At times, then, I am not a middle but instead behave as a bottom or as a top, depending on the context I find myself in. When I am with a junior doctor in my department she may consider me a top; when I am with the Chair, or CQC, I may feel like a bottom. However, irrespective of who we are, our tendencies to behave and experience emotion are driven by our place in what he calls the "system".

Secondly, Oshry suggests we tend to over-privilege the significance of our experiences to us as individuals. We read meaning into events in a very personal way. For example, I may have interpreted Julian's decision for not providing me with more resource for my role as a personal rebuff ("He doesn't believe me!" or, "They don't appreciate my hard work") when he and Simon were under pressure from *their* line managers not to increase expenditure for other than front-line services. In that sense, I was seeing him as a top but he (and Simon) could also be viewed as middles themselves. This way of seeing helped me to empathise with both my line managers and to see things a bit more from their perspective.

Was this what was happening to me when repeatedly finding myself in similar difficult situations, especially with Julian? I wondered if I could use this understanding to positively change my relationships with others and to reach out to them. This theory also became important to me in giving me some personal resilience, as I will explain later.

Becoming more appreciative

Appreciation:
1) Recognition and enjoyment of the good qualities of someone or something
2) A full understanding of a situation

Oxford English Dictionaries

At about this time, I had also become interested in the power of making appreciative gestures to build relationships, and to shift the local culture to be more conducive to quality improvement. My organisation had adopted an almost exclusively deficit-based approach to improvement. We had critical incident reporting, root cause analysis, serious untoward incident investigation, and even a weekly meeting, chaired by one of the executive team, which acted upon failures of care.

> Appreciative Inquiry is the study of what gives life to human systems when they function at their best. This approach to personal change and organisational change is based on the assumption that questions and dialogue about strengths, successes, values, hopes and dreams are themselves transformational. In short, Appreciative Inquiry suggests that human organising and change at its best is a relational process of inquiry, grounded in affirmation and appreciation.

(Whitney and Trosten-Bloom 2010, p. 1)

I had read a little about appreciative inquiry as a method for improvement, and I began to experiment with specific appreciative gestures to others. I was impressed with the power a seemingly small gesture may have. For example, at the end of one particularly long twelve-hour operating list, I asked the team if we could have a debrief. The nurses began with talking about what had not gone so well, with rather downcast body language, drooping shoulders and looking down. I chose this as the moment to experiment. When it was my turn to speak, I praised each of them individually for a specific thing they had done that day which had improved a patient's experience (such as being a reassuring hand-holder), or which had enabled the list to run smoothly with no patient cancellations. The change in their body language was as instant as it was surprising. They were so thankful, and so energised, they looked ten feet taller! I overheard Helen say as she walked down the corridor for home a few minutes later, "That debrief was really good. I'm actually looking forward to coming to work tomorrow to do it all over again!" It made me wonder how the care each of them would deliver the next day had been changed by just one conversation.

It struck me then that being appreciative meant more than thanking people. It was also about empathising with another's point of view, their position, their pressures, their anxieties and concerns. Could I use this to liberate my strained relationship with Julian? Could I make a gesture that would start to shift the stuck pattern we were in?

It was during a meeting about the pre-operative surgical pathway that I first made an appreciative gesture to Julian, specifically thanking him for his useful interventions during the meeting. This was not easy for me in view of our history, but I was utterly genuine in what I said to him. This was not a cynical or manipulative gesture on my part. I was not being a Fox; I really meant what I said. I was surprised in the following days to notice Julian also thanking others in meetings, and the meetings involving the two of us felt more productive, as though our agendas were more closely aligned. It wasn't just me that noticed this. One of my consultant colleagues, Sarah, also remarked that Julian was making more appreciative gestures to others. Was it my appreciative gesture of him which had prompted this change, or was it a coincidence?

Me in the middle

Just when my relationship with Julian was beginning to improve, things were complicated further. Julian announced that the pre-operative clinic (which was managed within my department) must move to free up space for additional in-patient beds. Furthermore, because there was little additional estate which could accommodate the clinic in its entirety, pre-op would have to be broken up into multiple sites, and Julian made it clear there was no additional resource available to support any of this.

Mandy (the pre-op matron) and Bill (the consultant lead for pre-op and one of my consultant colleagues) were horrified. Bill was concerned that duplication of services on two or more sites without additional resource would lead to a worse patient experience and safety risks. Mandy was worried how she would cope with staff sickness across multiple sites. They feared a regression of the improvements they had worked so hard over the last two years to achieve, and they were asking me as Clinical Director for help to avoid splitting the clinic. They wanted me to fight their corner.

And so here I was again, in the middle between the competing and seemingly incompatible and uncompromising positions of others. I used my new insight of tops, middles and bottoms to give me an understanding of the situation and used this to help me consider my next moves.

I realised that Julian, as a top, was under pressure from the demands of *his* tops in the executive team, who were demanding improvements in care group activity and fiscal balance in the face of budgetary cuts and increasing expectations from patient groups and regulators. I read that tops often see suggestions as criticism. Was this what was happening to Julian in meetings, when he rebuffed concerns and views from others? The challenge was for me now as a middle to help Julian address his issue, and to help him share his responsibilities with others.

The bottoms, in this case Bill and Mandy, I read as feeling that they are invisible, vulnerable, and without a voice or control over their environment. They saw things as being done *to* them rather than being *part of* change. The challenge for me was to try to reduce their sense of vulnerability, and to encourage them to take more responsibility.

Both patterns are examples of habitual behaviours and feelings invited by our context. We are often unaware of (or blind to) the choices and opportunities available to us and often have negative interactions as a result. In this dysfunctional dance, the drawing of responsibility up to the top has a disabling effect on bottoms, reflected in Bill's comment to me:

"What's the point of being the pre-op lead when Julian doesn't listen to what I have to say? They just take decisions without talking to the stakeholders."

I decided to experiment with Oshry's theory, to try to develop my role and influence by encouraging Bill and Mandy to take more responsibility for their role in the system, and by encouraging Julian to trust others and relinquish some responsibility to the team.

Creating partnerships and collaboration

I asked Julian, Bill and Mandy to meet with me to discuss the imminent changes for the clinic. It was a meeting arranged in a hurry as Bill and Mandy sensed that they needed to quickly reverse Julian's existing decision before it became an accepted decision for the care group. At the meeting, Julian said he had asked for an options appraisal to be written by his project manager. Bill was sceptical of the motive behind this. He thought it was a pretence at examining other options, and the decision had already been made.

I suggested Bill and the pre-op clinic team might be involved in writing the options appraisal with Julian's project manager, particularly given that they knew the service better than anyone. Julian agreed; how could he not? Bill said to me afterwards that this was a step in the right direction and he now felt part of the decision-making. He said he still felt that he didn't trust Julian. I suggested he give it a chance to work. I felt palpably less torn now that the tops and bottoms were working together, and looked forward to reading the options appraisal.

Bill asked me for help with writing the paper. Mindful of wanting to reinforce the sense of Bill having increased influence, I took a neutral stance about the options, and gave him challenge during his writing (as a middle should do), encouraging him to gain a spectrum of views from pre-op clinic and more widely across the care group (from our internal "customers", the surgical business units). It felt important that I resisted any temptation to become the Rescuer, leaving Bill as an Adult, in charge. I also suggested he should write a recommendation at the end of the paper. Trust was developing slowly, and so too his sense of being part of the decision-making. I wondered whether Julian was feeling we were giving him help, or whether we were interfering.

Sharing a confidence

Julian asked to meet me to discuss some other issues unrelated to pre-op. However, the meeting took an unexpected turn. Julian came to my office and explained he had just had a very difficult meeting with the Executive Operating Officer during which the downturn in elective activity in the care group (resulting in a £1m loss in a month) was discussed.

He shared with me that the Executive Operating Officer had interrogated him directly about the plans he was going to put in place to reverse this downturn in surgical activity. Julian told me confidentially he was feeling anxious and feared for his job. This show of personal vulnerability *in my office* took me by surprise, a side of Julian I had not seen. I recognised this as a gesture from him to reach out for help, a gesture that shifted the nature of our relationship in that very moment. I paused, took a breath, and expressed my thanks for sharing what could not be easy. It felt so important to acknowledge and appreciate him showing that vulnerability. I felt trusted by him.

I also spoke of my willingness to work together to improve divisional activity, and that I had some ideas as to how we may do this. It felt like we were suddenly on the same page, on the same side as each other. I also told him I thought his grasp of the finance and business side of the work was very sound; that he had real talent for this (which I sincerely believed to be true). I asked him if in the future, when the timing was right, he could give me some help with this. This appreciative approach seemed to help and was in effect a reciprocal show of my vulnerability (and my wish to learn from him). How things had changed from when we first met during the interview twelve months before!

He told me then, almost as an aside, that he had seen Bill's options appraisal which made perfect sense, and that he would look for other sites to relocate pre-op clinic to in its entirety. Reflecting on this event, there was a growing recognition from both of us of the need to work co-operatively. By me being more appreciative of not only Julian's leadership contribution but also his context, I was able to recognise and return his gesture. I began to consider whether my previous negative view of him represented me seeking certainty, polarising my view of him, and whether his behaviour in fact originated from his position in the system (or how he perceived it) rather than representing who he was. I also wondered whether in fact in a broader sense Julian was being used as a scapegoat for poor divisional performance, and that this pervading narrative from clinicians, clinical directors and business managers was one I had unwittingly become a part of. I was beginning to see that perhaps I had made some assumptions about him which I was now questioning.

Understanding others

I asked to meet Mandy to discuss the process by which we were making decisions about the pre-op service. Mandy said she thought my suggestion that she and Bill help write the options appraisal was an important inter-vention. Our conversation slowed and deepened. Mandy confided in me that she has a strong drive to succeed in her work due to a significant childhood event. Mandy's mother died when she was 10 years old, and Mandy was forced to leave school early and, with her father, bring up the family. Without much of a formal education, she had become a nurse, then ward sister, and then matron, before working now as the sister managing pre-op clinic. I was moved and humbled, both by her story and her trust in sharing it with me.

She went on to say that she has a strong desire to please authority figures and that she could easily fall into Child mode, in TA terminology, and felt that Julian had taken advantage of this when he told Mandy pre-op clinic must split, saying, "Come on Mandy, I'm disappointed in you, you know we need to do this." Mandy said she really resented this as she felt manipulated into doing something she thought was not right for the patients in pre-op clinic. She valued the support she felt she received from Bill and me, and that her voice could now be heard. There seemed to be a growing sense of us all being able to understand each other better, our agendas and needs. Our relationships were beginning to work better too, for the service and ultimately for patients.

Since this work, I have noticed that my ability to influence change more widely within the division has increased. My relationship with Julian has changed, and we have become more powerful together in helping others to appreciate and work with the challenges of our context in areas beyond pre-op clinic. Not only have these insights helped me, but I have introduced

Oshry's theory into conversations involving Mandy and Bill to help them understand and depersonalise their negative feelings. I believe this has helped them to set aside their prejudices and to work better with Julian.

Maintaining resilience

I am sure I am not the first leader to at times doubt my abilities to lead a team in the NHS during a difficult period with so many pressures upon us. As I reflect on my experiences, I think an important quality I have worked hard to develop has been my personal resilience. As a leader it is all too easy to take things personally; too easy to give up and not say the things which need to be said to shift relationships, to encourage others to think differently, to shift the local culture.

There are many aspects to maintaining my personal resilience, such as having a supportive family and time and interests outside work. These things cannot be learned on a course and are self-evidently true. However, I have also found knowledge of theory to help me be more resilient: to realise that I am not unique, nor alone in my experience, to understand why things might happen as they do.

Through learning to reflect upon my experience and to take my own experience seriously, I have often noticed how my initial intentions do not lead to predictable consequences, and that along the way I am buffeted by unpredictable events. Some of the changes described above are an example of this. Complexity thinking has helped me make sense of this, to see in practice the idea of people like Ralph Stacey (2012) that organisations are composed of groups of individuals involved in complex social interactions in which even small gestures may have profound and unpredictable consequences.

With Stacey, Oshry shares the view that there is complexity in our organisational lives, and in the world outside organisations, as these too are made of human groups. Humans have difficulty tolerating uncertainty and ambiguity in response to a complex environment, and instead can adopt fixed polar positions as a reassuring veneer of rules, procedures and organisational policies. Considering events from a complexity perspective is part of my personal leadership transition, and reassures me that the context in which I lead is not as predictable or controllable as I may sometimes wish.

By building relationships, even with those who we may initially feel we cannot work with, we are stronger and more powerful in leading change, because change, and improvement, is fundamentally a social pursuit.

CHAPTER 11

Now for Something Completely Different

The starting line

It's the other hospital site. I've wandered around for a while feeling a bit lost, choosing to walk around the outside of the buildings rather than get stuck in the maze of corridors until I find Trust Headquarters. It's before 8am so I must use my swipe card to get in. As I start to walk down the Headquarters' main corridor, the lights come on automatically. It's a bit disconcerting. I find my new office; my name is on the door already; the key works; the lights turn on as I walk in. Lots of doors I've walked past are open – or have colourful moveable signs on the door that say things like: "Busy", "Can be disturbed if urgent", or "Free for a chat" – clearly open door means open door. This all feels very unfamiliar. Although I am only doing this new role for one and a half days a week, my diary has already been filled with 26 induction meetings and a number of 1-2-1 meetings. I have never given away control of my diary before. Who are these people? What am I going to say? What are we going to talk about? What on earth is a 1-2-1?

I was here because several months previously I had seen an email from the Chief Executive of our Trust...

> *We are seeking to appoint a medical colleague in a medical champion*
> *role as Head of Faculty for Medical Leadership in the new Academy.*
> *The Academy will bring together current expertise in service*
> *improvement, organisational and leadership development. The*
> *successful candidate will also play a pivotal part in informing,*

designing and delivering organisational development solutions to support individuals and teams to deliver excellent, caring, safe and thoughtful health care.

This new role will provide a medical colleague with the opportunity to represent our medical workforce and shape how we develop our organisational specialties, teams and individuals over the next two years.

The context

At this point I was a consultant, working at the front line, in a large acute trust struggling with the four-hour access target and a financial deficit. I had been a consultant for three years, had a clinical lead role for a small department and was involved in service improvement work. I was also 12 months into a leadership programme called GenerationQ and was just about to start my Masters dissertation. I had no idea what organisation development (OD) was but I thought that the advertisement was an opportunity for me to step up as someone interested in leadership and quality improvement. Re-reading the email from the Chief Executive's office late one night, it seemed to be an opportunity to be seen, but clearly not a job I was going to get. It was a role for someone more senior, with more experience than me. As I was not expecting to get the job, I enjoyed the interview. I had felt confident pushing back against what seemed to be a rush to create a leadership course, as if that would solve everything. In response to another interview question, I had challenged the notion of implementing a solution before we knew what the issue or question was that needed solving. I had not felt too in awe of the senior colleagues around the table and had become totally immersed in what had become a group discussion. Without being aware of what I was doing, I was already, in a light touch way, challenging some of the dominant cultural patterns I knew only too well in the organisation. I had nothing to lose... I got the job.

The job put me in an unusual position of being a clinician on the inside developing medical leadership with the Organisational Development team, rather than a clinician on the receiving end of developments. It was a position that required me to work across two distinct subcultures, that of clinicians and that of "corporate". I also used the new job as an opportunity to experiment with what I had been learning on GenerationQ. I was attracted to complexity thinking and the idea of conversation as a way of shifting patterns of behaviour and helping people to think differently, something which, looking back, I had begun in the interview.

I was going to be doing the new role part time, alongside my clinical role. Before I started, I met with my two line managers, one from Human Resources, the other from Organisational Development. They outlined what they and the executive were expecting from me in the role.

"We've got nursing leadership training and manager training but no leadership or improvement training for doctors," said the OD person, "and additionally we're finding it really hard to find clinicians who want to lead and become Heads of Service."

"Yup," said the HR person, nodding in vehement agreement, "we sure have. No one seems to want the job; people who are in the role suddenly give up and of course consultants can be difficult and hard to engage."

They both sighed and nodded. Here already was an insight into some of the different assumptions people like them (corporate) had about people like me (doctors). It almost felt as though they were talking about doctors as though they (we) were some alien tribe, who were different and difficult; as if they had momentarily forgotten that I too belonged to that tribe. Here already was an example of what I had been learning about on GenerationQ – the way subcultures are maintained and reinforced because of the way people talk about each other.

Working in a large, acute hospital, my experience of change was that it tended to be solution focused, programmatic, intervention heavy and data driven. It was nearly always top down imposed change as if the organisation were a machine, being controlled by the driver at the top. Ralph Stacey and other complexity thinkers suggest change happens through having different conversations. His writing is a bit opaque, but in my view this is the essence when he writes:

> Organisations change when the themes that organise conversation
> and power relations change. Learning is change in these themes.
> Knowledge is language and meaning emerges as themes interact to
> form conversation (Stacey 2011, p. 478)

This quote helped remind me about my intentions in taking up the new role and my chosen approach: to use the idea of conversation as a way of shifting patterns of behaviour and helping people to think differently. This chapter tells the story of these conversations, of the value of difference, of navigating subcultures and the emergence of my own personal power in the context of trying to support and develop colleagues' leadership. It's the story of gestures made with the intention of starting to shift the cultural divide between Corporate Land and Clinicians' World.

Same word different language

What does the word champion mean or evoke for you? For me, the first thing that comes to mind is the Queen song, and then sports. Yet I was expected to be a 'medical champion' in my new role. The words had no meaning, intrinsic authority or position for me in a work context. However, if I was going to "go out and about" and have a series of conversations around the organisation, I felt I needed to have some form of implied authority and positional power, to have a proper title with which I was comfortable, especially as I was very aware of my own tendency to feel junior and dislike labels (categorise and stereotype me at your peril!).

I had a pre-meeting with my two line managers (to be known subsequently as "the accountant", HR, and "the professor", OD)* before I officially started. I made an important first move, requesting that the name of the role was changed from clinical champion to Head of Medical Leadership Development. In this early conversation, some of the differences between clinical and corporate cultures in terms of language, thinking and assumptions became apparent. For the accountant and the professor, champion is meaningful and has intrinsic status at work. They were surprised that I didn't see things that way. It also made me aware for probably the first time that what we are called matters, in terms of the power a title holds. In this context, shifting to a title that had a better fit with the clinical, rather than the corporate hierarchical language, conferred power on me for when I was talking with other doctors. It also enabled me to feel more comfortable in inhabiting and owning the role. This conversation, before I had even officially started the new role, was the first of many that revealed subcultural differences in language and assumptions. It was like unscrewing a bottle that you thought was still water and finding it was fizzy. It is water, but it is also not what you were expecting.

Something else I was not expecting was to find 26 induction meetings in my diary when I started the new role. As a doctor, I had clinical shifts and on my few non-clinical days, I might have timetabled a few of my own meetings, but finding my diary being managed by other people to this degree was a

---

* These descriptors are used for anonymity and to enable you the reader to conjure a picture of these individuals, which makes it easier to place them in the rest of the chapter. Whilst, as the author, I am aware these could be seen as stereotypes, this is also intentional. An offer is made to notice what you picture in terms of gender, ethnicity, age and so on, and consider that this may be completely different from what others picture, offering an opportunity to view the subsequent theme of difference and diversity in a way that an explanation alone could not give.

shock. With so many meetings, all of which were an hour long, it also felt intimidating.

The professor and I had regular conversations about this experience and much more about what I was noticing and what was being noticed by others about me. These became opportunities to highlight aspects of being and working which seemed normal in organisational development / Corporate Land but seemed totally alien to me from Clinicians' World, and vice versa. It also gave me an opportunity to use what I was noticing and feeling myself about starting this new role as an insight into how clinical colleagues may feel when stepping up into leadership roles like Head of Service. Perhaps they feel like me – not knowing what I was doing, feeling junior, anxious, lost, defensive, unsure what the job title really meant and what, if any, power I really had.

I valued greatly the conversations with the professor and they were an important form of support in the early days of the role. The regular 1-2-1 conversations (notice my use of language is already shifting!) with the professor also became opportunities to co-inquire into what we all understood by the notion of medical leadership development. Before starting this new role, I had struggled with reflective practice. In this new role, there were now so many small but significant observations to be noticed and remembered that writing even just once a week in my journal became a really important discipline. It gave me an opportunity to stop and notice the difference in subcultures, and to incorporate this learning into what we subsequently developed.

Meetings as conversations – part one

As for the 26 induction meetings, I wasn't sure what I was supposed to do – a meeting for me was something formal with an agenda, a discussion around tasks. Without a task, I chose to make them conversational, asking people: "What do you do? What do you think I should be doing? What do you think doctors in leadership positions might benefit from? Who else should I talk to?" It gave me an opportunity for inquiry – to really hear what was being said, free from any assumption on my part as to what the answers were going to be. I concentrated not only on the answers to the questions, but also on noticing any difference both in terms of my experience and their ideas and viewpoints, making notes throughout. I enjoyed some great conversations that strayed in all sorts of directions, and through which emerged some key themes around leadership in the organisation, and aspects of organisational culture affecting leadership. I remember thinking at the time, is this real work, having great conversations? Can I really believe this to be the case?

The lack of diversity in the organisation, from board level to patient representative level was highlighted to me in one conversation. The board and executive team are predominantly white, male and over 50; the patient representatives are primarily white, female professionals over 60. These groups were not diverse in terms of age, ethnicity or gender, and neither were they reflective of the diversity of the populations they were representing – the hospital workforce was *not* predominantly white men in their 50s and the patient population was *not* primarily highly educated white women in their 60s. Some of my corporate colleagues felt that doctors were less aware of equality and diversity issues. However, I was able to draw their attention to something that had struck me, but they had never noticed – leadership training for BME colleagues (and other protected characteristics), was available to all professions in the organisation, except doctors. Small differences like this collectively add to the development of subcultures and tribes, or perceptions that can easily be reinforced into prejudice and stereotypes.

Diversity and difference became key themes for me throughout this process. I knew that my approach to change was counter to the dominant model of machine-like, top down change. Secondly, and perhaps more importantly, I was wanting to explore the way difference and diversity of thought supports the generation of new ideas. I thought conversations could play a key role in enhancing this: more conversations of different forms, with different membership.

Experimenting with different approaches and reflecting on what worked and what didn't was one of the things we were encouraged to do as part of GenerationQ. With this in mind, I decided to re-arrange all the individual induction meetings with the HR managers and have one group meeting instead.

I started off the group meeting talking about my hopes for the session. From the conversation that followed there seemed to be a general consensus that the doctors who were heads of service were struggling to lead well, although it wasn't clear what "struggling", or even "leading well" meant in practice. I wanted to inquire more deeply.

"Do you feel that consultants understand the role of HR managers?" I asked. There was a unanimous "No". In fact, they all felt that consultants could benefit from shadowing them. I agreed.

"To be honest, I'm not sure I know what you all do," I admitted.

"Do you know what consultants do?" I continued. There was another unanimous response – this time "Yes!". I consciously looked a bit surprised.

"Does that mean that shadowing doctors wouldn't be useful for you?" I asked, knowing that one of the HR managers, Lynne, had told me earlier she thought this a great idea. Most replied quickly that it wouldn't be useful, a lovely example of the way homogeneous groups make collective assumptions without even considering alternatives. However, Lynne then spoke up and said she was about to shadow one of the newer Heads of Service. This seemed to give another manager the confidence to say that maybe they didn't actually know what consultants did, or how they fitted in everything that was asked of them. My admission that I didn't know what they did, alongside an awareness that one of them didn't know what her clinical colleagues did, enabled an alternative viewpoint to be heard within the conversation. This resulted in a much wider and more granular discussion around the multiple expectations of clinical leaders, and whether these expectations were realistic in the time given. Can one Head of Service really be an expert in HR, finance and change doing the role four hours a week whilst maintaining clinical skills? We then discussed that if these expectations and time limitations were not understood, how it might instead be interpreted as poor leadership – bridging the cultural gap between corporate assumptions and clinical reality (and vice versa). We ended the conversation in a very different place than we started.

"Just" more conversations

The induction conversations were one thing, but now I had to start addressing the issues that led to the development of my role: that Heads of Service were struggling (or perceived to be struggling) to lead services. Having found the induction meetings easier, more enjoyable and more useful as conversations I decided to continue with this approach, but shifting the focus to clinicians. In the induction meetings I had asked:

> Who do you think I should talk to who is, has been or could be a
> doctor in a leadership position – not necessarily someone who you
> feel is successful, but someone it would be useful for me to speak to, to
> get a range of viewpoints?

I developed an email that invited consultant colleagues to have a conversation about doctors in leadership positions. I sent the email to 18 colleagues, a mixture of doctors in, and no longer in, leadership roles, and got 14 replies, all agreeing to meet me. I was pleased and more than a bit relieved. At least they wanted to talk!

I started each of the conversations with a similar introduction to frame the conversation, namely, that I was focusing on support and development of doctors in leadership positions. I had expected to need prompts, but after this framing the conversations seemed to just start. I had a list of potential themes in my notepad as a reminder, but I never needed them. The conversations flowed, lasted about forty-five minutes and seemed to conclude naturally.

I discovered that the gesture of having a conversation itself, without an agenda or intended outcome in mind, with an open-ended inquiry focus rather than a solution focus, was enabling issues to be raised and heard that hadn't been before. Organisational issues around governance, structure, accountability and responsibility that were impacting the ability of doctor colleagues to lead were being raised and discussed alongside their own developmental needs. Instead of just reading about change as conversations I was getting a practical, tangible understanding of a theory. I also hoped that these different conversations would prompt others to have conversations so that the ideas would go viral and spread, with changes emerging. I was also beginning to realise that organisational development and leadership development can be two sides of the same coin; that leadership development doesn't happen on a training course, at least not without something else going on alongside.

The challenge of conversations

Do you ever go to parties and find yourself serving the drinks, or playing with other people's children, rather than doing small talk and having conversations? Do you ever dread conferences, mostly the networking sessions, as this means that you will need to introduce yourself to people you don't know and have conversations? Until relatively recently, and on some occasions still, this is me. Hearing this, you can see that choosing to experiment with "conversing as organising" was not an obvious fit for me. In addition, I am someone who worries about being too junior for the role (any role), about not understanding the politics and having the tendency to be a sheep. I am also wary of hierarchy, so going out to speak to senior colleagues about potentially difficult topics was quite a significant step out of my comfort zone.

Then there is the biggest practical challenge of time: (a) finding time to fit conversations into my working week, around clinical work, coordinating colleagues' diaries and my own, and (b) the time it takes to get an outcome, which is uncertain and emergent. The organisational context for my Trust, which was struggling financially, was that this role was only funded for two years. This created significant tension for me. I wanted to allow meaning to emerge through conversations, and yet I knew I needed to produce a tangible outcome that kept my OD colleagues employed and made a difference to clinical leadership, patients and the organisation. I felt I needed to push back and up; if the Trust were serious about making a difference to clinical leadership then they needed to be serious about supporting the time it takes to get it right. I was also, however, caught up in the tension, worried that a more structured approach or developing a training course would be seen as more successful, faster and less vague than what I was doing. As a front-line clinician used to rapid decision-making and delivery, holding to this approach and to this uncertainty was again challenging for me.

As mentioned earlier, I was also curious about the importance of difference to the generation of new ideas. I was keen to understand whether the difference of me as a clinician in Corporate Land impacted the themes and ideas that emerged in conversations. Perhaps the act of having conversations with not just "the usual suspects" would be enough of a difference in itself? I am not sure whether I answered these questions, but certainly instigating conversations with a myriad of colleagues, inquiring differently and pushing back against the expected approach, did seem to make visible some cultural and organisational issues that were previously hidden. The professor remarked that "Previously people have turned the stones over and then put them back down, you are turning them over and leaving them upside down and exposed."

This however, also has risks. What happens to me if people don't like, or don't want to see, what is exposed?

What was exposed?

A series of conversations and meetings over the first three months of my role identified some clear developmental needs for consultant colleagues in clinical leadership roles, including improved understanding of HR, finances, improvement methodology and performance management. However, what surfaced and were seen to impact much more heavily on colleagues' ability to lead services were cultural and organisational issues. Most Heads of Service were expected to be experts in everything in a very limited time, with no induction or handover into the role. There were no job descriptions within the organisation, and therefore limited consistency about what the role entailed across different services. This also meant no clear deliverables, accountability, processes or support for the role – colleagues felt they just "collided with stuff" and tried to muddle through. There were significant issues highlighted around performance management, and lack of support from senior medical colleagues in managing performance or behaviour, such that "Why should I change if there are no consequences for doing so?" and "What do you have to do to get told off around here?" were phrases that came up more than once in my conversations.

There was also a strong feeling that "executives see consultants as the problem". This echoed the early meeting with my two line managers before I'd taken up the role. There was a cultural pattern going on that I'd learnt is called the drama triangle. One group (clinicians) were feeling blamed for being poor leaders by the executives, so the clinicians were seeing themselves as victims and the Exec and those in Corporate Land as the persecutors. My role was not to rescue but, through conversation, to help each side see things from the perspective of others. For instance, another common theme talking to clinicians was that if the organisation was not seen to value clinical colleagues in leadership roles, then colleagues could drop the roles and just go back to clinical work: "If it isn't valued I won't do the work". Silo working was the final issue that was voiced – we do not lead as individuals, we lead as teams, and patients don't access one service or group of staff they access multiples, but we teach, train, learn and lead in role-defined or service-defined silos – something we need to do differently.

Being a doctor, still working clinically, enabled other doctors to talk to me in a way that they wouldn't readily talk to corporate colleagues. Equally, coming at the conversation from within a corporate role enabled me to ask questions and focus the conversation on areas that I wouldn't have done as "just" a clinician. At times it felt like I was translating language and forming a bridge between two subcultures, allowing different and more traffic to cross the divide than usual. Part of this was an almost physical bridging with one foot on each side, by virtue of a role in each, but the rest of the bridge was built via the act of inquiring openly, hearing the responses, allowing the outcome to emerge, and by trying not to place more value on the responses from one group / tribe / subculture over the other. I had to learn to stay truly open to all that I heard.

Meetings as conversations – part two

My first attempt at feeding back these organisational issues was an update meeting with the accountant and the professor that had been in the diary for a while. This wasn't an easy meeting. The accountant was at times very defensive on behalf of the executive team and the Medical Director. I responded to this defensiveness by focusing on the fact that I was summarising perceptions of, rather than intentions of the executive team, so this wasn't about apportioning blame. I was able to stay in Adult and not get caught up in the drama triangle myself in the meeting. The professor helpfully corroborated what I was saying, having picked up similar themes. The accountant to his/her credit, calmed down and was able to really hear the issues. The three of us agreed the issues needed to be formally addressed. This meant a meeting with more senior colleagues. The first of these was with the professor, the accountant, the Medical Director (MD), the Deputy Medical Director (DMD) and me. The prospect of feeding back to the MD specific organisational issues, which included his perceived lack of support and management of clinical colleagues, made me rather anxious, unsurprisingly.

I discussed my anxieties at a coaching session. I was increasingly aware that my tendencies to "feel junior, not be good enough and be solution focused" could potentially derail this meeting. However, my coach reminded me that the conversations I had been having with more senior clinical colleagues had not elicited "feeling junior", and that perhaps this was a story I needed to change for myself, so I decided to try and run the meeting as a conversation rather than as a formal PowerPoint presentation. I planned the following introduction which enabled me to go into the meeting knowing how I wanted to approach it, feeling more confident. This was my framing introduction:

> *This meeting gives me an opportunity to update you with my findings from my role so far. I gained this information through conversations, so thought it would be good to continue this by having a conversation about the key themes and where to go next. Some key areas of knowledge development have been found. There are also some wider issues around value of and support for clinical leadership roles, that have as big, if not a bigger impact on colleagues' ability to be successful in these roles.*

The meeting went well, the MD did not spend time on his phone or computer or reading other papers. He made eye contact, nodded a few times, made a few notes and even spoke – all very positive interactions I subsequently discovered. I was able to bring up all the issues including the need for accountability and executive support for performance managing clinical colleagues.

Having the meeting as a conversation enabled me to not feel junior, and for there to be a less defensive or critical response from the senior players in the room. It felt as if we were in the conversation together, as equal parties with a shared interest, power differences dissolved. I was not set up to be the expert, selling my expertise to an audience, inviting a win-lose debate. I think we achieved real dialogue. I came away with future actions that would hopefully impact my colleagues positively and thereby patients and the organisation. The difference in this meeting was not only the meeting style, but also not shying away from feeding up the issues – something I replicated in upcoming meetings (conversations) with the DMD (who couldn't come to this meeting as planned), the Deputy Chief Executive and the Chair of the Board. The accountant was very helpful afterwards, reassuring me that the meeting went very well with what was significant engagement from the MD, despite his appearance of being disengaged at times. The accountant specifically highlighted the obvious preparation I had done and the introduction to the meeting as being critical to its success. It is a reminder to me that leading through conversations still requires being thoughtful and intentional, thinking about how to ensure there is dialogue and that people are not defensive. It's not the same as just rocking up unprepared for a random chat!

Organisational impact – known or unknown?

Taking a complexity approach and working in a complex organisation it is hard to know exactly how these conversations, the ripples from them, the voiced themes and "exposed rocks" had a direct impact on subsequent organisational changes. Did they create a shift in understanding and appreciation of the different subcultures of Corporate Land and Clinicians' World? Certainly, new combined job descriptions for the service management teams (doctor, nurse, manager) rather than individuals, were developed. All new Heads of Service, and the majority of those in post, have been given eight hours a week, rather than four hours to do the role. Within a few months we underwent a process of organisation restructure with the intention to move decision-making nearer the front line, making lines of accountability and responsibility clearer, simpler and more efficient. If I hold onto the idea that organisations change when the themes that organise conversation and power relations change, as outlined by Stacey (2012), I think that it is likely that the conversations I and others had resulted in some organisational and cultural themes becoming more visible than they were before. I feel that these themes then fed into changes, some of which may have happened anyway but potentially the emphasis was differently placed than it would have been without the conversations. It could be argued that it wasn't the process of conversations that has resulted in these themes being visible, but that these issues were so close to the surface that they would have come out anyway. I do know, however, that a corporate colleague's Masters' dissertation on medical leadership, done a few years earlier, raised similar concerns but they were not heard more widely in the organisation. The professor commented that "nobody has taken the time to say this sort of stuff before", whereas I knew my colleague had, just not using a process of conversations.

I am also struck by the "legitimacy" afforded by undertaking a Masters, which gave me the confidence and framework for using conversations as a methodology of inquiry. This approach enabled me to voice what was being said by others. Although having conversations takes time, the process of conversing as organising, if the concepts matter, can be fast. Whilst I can't know whether the conversations I have are organising change, or whether change is influencing the conversations, it probably doesn't matter if changes still emerge.

Personal impact – difference and power

I was very aware throughout how it felt for me being different: a clinician in a non-clinical team, in a non-clinical environment; and how that experience of difference was useful in understanding how colleagues might feel. It wasn't, however, until I made a "non-significant" decision about taking part in an OD meeting about NHS Change Day that I realised the impact of this difference on the OD team. I was in my office when the OD administrator walked past and asked me if, as I was part of the OD team, I would like to come and join their meeting about NHS Change Day and the pledges they were going to do. I didn't have any other meetings booked and thought it would be interesting so said yes and went along. We discussed potential team pledges, decided on a direction to take, and had a team photo taken under the tree at the front of Trust HQ where we had also decided we would hang the pledges on Change Day.

At my next meeting with the professor I was thanked for agreeing to be part of the session. I was surprised – it was something the team were doing and as part of the team I hadn't considered not doing it. However, I was unaware till then that this gesture had resulted in a real shift in opinion of the team. Not only were they discussing that perhaps consultants aren't difficult to engage but, more surprising to me, they felt they were more credible by having a doctor on the team. They felt if I, as a doctor, valued the team then the team must have value.

In a subsequent conversation with the professor, it seems it is not just the team that feel this. I often start our meetings with "Hi Boss", as I consider the professor my senior in almost all arenas – OD, the organisation, position, knowledge, experience and so on – and I use it as an informal, light-hearted reflection of this. I found out that this makes the professor smile every time, not just because I am considered an equal member of the team but "imagine a doctor calling me boss". Even the professor's Mum was impressed: "You have really achieved something having a doctor on the team." I had never been in a work situation before in which I had become aware of the power and status that just being a doctor has within corporate parts of the organisation.

I am now significantly more aware of the power that comes with certain roles, whether those individuals are aware of (or want) that power or not. Prior to starting in this role my "power" was very much based on my clinical role – clinical credibility gave me a leadership role as did the improvement work I undertook in my clinical area of expertise. This new role within Corporate Land has meant that clinical credibility is no longer the mainstay of any power that I have. My power in this context is related to speaking and acting authentically, speaking up, focusing on values, focusing on difference, being different and having conversations – a much less defined and much more personal power. This brings with it very different and exciting expectations and opportunities, but also increased risk: if the power is more personal then so is the risk should projects not work, or if the exposed stones are too big.

Was it something completely different?

In keeping with the idea of complexity theory and emergence, I think the answer to the question of "Was it something completely different?" is still emerging and evolving. Having a clinician who works both clinically and as part of an organisation development team was different for our organisation, different for me, and is relatively uncommon across the NHS, as far as I am aware. This working across subcultures has been incredibly valuable in shifting learning, expectations and understandings for a variety of individuals in those teams including myself, the accountant and the professor, but also for the wider organisation development team, and I hope for the clinical team within which I work.

Choosing to undertake a change and development project via conversations was different again for me, and I think brought some ideas and themes into greater visibility than they would have been if a more expected approach of training needs analysis, focus groups and improvement methodology had been used. This difference of approach was, however, I suspect not visible to the organisation as much as the outcome, and perhaps had I been braver in articulating the concepts behind my approach this would have added another layer to the conversations and potentially the impact. It may have also made it an approach and ethos that could be used more by others and made the "personal power" less personal and more collective.

I have a very different network within the organisation now than I would ever have had without this role, and have subsequently become involved in cross-organisational projects that I would have been terrified of, felt too junior for, and not known how to approach without this. It transpires that I can do conversations and that this works for me, but I have also realised how complex it is to remain focused in this methodology, to hold the uncertainty of outcome for myself and others and to trust that the ripples of conversations and upturned stones will deliver a change.

My understanding of leadership has also shifted. I now see leadership as a process of inquiry through conversations. It's not about control. Language matters. How we talk matters. It is about planting a seed and waiting to see what happens. It is not bonsai or topiary. I have a much greater awareness of the role of language in shaping the whole process of quality improvement, leadership and organisations, as well as the day to day medical work we do – what a different expectation we would all have if we worked in *illness care* not *health care.*

CHAPTER 12

Choosing Wedlock Over Deadlock

Setting the scene

If merger can be characterised as a marriage, then this one was more like a shotgun wedding with a room full of family and friends all loudly stating their objections. Yet this is also a story of hope which testifies to the power of involving those same families and friends in a process of co-designing a joint future. It highlights that, even with fraught beginnings, where there is will, mutual respect and a willingness to forgive, a union can become greater than the sum of its parts.

This is the story of the merger of three different improvement support services, each with their own unique cultures, a strong attachment to different approaches and methods, and with different client experiences, although largely in the health and care sector. That's a gross oversimplification that I hope those involved will forgive as, for the purposes of this story, it highlights some of the key differences and tensions that we had to face and address through the process of merger.

I don't know if this story will speak to you the reader, but perhaps it will echo the feelings and capture the imagination of any who work in a system where there are different corporate, regional or national teams with different philosophies about how to enable improvement, and different cultures and ways of working.

A subjective account of our engagement and wedding

I pick the story up at the point where the engagement (decision to merge) has been publicly announced. The context is one of mistrust and anger from a range of key stakeholders about the way the issues have progressed to date, with a number feeling that the decision to merge the three services was made behind closed doors without appropriate involvement. In particular there are concerns about the decision that my service will govern the new merged entity and a fear that we will simply take over and impose our way of doing things.

What I go on to describe is a snapshot of my experience of the process that followed. There are elements that are factual. However much of this story will be coloured my own subjective views and experiences, alongside decisions about what is helpful and appropriate to share in this context. The fact that I led the improvement support team already situated in the service that would lead the new merged entity is also vital context that inevitably led me to experience this process differently to the leaders of the other two services. I recognise that the experiences of others may have been very different.

A good relationship counsellor sets you up for success

Following the formal announcement of the merger, Nadine and Petra, the leaders of the other two services, approached me about the possibility of co-designing the purpose, functions and approach of the newly formed improvement service, with a desire to include key stakeholders in the process.

We quickly secured the support of our commissioners for this approach, I think largely because it was a joint proposition that accepted that merger was a given, whilst offering to work with stakeholders to address the highly contested questions about what this new service would do and how it would function. It offered a solution to the commissioners' challenge of agreeing next steps whilst at the same time securing a voice for those who, up to now, had felt disempowered by the process to date.

Very early on we agreed that, given the contested nature of the territory ahead, there would be significant benefit in commissioning an independent Organisational Development expert to support the three of us through this process. We quickly agreed on an individual known and respected by all three of us whom, for the purposes of this story, I will call Irene.

Finding a time to come together as a group of three when she was also available was challenging. Being pragmatists, we proposed that the initial scoping/contracting meeting would be with just two of us, and asked her to meet separately with the third member. Much to our surprise, Irene refused to work with us in this way and later reflected:

> The way I get invited in as a consultant tells me about the work which needs to be done. It matters how things begin as it creates from the outset the conditions for the work.

She later explained:

> The way three of you interacted with me initially highlighted to me that you had issues around clarity of task and around commitment to integrate. There is no such thing as integration without shared meaning, so your success was dependent on your capacity to get in the room together and set the agenda. You had to integrate in order to integrate.

With Irene's challenge on the table, we managed to rearrange our diaries to all come together for the initial contracting session. We committed to meeting for two hours every other week for the next six months whilst we jointly led the work of co-designing the new service. I refer to these sessions going forward as the integration leadership meetings. It wasn't easy to protect this time, and there were always good reasons that any one of us could have used to cancel. However, Irene made it clear that our success depended on our choices as leaders to prioritise meeting together and, with these conditions clearly laid out, the only no shows happened when someone was too ill to come to work.

Irene's willingness to walk away from the commission if we weren't willing to prioritise time to come together on a regular basis was key to creating a context that was conducive to success. This is a lesson that has growing resonance with our current improvement work, yet one that in truth we find hard to apply in practice. The predominant culture in many health organisations seems to drive us to "do something" even if the "something" has little chance of delivering sustained improvement. Irene highlighted in practice the power of taking a stance about what mattered, and by doing this, enabled us to create the key conditions for future success.

Making time to get to know each other, warts and all

One way of thinking about the merger process is as bringing together three groups of staff, each with their unique social identities. In his work on social identities and intergroup relations, Tajfel (1971, 1978) highlights just how powerful group dynamics can be, and how natural it is to try and enhance our own group identity by conceptualising the other as inferior. I learned on GenerationQ that it is a natural human tendency to divide individuals into for or against, good or bad, them and us, a process that is called "splitting".

If we add into the mix the fact that merger and acquisition activity is "an extraordinary and destabilizing life event requiring considerable personal adjustment" (Cartwright and Cooper 1996, p33), then we have the perfect ingredients for a negative spiral. Initial poor behaviour caused by stress can lead to unhelpful and unsubstantiated judgements about colleagues from the other service, which has the potential to create a filter from which even neutral actions are interpreted negatively, leading to an ongoing spiral of deteriorating relationships and the creation of a toxic culture. Phew!

I think we largely managed to avoid falling into this trap and key to this was our integration leadership meetings. Reading through my reflective journal, I note myself constantly fighting the tendency to assume my colleagues' words and actions were underpinned by ill intent. The bi-weekly meetings provided a regular opportunity to recalibrate my internal dialogue and remind myself that I wasn't engaged in a venture of the good (my service) integrating with the bad (the other two). Rather we were three groups and three leaders with equally good intent caught up in a complex process of integration.

The regular time together helped us to "get real" and discuss the issues that normally stay off the table. We recognised that, as we sought to understand each other's positions, we were in fact generating key insights and enabling ourselves to better lead the wider system through the process of integration. At one point Irene noted:

> When something becomes overwhelming individuals can go into
> passive mode but you three didn't, you came to session and shared
> how you were all feeling and then you acted on it there and then.

By doing so it opened up relationships between the three of us in the group and helped us to create deeper connections. It served as a way of preventing us from entering our fortresses and firing arrows from a distance. I think that key to this was the fact that we weren't meeting as a team development exercise, our sessions were always full of tasks to do and key issues that had come up over the last two weeks that needed discussion. The development work was woven seamlessly around the practical work of change.

But I am in danger of making it sound like it was easy. In truth there were many difficult and challenging moments along the way, including key insights and learning about my own behaviours in these circumstances.

In the past I found it really difficult if anything I did or said evoked negative emotions in another. If the person was angry, then my assumption was that it was my fault for not handling the interaction skilfully enough. If they were sad then I assumed responsibility for *rescuing* them from that sadness, even if that then detracted from whatever I had said that led to the unhappiness or tears (see Drama Triangle: Karpman 1968).

Needless to say, it simply wasn't possible to effectively jointly lead this co-design process without facing up to some challenging issues and some difficult conversations. The support I received through GenerationQ helped me to realise that I am not responsible for how people react to what I say and do, and that when my gesture generates a negative reaction I have a choice about how I then respond. I don't have to kick into an automatic pacifying mode. Indeed, Transactional Analysis theory (Lapworth and Sills 2011) has helped me to understand that moving into Rescuer mode can actually hinder both individual and organisational development as it can push others into the role of Victim, detracting from their freedom and responsibility to manage and work through their own responses. This insight has been key to enabling me to get a better balance between my own and others' responsibilities for resolving difficult situations. However, I suspect the urge to "rescue" is one I will continue struggling with for the rest of my life.

Co-creating our future with family and friends

So, what does it mean to co-design a new merged service? I am not sure that any of us really knew when we set out and it is easy to forget just how scary it was initially. I found myself reading back over my reflective diary and finding this entry at the period where we were agreeing to go into this process:

> I want a process of co-design that ends up delivering what I want – I'm happy to have my views changed through the process – but not happy if we end up with something that feels like a compromise. I'm nervous about entering it.

And then at one point in the midst of it I noted:

> Feeling utterly overwhelmed, scared as to how to make sense of it all, not sure what to do in response, feeling like I have lost control around the process. I feel inadequate for my role and scared as to how we deliver.

Both entries were a surprise to read as I had forgotten just how vulnerable I felt at moments in the process.

In hindsight I can lay out a clear and rational process, but in practice we didn't start with a project plan with each step mapped out. We weren't taking a machine-thinking approach to the task of integration. Instead we started with a clear purpose and intention, and an agreement that we wanted to involve our staff and our stakeholders in the process of working out how to get there. Our approach evolved over time and included key stakeholder interviews; a number of workshops with staff from the three existing entities; a stakeholder co-design day; critical friend review of the draft proposals, and discussions at a range of existing meetings and forums. And, of course, the regular integration leadership meetings where we came together to reflect and agree next steps.

Along the way, I learnt the importance of placing the stakes in the ground when doing the work of emergence. What do I mean by this? Irene taught us that, when co-designing the future, you need to hold and contain individuals' anxieties so that they are able to engage in a productive way. This means you need a clear purpose and direction of travel, as well as clarity on the "givens", so that individuals understand what is up for discussion and what has already been agreed. This then provides a sense of containment for the work of co-design; it allows individuals to feel safe enough to engage in the work of co-creating a future.

As a practical example of a "given", from the very beginning we were clear that there would be a new integrated improvement service that would bring together the unique and common capabilities of the three merging services – this was not up for debate – it was a given. Further, Irene taught us the importance of continually restating those givens, so at the start of every engagement event we would clearly spell out the current set of givens, which grew over time as we progressed the co-design.

I also learnt that working in an emergent way doesn't mean you don't have structure or plans; indeed, every event was very carefully planned. But rather than planning something to deliver a predetermined outcome, the focus was on providing a framework that then allowed those present to engage meaningfully with the key issues and co-create the solutions. Working emergently also meant we had to protect the time to make sense together of what we were hearing and seeing; and on the basis of this joint sense-making, be willing and open to adapting our plans going forward. And, in reality, by being open to joint sense-making, you do end up changing your views through the process so that where you end up becomes somewhere you feel comfortable with. And if it's not, well as I will come to later, you stay in the conversation and keep exploring and inquiring together.

The power of appreciative inquiry to build understanding

I've already highlighted that this change process included bringing together teams and stakeholders with very different views on what delivers improvement. One of our concerns in leading this process was the potential for individuals to retreat into ideological corners where the focus became defending one approach as better than another, retreating into being different tribes. Further, I entered this change process with an already formed belief that the organisation would need to take a pluralistic approach, so one of my personal aims was to develop an acceptance of the value of different approaches.

Appreciative Inquiry (AI) provides a framework that focuses conversations on practical experiences of what actually works and is a way of building "positive change through increased co-operation among multiple stake-holders" (Barrett and Fry 2005, p. 23). It is "based on the simple assumption that every organization has something that works well, and those strengths can be the starting point for creating positive change" (Cooperrider et al 2005, p. 3). Hence it aligned well with the commitment from all three services to an "explicit aim of drawing from the respective strengths of their current approaches to create a coherent and integrated offer that meets the needs of the integrated health and social care landscape".

Rather than using the formal 4D AI method, we agreed together as a leadership team that we would weave an appreciative stance throughout the process. The power of this appreciative stance was probably strongest during our first joint staff meeting. A key exercise at the workshop was groups of three (ideally one from each service but the balance of numbers meant this was not always possible), a Storyteller, Note Taker, and Questioner. The Questioner used the following questions to prompt the Storyteller

- Briefly describe a piece of improvement work that your service has done that you are really proud of, and links in to one (or more) of the outcomes that you see listed on the table
- What difference(s) did this work make?
- What made such difference(s) possible?
- How did you know?

The exercise was completed three times so every person in that room got to tell their story.

One of the key reflections I remember being made at the end was that, despite the different improvement approaches, there was so much common-ality around what actually worked in practice. At the end of session, we went around the room and each person was asked to share three words that summed up their experience of the day. The following word cloud highlights the positivity of those three words. For me though, the most powerful moment was when one individual said, "No longer scared".

Figure 12.1

Speaking the same language but with different meanings

In addition to staff and stakeholder workshops, we also commissioned a set of semi-structured key stakeholder interviews to inform the co-design work. As we reflected together as a leadership team on the outputs of the stakeholder interviews, we identified that one of the key challenges in developing this new offering was that different stakeholders had different views on what was meant by "improvement", what enables it to happen, and hence what the new offering should do.

And to complicate matters further, "there are juggernauts of beliefs out there around what people think other folk do and don't do" (Local Authority Stakeholder). So not only did we have different understandings of "improvement", we were surrounded by misunderstandings about what each other thought "improvement" meant.

For me personally, a key insight from all of this was around the use of "improvement" as a shorthand for either improvement science or quality improvement methodologies. Indeed, I noted in my journal:

> I think it's arrogant of those of us* using quality improvement methodologies to use the word "improvement" as a shorthand for what we do. It implies an exclusive ownership of the "improvement" arena and may be subconsciously (and in my experience sometimes consciously) communicating that the only way to deliver improvement is through the application of quality improvement methodology. We are then, by default, passing judgement on the worth of colleagues who are contributing to improved outcomes through different approaches such as the production of evidence-based guidelines or the development of clinical skills.
>
> * When I wrote this, I was including myself in the "us" – as in truth I have been as guilty as anyone in using that shorthand.

Further, just the process of recognising and naming this issue turned out to be powerful as highlighted in the following journal entry:

> It is like it suddenly frees people up to engage openly in discussion and feels like I've taken a shackle off them that means they no longer need to defend why what they do is of equal value. This then enables them to engage in talking openly about what might help, including the potential value of using quality improvement methodologies.

I also realised that, as a leadership team, we had been holding the tensions around the different perspectives about what improvement is and how it is best supported. We agreed that we needed to move to a place where the different stakeholders owned both the tensions and the challenge of resolving them, and that we could use an upcoming stakeholder event to help with this transfer of ownership. This view was informed by Heifetz (2002, p. 139) who highlights how, with change that requires individuals to adapt their behaviours and beliefs, it is important to "place the work within and between the factions who are faced with the challenge" and "let people feel the weight of responsibility for tackling those issues" (p. 109).

The anecdotal feedback from the stakeholder day was very positive with a consistent phrase being used about the "buzz" in the room throughout, and I noticed that individuals were starting to talk more about the different meanings of the word "improvement". This was evidence that we were starting to see a change in the nature of conversation from "this is my position and I'm right" to one that was more interested in understanding and working with the difference.

Surfacing the core tensions

However, as we reflected together as a leadership group following the event we identified that, whilst there was an emerging consensus that the new offering would need to use a mixture of approaches and methodologies, there were still key questions around what that balance would look like in practice. There was also a need to ensure our own staff understood and valued the different approaches. We decided to focus the next joint staff session on inquiring into the tensions between the different approaches.

Through discussion in our leadership group we identified seven core tensions that had emerged from the work to date, and agreed that we wanted every staff member to spend a bit of time exploring every tension. As we explored how to do this, we realised that there would be a benefit in getting staff to fill in the strengths and weaknesses grid that comes out of polarity management (see Johnson 1992) as this would highlight that the strength of one usually addressed the weakness of the other and vice versa, thus making the point that we needed "both/and" not "either/or" thinking. We also thought it would be interesting to ask them individually to mark where on the spectrum they thought we should be, to get an understanding of the different perspectives in the room.

Imagine the event. We held it on neutral premises, a local centre for social innovation, in an attic room with sun streaming through the windows. About 40 members of staff were there, and I could feel the energy and the anxiety in the room. Both were palpable. As we introduced the polarities exercise everyone stood up and began to move and mingle at their own pace. It was both wonderful and scary to watch and be part of.

As a practical example, one of the tensions was between an approach that focused on running large-scale collaboratives versus offering bespoke support to address key local improvement challenges. The following highlights the difference of opinion in the room as to where our focus should be. As we explored further these differences of view there was a real sense of coming together and starting to recognise that our future may be in the world of both/and rather than the either/or. We really were co-designing our future together through every step that we took.

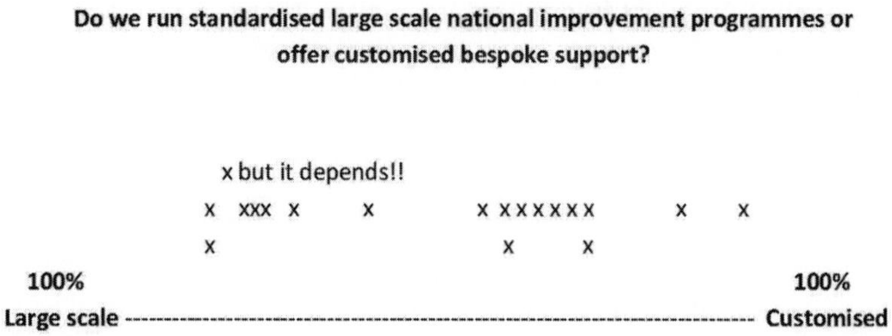

Do we run standardised large scale national improvement programmes or offer customised bespoke support?

```
                        x but it depends!!
          x   xxx  x        x            x x x x x x x        x     x
          x                              x       x
   100%                                                              100%
   Large scale ----------------------------------------------------- Customised
```

Figure 12.2

However, I left the session feeling very uncomfortable, and my journal notes:

> Anxious that we've taken some folk from being anti the integration to be really positive about it – yet they may not have a role in the new service.

Despite the positive excitement of the day, I slept badly that night and decided the following morning that I was going to share my concerns with the leadership team meeting that day. We started with check-in/reflection on the staff session and, following some initial positive reflections from colleagues, I went ahead and shared my anxieties. In response to this, one of my colleagues then shared her anxieties, and for the first time we started to get into the tricky discussions about who was going to transfer into the merged service. I reflected afterwards:

> There was a real sense of open and honest sharing from the heart which led us to jointly recognise some of the difficult issues we still had to face without necessarily seeking to find the solutions there and then...it feels like there are two conflicting values here – designing a service that is positioned in the best possible way for the future versus looking after the staff.

For me a pivotal moment in the process was shortly after this meeting reading Cartwright and Cooper's (1996) summary of the research into the impact of merger and acquisition on the individual. One statement they quoted from a research paper by Mangham (1973) into mergers has stayed with me ever since: "it wasn't experienced as seduction it was experienced as rape".

> This statement jumped off the page at me and it was like someone had just put a knife through my heart. In that moment I felt an overwhelming sense of compassion for the individuals in this process that simply hadn't been there before.

Despite all our efforts to co-design I realised that this had basically still been a process of "doing to" the staff, as the decision to integrate them was not one they had any control over. And hence some individuals' initial attempts to stop it from happening could be compared to the struggle to fight off an unwelcome attacker.

Yet, as leaders, we still had to balance that compassion for the individual with a focus on creating the best team for the future. This is an example of what Binney et al (2012, p. 116) refer to as balancing the need to get close to people with the need to maintain a distance so there is an ability to make the tough decisions. For me, it has been one of the most challenging aspects of the whole process as, despite our best efforts to look after individuals, difficult decisions had to be made and I know that some individuals have been hurt by the process. Some of that was inevitable, but I suspect that some individuals' experiences were more painful than necessary because of a lack of time and/or skill to handle it better.

One of the questions I've been asked about this process is how I personally managed that tension without completely closing off to the human impact of what we were doing. I am wary of giving advice as what worked for me may not work for others. I also recognise that some individuals may not have experienced my leadership as remaining connected to the human consequences. Further, I think it is important to be frank that I had many sleepless nights through it, not to mention a range of physical symptoms of stress. Nadine later told me that she also suffered physical symptoms of stress throughout this process.

For me personally, I think the combination of the following helped me through:
- Keeping a reflective diary throughout the whole process, which helped me to make sense of what was happening around me and to think about what I might need to do differently going forward
- Using the theory to make sense of my experiences, in particular Cartwright and Cooper's (1996) writings on merger, Stacey's (2010) writings on complexity and Buchanan and Badham's (2008) writings on working with politics and power
- The OD support provided by Irene which enabled us, as three leaders, to jointly make sense of what was happening around us and created a safe space to have the difficult discussions
- The willingness of Nadine and Petra to engage in this process in such a powerful and productive way
- Support from trusted colleagues and friends who more than once sat and listened as I downloaded emotions from a difficult discussion or meeting

- A genuine belief that merger was the right thing to do and keeping the endpoint in mind; which was developing an improvement support offering that made the best use of public funds to deliver the maximum possible benefit on improved outcomes for people using health and care services.

I also learnt from Stacey that "effective communication, therefore, cannot be regarded as a one off event because it is an ongoing process of negotiation. Effective communication requires staying in the conversation" (Stacey 2010, p. 145). This led me to conclude that my ability as a leader to influence was impacted in part by my willingness to stay in the conversation, no matter how uncomfortable it got.

There were many moments when I wanted to walk away and disengage from the difficult discussions, and one point just after the announcement of the merger where I simply avoided contact or discussions for three weeks. It didn't feel good and was probably the point in the process where I was most stressed, indeed I noted in my reflective diary at the time that the point at which I sought out conversations with both Petra and Nadine was the point where I could physically feel my stress levels lower. Reflecting on it now, it further emphasises the importance of the fortnightly integration leadership team meetings, as they created a structure that enabled (or maybe even forced) us to stay in the conversation.

Finalising the prenuptial agreement

One of the decisions we made as a leadership group was that each one of us should own every word in the final report recommending the purpose, functions and approach of the new integrated improvement service. This key constraint forced us to either work through the contested issues or defer them to the next stage of the process.

The initial draft of the report, which we recognised needed to be a living document, included an overall improvement framework that conceptualised our common approach. I was really proud of this framework and poured hours of my time into crafting it with others. I thought that it beautifully – perhaps over perfectly – weaved the different tools and techniques into an overall model. We sent a draft document to a set of expert critical friends and quickly received feedback from those in social care:

A model embedded within the health view of the world.

I was so torn in how to respond and, if honest, upset. Yet this was not the first time that I had to challenge myself to let go of what I had become attached to for the benefit of the overall process. We took the model out of the report and deferred it to the next stage, allowing more time to work through the differing perspectives. Inevitably, this led to criticism that we were ducking difficult issues as this was not the first matter we had deferred. However, we were learning that you can't please everyone in a process of change and held on strongly to our shared belief that we needed to broker sufficient agreement amongst all stakeholders. If the new service were to be successful, even if that took a little longer, imposition was not an option. Eventually, we achieved sign off from all our stakeholders. That was a good day.

The wedding

The story of the wedding and what follows would be a whole other chapter. Suffice to say it went ahead and we achieved a successful first year of operation, though not without having to face some significant challenges along the way. We experienced first hand the fact that much of the real work of integration is done post marriage. That marriage is just an important symbolic beginning.

Summary

I have used the analogy of a wedding throughout this chapter. When two (or in this case three) parties commit to each other, there has to be a giving up and a taking on, as well as both parties offering and pushing for something. I felt throughout this process that we were trying to deal with apparent tensions and polarities across many different dimensions; yet so often the solution was not one or the other but learning instead to live and work with both/and. Maybe improvement work, or any change, is always like this, and we need to become better at moving between different world views and living with the complexity and messiness of both/and rather than either/or thinking.

Finally, none of the above would have been possible without the willingness of Nadine and Petra to stay in the conversation and work through the difficult issues, to forgive me for the many mistakes I made along the way, and their ability to put their own needs secondary to that of the wider system. I suspect it would have been a very different story if any of the key actors hadn't engaged with such integrity throughout the process. Thank you.

CHAPTER 13

Quietening the Wind

I was sitting in the interview, across from a panel of eminent looking men and one woman. I had just given an answer to one of their questions which felt truthful and congruent with how I see things. I had described a situation where we had, as a team, worked hard together to redesign a patient pathway. One of the panel members, an impeccably dressed non-exec, gave me a look, a slight rise of a white, perfectly groomed eyebrow as he settled himself further back in his chair. I knew then that I hadn't won him over. It felt like he was looking down on me from some vastly superior height even though we were only across a table. The look said, "I know better", "I am older and wiser than you", "You are small". A power move communicated without uttering a single word.

And I didn't get the job, even though I was the only person called for interview.

I was disappointed but not totally surprised. In the feedback, the HR Director told me how well the general stakeholder presentation had gone. She was complimentary too about my experience, skills and track record. However, apparently several members of the panel thought I hadn't done enough as a leader myself.

"You talked a great deal about 'we', not about 'I'," she said.

This felt a real misinterpretation of my skills and approach, because I don't believe in pretending to be some macho, heroic leader, taking the credit for everything and making out it was all about me, me, me. To do so would have felt disingenuous and totally contrary to my values.

A week later she came back. "Would you consider taking on the role as an interim?"

I chatted with a few people – colleagues and my wife – to help me think through my response. It felt a risk, but I knew paradoxically that this would also be a strong motivator for me doing it well. The job was interesting. I also believed I had the leadership skills for the challenge of the role and that they had misread me. Lastly, I'm usually up for a challenge as experience has taught me that although things may not work out how I anticipate, they usually work out well.

I agreed to take the role as an interim, even though it was initially for just a year. This is the story of what happened next. On the GenerationQ programme, I learned the phrase "first steps are fateful", in the sense that they often shape what eventually happens; small seeds that hold the potential for the future, for what happens next, but whose significance only becomes apparent much later. It has been a journey of shifting a culture from one that was seen by most people, internally and externally, as arrogant and intimidating, to one where collaboration has become much more the way we work internally and how we work with a network of partner organisations. It is a story of creating a culture where gradually, often through conversations behind the scenes, the norm has become to talk about "we" rather than "me". At the same time, it is also a personal story about what I have learned of myself as a leader – what enables me to keep going, my values and the choices I make both in my role within the network and my role as a clinical lead.

The organisation I was joining is linked with a prestigious university and has a history of being intellectual and competitive, not just regionally but internationally. With the benefit of hindsight, I can see now that eventually I was able to do something others in my organisation could not have done, because they were approaching working with the network from a very different mind-set to mine. When I first started the job, I would sit in meetings in my own organisation with senior folk and somebody would invariably say "Our organisation is head and shoulders above any of these other organisations in the network. We've done so much more. Why would we want to waste time working with these people when all they'll do is slow us down? We're leading here, and those sorts of collaborations are either just going to be at best distracting and at worse will tarnish our reputation." That was the mind-set, and actually for some people probably still is the mind-set. The way you think, and the way you see the world, shapes what possibilities you see and what actions and moves you take. For many in my organisation, success was around being linked to a university that could bring in big grants, and being associated with academics who had national and international reputations. For me, true collaboration is about bringing out the best in everyone with consequences which can often be transformational – you just can't know about it until you're in those relationships.

The "we are the best" cultural assumption was amplified by the fact we were housed in a brand-new building, all glass and marble, on the University campus; so quite different from the NHS real estate of some of the partner organisations in the network, and a significant cultural artefact. The most senior players were all intellectual heavyweights, publishing papers, invited to be part of government think tanks. Robust debate rather than conversational dialogue was the norm, where contributors vied to defend their own points of view, or to shoot down others. It was stimulating, but had the cut and thrust of debates at the Houses of Parliament, where sometimes making a point seems to be more important than the content of the point.

The very first meeting of the network I attended was awkward, and made worse because it was the first time anyone had come up from NHS England. This contributed to an edgy atmosphere. As the round of introductions began it became very apparent that everyone else had a bigger (and often longer) job title than I did. When it was my turn and I introduced myself, people looked confused, saying things like "Yes, but what do you do? Who are you? What's happened to Bill?". Nobody in my organisation had bothered to tell them that my predecessor had left.

In the break for coffee I learned that the meaning that most in the room were inferring from my organisation's behaviour was "You partner organisations aren't important because we haven't even had the courtesy to tell you about this new guy; we can't be bothered to send along someone of the right level, so we've sent along someone who's obviously just filling the seat". It reinforced people's perceptions of the arrogance of my organisation. It also meant that, in terms of power, I started out with no positional power because not only was the role interim, I didn't have the same job title as others. On the upside, it also meant people had limited expectations of me and I wasn't seen as a threat. This allowed me to be more of myself.

As I was genuinely curious about what the other organisations in the network were doing, I made it my business over the first twelve months to build relationships with as many of the partner organisations as possible. I didn't just rely on the formal monthly meetings. I went and had conversations with people with no specific agenda other than to connect and get to know them. Not everyone was up for such a meeting, so with some I just tried to connect a bit round the edges of the formal meetings. From what I picked up, the approach was very different from my predecessor's. I did not know what would emerge, but I was absolutely certain that doing things differently, being more relational, was important for shifting the tense dynamics between the different organisations in the network. I also believe that partnerships between organisations only work when there are relationships at a personal, individual level.

Perhaps it's helpful to say a bit about me at this point. I'm comfortable saying what I need to say in big meetings but I also enjoy one-on-one conversations. It was therefore really affirming on the GenerationQ programme to find out about the importance of leaders working on what organisation researchers call the back stage, as well as the front stage. The front stage comprises big set-piece meetings, such as the first network meeting I attended. In my experience, and perhaps in yours too, they can feel very stilted, very formal and guarded, which can encourage posturing and nothing much moves forward. The back stage is where people can be more themselves, able to say what they really need or think, without worrying whether this is the right thing to be voicing politically. This is leadership work too. Certainly through building relationships back stage, one conversation at a time, I became an integral part of the network rather than an outsider. I was seen as someone who wanted to collaborate rather than compete.

There were two other significant events in that first year, one planned, the other a complete surprise. Firstly, I persuaded my organisation to host one of the pieces of work the network was supposed to be delivering. It was quite a big risk as there were many unknowns involved. The significance was not that we offered to host it, but that we then shared the initiative. And I say "we" here because I had now managed to recruit a couple of great people who could support me in doing some of the work; writing presentations, preparing documents, meeting people. This didn't just help me with the work load, it began to shift the culture within my own organisation, as I had specifically hired people who had similar beliefs and values to me in respect of collaborative working. We were building a bit more critical mass in terms of approach and style, at least in my part of the organisation.

In inviting the partner organisations to join we were genuinely wanting to be generous and collaborative, but it was still immensely difficult because many people remained suspicious. There was a lot of history and assumptions based on the past. How often does that happen when trying to merge departments or organisations? Some were still judging me on the dominant culture and track record of my organisation rather than me as an individual. They were saying "Yes, but what are you as an organisation planning to get out of this? Why should we help, because in the long run it might act against us?"

My team and I kept going back to them, having more conversations, listening, sharing ideas, exploring and, just by sheer doggedness and attrition, we got a couple of the partner organisations to join the work. Then a couple more. If I had been confrontational with any one of those people, pushed too hard, they would have probably dug their heels in, if only as a point of principle. It felt important to me that they felt invited, pulled towards us, and that it was their choice to join. It's the concept of the leader as the sun rather than the wind: people will take off their coat voluntarily in the sun; they hold on more tightly when the wind howls louder! We were shifting the culture through conversation, through relationship, building some momentum. It had taken twelve months.

However, there were still two key people whose support we needed. At the next meeting, I did a presentation articulating all the benefits from collaborating on the work. Greg, a clinician, had up till then been one of the most negative about the proposals. He was a rather portly individual who often appeared to be asleep in meetings, but he was formidably clever. He would suddenly stir and laser a weakness in an argument with the precision of a neurosurgeon. This made him highly respected, as well as slightly feared. Having had so many conversations with others, we had now really honed and improved our presentation (a benefit of engaging with, and listening to people who others might label as resistant!). The presentation was much more robust now, with more data. This time, Greg was persuaded and actively supported the proposal. Interestingly, he has now become one of its biggest advocates. The other negative person was absent from the meeting – by luck or design, who knows, but we now had everyone signed up. To reach this position had taken a great amount of work for myself and my team, what with having conversations, writing documents, putting together business cases. It had taken just over a year. The programme became the first piece of work all organisations in the network successfully worked on and delivered, together. This was important practically and symbolically as, on the basis of this success, the network then got funding for further work.

My team and I were having a well-deserved celebratory drink in the pub. Gemma, one of the newer members of the team, asked me,

"How do you stay resilient? What helps you keep going?"

It was a good question and one I'd pondered myself.

I told them about the support I've had from a non-exec on the board who has become my mentor. We sometimes have breakfast meetings, or he'll be available on the phone if I need to talk to him. I've been able to be very honest with him about things and to share with him some of my moments of doubt. People can rarely give you the answer, and frankly it wouldn't help if they did as we each need to find our own way, but having a sounding board has been useful. I know rationally that things usually work themselves out, but in moments when I experienced self-doubt or worried about things, it has been good to turn to him for wisdom as opposed to knowledge. And over time the bad days get fewer because you take on that wisdom and learn how to work with people better across all sorts of complexities.

I also recounted an incident in my childhood. In my family, there was an expectation that when you turned 10 or 11, you would get a job to earn your pocket money. One winter morning it was dreadfully cold and I was doing my paper round. There was a residential home with a pond. I took the papers out to get them in the right order when a sudden gust of wind whisked five papers out of my chapped red hands and they landed in the pond. I can remember the iciness of the water seeping into my socks and shoes when I waded in to get them, as I still had to deliver them. They were completely sodden of course. Next day, the shopkeeper told me he had received complaints and was docking my wages. I still had to do the paper round that day, even though I was essentially doing the work for nothing. I could never have gone home to my parents and said, "I've given up that job". It wasn't that our family needed the money, it's just that's what you did. You earned your pocket money. And I think I learned about resilience and not giving up. There's a balance, of course. Important things do sometimes take a great deal of effort – having to attend many meetings, having to write documents, ignoring some of the voices in my own organisation which, when I said I was involved in these meetings, would say, "That's a waste of time. That's never going to happen." But we kept on doing it, and actually what's happened seems to have massively paid off. The point of it is the perseverance. I saw one of those "Thoughts for the day" on the Underground recently that summed it up: "Success is the sum of small efforts repeated day in and day out".

What else have I learned about myself from getting the network to collaborate? On GenerationQ we were introduced to the idea that we all have different approaches to how we deal with people who hold a different opinion to ourselves. People whose preferred style is to compete are those who are primarily interested in their own agenda, their own views. They tend to ignore those of the other party. This style can be experienced as powerful and authoritative, sometimes aggressive. It's a position of win-lose. That was certainly the style of my predecessor and my organisation when I joined. For a collaborative approach, there needs to be a willingness to engage in listening and exploring the other's agenda, and to find ways to meet both, which takes time. This goes beyond compromise, which is a style when both sides do a deal that doesn't quite meet either's requirements. Collaboration takes the position of win-win which fits with my personal values and I believe can yield innovative and creative solutions to highly complex challenges. It also holds the possibility to grow collective power and to get more done. However, I know from my own experience that it takes time to build relationships, to encourage others to lay aside their initial assumptions. Hence the importance of all the back stage conversations.

Collaboration also requires trust, and towards the end of the first year, before everyone had agreed to work together, something else happened which I think may have shaped how others saw me and my organisation. It wasn't something I had planned but my response was. One day, I was busy writing a report in my office. There was a knock at the door, even though the door was open. It was Deidre, a feisty ex-nurse from Northern Ireland. She worked for one of the partner organisations in the network and was responsible for a prominent funding stream. She sat down and launched straight in, dismissing my offer of coffee.

"I don't know how much you know," she said, without pausing to hear my reaction, "but there are various inter-personal problems going on in my organisation and I don't really like the leadership. I don't like how things are running."

I was about to express regret and ask her to say more but she was unstoppable...

"I've an offer to put to you...I can take this funding stream and arrange for it to be taken over by your organisation."

I was completely shocked. She must have seen this on my face because she paused, looked at her watch, and then said, "I'm going to another meeting. Have a think and let me know", and then swept out. She was like a tornado, whirling in, stirring everything up, and vanishing. I certainly needed a coffee at this point. My immediate, gut level response was simple: "That's just not on".

In the short term, taking the piece of work would have delighted some on the board in my own organisation. However, it would have signalled to everyone in the network that we were still a highly aggressive organisation, prepared to do any deal for individual gain, an organisation without ethics. I would have been seen as a 'Fox', untrustworthy, using political knowledge for personal gain.

Instead, I contacted the chair of the network, explaining what had happened and that I had decided to turn Deidre's offer down. I phoned Deidre and told her too. I had hoped that the work would be offered in an open and transparent way to all of us and then I would have made a bid for it, but things don't always work out as you'd like them to. In fact, I never knew what happened with that particular piece of work. What I do know is that having demonstrated that I was prepared to do the right thing from the point of view of the network, there was a shift in the dynamics in my relationship with some key individuals, including the Chair. They knew they could trust me because when I was given the opportunity to do the right thing, I did so.

Shortly after this, a very important role came up on a National Board and although it was competitive, I was asked to represent the regional network. I think it was on the basis of "Well we can trust him to represent us fairly". I couldn't have predicted this, yet I do believe that the reason that you get chosen often goes beyond because you just grab it. People need to believe that you will act with integrity and do the right thing. For me, that's an important part of my life as much as my career.

Whilst all of this was taking place, I still had a clinical role. Historically I have tended to avoid conflict, worrying I might lose control of a situation or a group. However, one of the main learning points for me through the Generation Q experience has been the realisation that, dealt with properly, conflict and difficult conversations are absolutely critical. They can be the means of preventing problems rather than creating them, of building respect and relationships if both sides can talk in what, in Transactional Analysis (TA) terms, is Adult-Adult. Without having such conversations, I've seen misunderstanding and miscommunication result in far worse outcomes.

As lead for a clinical team, I was responsible for dealing with complaints from patients or relatives. In this particular case, a patient was on a life support system with an extremely poor prognosis for any meaningful recovery. A decision was made, following discussion with the family, to withdraw life support and to provide palliative care. Two days later the patient died. The patient's daughter complained that my colleague had been insensitive to the family's distraught condition during the discussion, and had "bullied" them into making a decision to withdraw life support earlier than they would have wished. The family were calling for disciplinary action.

I arranged for my colleague, Rajan, and I to meet in my office. He accepted my offer of coffee. I had briefed him that we were going to need to discuss a complaint that had been made about him. When I mentioned the name of the patient and relative who complained his first reaction was,

"So, the Trust are going to automatically side with the relatives, are they?"

I explained that was not the case, and that the first step was to have a clear account of his recollection of the meeting with the relatives. This in itself was helpful since it provided some important context. He had had previous discussions with other family members about the severity of the patient's illness and had assumed that this had been conveyed to the whole family. However this had been his first communication with the daughter who subsequently made the complaint.

The other strand to our discussion, which was evident from his body language and tone, was that he was clearly annoyed with me. I did not explore this with him at the time since I was focused on obtaining the facts and his version of events. As we finished the first meeting he asked me,

"Am I going to be disciplined over this?"

I said I needed to speak to other members of staff and that we could then meet again.

However, I reflected afterwards on the dynamics of what had been a difficult conversation. Rajan seemed to have adopted the Child ego state in TA terms, feeling that he was being told off by me, even though this was definitely not my intention. I could see that in some ways I had also fallen into the Nurturing Parent role where I was trying to both control and protect. I may also have come across as an authoritarian figure, passing judgement on the situation and on his professional conduct. I realised I had probably also come across as quite detached when my role should have been primarily supportive, helping Rajan to explore how he could improve his communication, demonstrating the compassion I know he has. A resilience questionnaire I had completed on GenerationQ suggested that when dealing with conflict and difficult conversations, I score highly on emotional control but poorly in my awareness of others. I needed to put myself in the position of my colleague. How would I have handled the situation? The fact is that I would have probably made the exact same miscalculation of judgement, assuming that having had a conversation with some family members I had communicated fully and effectively.

I scheduled another meeting. I started off by thanking Rajan for giving up more of his precious time and also said that I wanted to thank him for helping me learn something about myself. He was clearly rather taken aback by this. I explained that after our first discussion, I had placed myself in his position and realised I would have done exactly the same. I then said,

"I guess one learning point for both of us here is that we can't take clear communication with relatives for granted. Every time I sit down with relatives now, I will make sure we are all starting from the same place and have the same understanding of what is happening."

I was very aware that I was showing my own vulnerability by admitting I too had a similar mind-set and had got it wrong in communication with relatives in the past. I was starting to realise that vulnerability can be an important part of resilience. I noticed that his body language and way of speaking were completely different from what I had seen at our first meeting. He smiled and said,

"Well it's good to see even very senior consultants get it wrong sometimes as well."

He had changed from a very adversarial position to recognising that he could have done things better, and was prepared to accept that he was partly responsible for the situation that had arisen. We were both in an Adult-Adult state; what could have been conflict, each holding onto competing positions of right and wrong, had become a collaborative endeavour from which we both learned, and which strengthened our relationship.

The meeting came to an end with his suggestion that he meet up with all the relatives again to apologise and explain how there had been such an unfortunate misunderstanding. Before he left I asked him,

"Did you find my way of handling this meeting more helpful than our first one?"

"Yes," he answered. "You haven't been on a management course in between, have you?" he asked.

"Sort of," I replied.

The family accepted his apology and dropped the request for disciplinary action. It was also an important example of trying not to take sides, but rather to see both sides.

In conclusion, I have learned, in both my leadership role with the network and in my clinical lead role, that it is possible to develop a collaborative way of working, to go from everyone talking from their own perspective to creating conditions where there is dialogue, trust and relationships. In one of the books we read on GenerationQ, the author says "Don't get trapped into dividing everyone and everything into for and against, good and bad" (Binney 2012). That sums up my story.

Constructive Resistance

In this section we share another important theme to emerge from the stories, that of constructive resistance. In much of the traditional change literature, resistance is portrayed as something negative, associated with Luddites and those standing in the way of change. It is typically seen as a force that is stopping and holding back progress. However, this can be an unhelpfully restrictive and narrow view of resistance. Sometimes the pressures to find a solution as quickly as possible can create a culture in which everything is swept aside in the rush to meet deadlines or targets. Or, if power is concentrated and held by a few, a culture can be created where alternative points of view are suppressed, even unwelcome, where it is "my way or the highway".

In such circumstances, an important leadership role can be to challenge what appear to be top down diktats or commercial imperatives at the expense of all else. What can be required is to hold up a metaphorical hand and say pause, wait, we haven't considered all options, we are overlooking some important considerations, we haven't involved the people who are closest to the issue. It is sometimes appropriate to stand up for what needs to be protected rather than acquiesce to what is being suggested by others; to remind that there are moral priorities as well as organisational and political priorities. The intent when making such moves is to be helpful, hence the idea that this is constructive. However, such gestures may not always be seen as such by those driving for a solution, so such leaders may be seen as resistors by some.

Working in this way requires supreme relational and political skills, much courage and a great deal of self-awareness. It is a place where as a leader you are continually making judgement calls about how much to challenge, and when persisting in doing so will risk alienating key others. It is about knowing when to toe the line and when to walk the line. It is about being able to reframe challenge as a source of productive energy; to show that difference is not the same as disloyalty; to keep the conversation going and in play to allow other views to be explored. To use the back stage to gather interest and support. In these cases, what is required of leaders is *standing firm.*

To stand firm requires being aware of your own motivations and emotional drivers, so that you can notice and moderate your own behaviour. Sharing your emotional response can persuade others of your care and commitment. However, again the skill is to show this without over doing it, as too much may risk being too counter cultural, clouding the reasonableness of your argument or being perceived as a donkey in political terms. It requires understanding when a compromise is needed, even if how to get there is not yet clear.

There are two stories in this section:
- The first, *Creating Space*, tells the story of a clinician choosing to challenge a top down change that would have had a detrimental impact on the quality of care in one service
- The second, *Owning our History – Changing the Story*, describes what happened to an organisation that was being defined by external regulators and had lost sight of all else until a manager stimulated the creation of a counter narrative.

CHAPTER **14**

Creating Space

Setting out

What seemed to be an ordinary Tuesday afternoon brought the first inkling of the bruising organisational dispute that would come to define my leadership career.

In the thick of a messy and acrimonious conflict, I was fortunate to be a Fellow on the GenerationQ programme. This gave me thinking space to try to understand what was happening. I have no doubt that it helped me to choose how and when to act, enabling me to acknowledge my own emotions without becoming enslaved by them. Being part of a supportive learning community, having a coach and, crucially, my wonderfully patient and unconditionally supportive partner, also gave me the resource and resilience to keep going. I could very easily have given in to the pressure to toe the line, colluding in a decision that I knew would be disastrous for my service. Yet I didn't.

Reading this account, you may think that it was all a storm in a small specialty teacup, which of course it was, but it reveals much about cultural patterns in the organisation where I was working. It had become a place where important decisions were made without involving those who might have an alternative view and solution; where there was limited opportunity for dialogue, and where I experienced an almost irresistible organisational pull to closure and conclusion. It was a culture that privileged top down change and saw alternative views as disruptive resistance, negative, something to be overcome.

When I was invited to contribute to this book, I had mixed feelings about revisiting that time in my life. Now several years on, I'm working in a different organisation with a different and, I believe, healthier culture. Did I really want to go over it all again? At the time, I knew that all the players in the story were good people, trying to do their best. But with hindsight I'm sure there are things we could all have done differently. I will leave it to you to decide how I could have exercised greater wisdom and to better effect. I hope it offers you a vignette of organisational life within the NHS that will help you find the personal resources to stand firm for the values and principles you hold dear, question decisions that you know to be wrong when your certainty comes from a deep understanding of your service, or as Deming (2000) puts it, from "profound knowledge" acquired through years, perhaps decades of experience.

I was happily going with the flow of organisational life. I had an awareness of what was happening in other departments but didn't appreciate how their turbulence would affect me and my service, until the strong tide of their need was about to overwhelm us. Then it was time to stand firm as a rock.

An unusual Tuesday

I'd come to cherish the Tuesdays when I hadn't been on call on the Monday night. Perhaps it was the luxury of a full night of undisturbed sleep that filled me with enthusiasm for the day, as well as the opportunity to catch up on the infinite email in-box. I'd been in post as Deputy Medical Director for Women's Services for over 10 years and enjoyed the challenge of balancing between the clinical and corporate worlds. I was good at both roles and respected for what I did. I had good relationships with clinical and corporate colleagues across the organisation. The previous summer my partner and I had attended the Royal Garden Party, no less, nominated by the Chairman! And the CEO was my sponsor for GenerationQ. Looking back, perhaps I was a bit too comfortable, a bit too self-satisfied. Perhaps the sharp antennae I needed to maintain organisational and situational awareness were dulled by cosiness.

We had just eight months to go before our big move to a brand new hospital building several miles away. On this Tuesday afternoon the New Hospital Planning meeting was dragging. Suddenly, without knowing quite why, I was alert. What was it that Barry Hughes (General Manager for Medicine and Surgical Services) had just said?

"I'm sorry to say that we're looking at the gynaecology ward for the additional space we need for Acute Receiving."

I wondered if I'd heard correctly, "Sorry Barry, what are you talking about?" It didn't make sense.

"There is an urgent meeting tomorrow at nine o'clock to decide what we need to do. There is no alternative. We need all of the ward area that was going to be gynaecology. Check your emails. Terry is sending the papers out today."

He wasn't meeting my eye. There was something not right at all.

I liked Barry, a large amiable man who was always friendly and reasonable. I was aware that there was a serious concern about floor space in some clinical areas of the new hospital. The building had been planned before the universal exponential rise in emergency attendances. This meant that even before we physically moved in, the capacity of Acute Receiving, the first point of contact for all emergencies, was already only half the size of what was required. Although, in my awareness, I hadn't expected this to have any great impact on us in the Obstetrics & Gynaecology (O&G) service. We were, after all, completely on track in terms of our planning for the move. We were a good team. We'd worked long and hard on capacity and service improvement for over four years. We were ready to move.

As part of service redesign, we had significantly reduced hospital stay for O&G patients, providing safe out-patient management as an alternative. We had reduced inpatient beds in gynaecology by 30 percent and maternity by 50 percent. The changes we had been making were the sort of changes that others, particularly surgical specialities, needed to make to help address the capacity issues: reducing lengths of stay, more day case work, more direct consultant involvement in emergency care.

In the early days as Deputy Medical Director I had felt I could influence colleagues in other specialities by demonstrating what we could achieve in O&G. This just seemed to irritate my predominantly male colleagues. Our achievements were often discounted: "It's only O&G, you aren't affected by the same pressures. What do you know about the struggle to find patients a bed before you start a theatre list? You don't have sick patients. You have plenty of nurses." I had learned to stay quiet about what we were doing and didn't get involved in things I didn't seem to be able to influence. With the pressure of the countdown to the Big Move, the different medical tribes were even less interested in learning from our experience. Terry, the Deputy CEO, had once publicly added to this sense of being discounted by talking about Women's Services as "the cat flap". Even Jackie Craig, the new Women's Services' General Manager, who never missed an opportunity to ingratiate herself with Terry, had balked at that comment.

As well as working on the capacity issues, the other important thing we had achieved in our old buildings was to move the gynaecology ward closer to the labour ward and the maternity inpatients. The two areas had previously been separated by a maze of corridors, busy during the day and eerily deserted at night. The most important benefit of having the maternity and the gynaecology clinical areas "co-located" was patient safety. From past experience we knew the risks, particularly out of hours, for one team of medical staff trying to manage emergency patients in separate locations. Inevitably labour ward took precedence leaving gynaecology the poor relation. There had been some close calls and serious complaints to answer. In the planning process this "critical adjacency" was repeatedly stated. It was non-negotiable. Suddenly, from what I thought was a clear blue sky, on this Tuesday afternoon, the critical connection was under threat. In fact the whole of the gynaecology service was under threat! And maternity care would also be compromised.

Terry Murphy, deputy CEO, was in overall charge of the new hospital project and a career NHS manager. He was small and wiry and yet had a powerful presence, and a liking for dark suits and flashy ties. He had played a significant role in the success of getting our new hospital proposal signed off by the Government. It wouldn't have happened without him. While there was much to thank him for, his Achilles heel was the difficulty he had engaging with the senior medical staff. I think we were too disrespectful of corporate authority, difficult to manage. He also seemed to find dissenting views and uncertainty hard to live with, making it very difficult for anyone to offer views at odds with his own.

It also seemed to me that Terry had transient favourites among the medical staff. A newly appointed consultant often had "the answer" to whatever issue was top of the agenda. The latest favourite was a young, dynamic A&E consultant, Chris Taylor, who had been working with external management consultants on patient flow, wrestling with the recurring crisis of bed capacity, trying to maintain a safe service in our old buildings, as well as getting ready for the Big Move and the new model of one large Acute Receiving unit for all emergencies.

Returning now to that Tuesday. Everyone had left the meeting, Barry making for the door before I could collar him. I went to find my General Manager, Jackie. Surely, she must have known this was coming. Why hadn't she told me? The urgent meeting the next day was very worrying.

I'd known Jackie for a long time, but we didn't get on particularly well. She prided herself on managing up and she liked to collect "gold stars" from the CEO for coming in on budget, sometimes to the detriment of the service. Jackie was a large woman with a big voice, somehow able to suck the time and oxygen out of any working day. She ran the department by email, which saved moving from the comfort of her office. I had learnt not to open her emails or arrange a meeting with her after 5pm if I was to preserve any quality of life. Now at 5.30pm I really wanted to find her. Where was she?

At 10pm that evening I found the email from Terry, the deputy CEO. There it was, the threat, couched in portentously opaque language. We were being asked to "meet to confirm resolution of issues previously discussed regarding New Hospital accommodation for increasing numbers of emergencies presenting to secondary care". Nothing had been mentioned or discussed with me about this. As I read and re-read the email, in light of the meeting, I felt stunned. How could I have been so naïve as not to have seen this coming?

The next day

The next morning, Barry chaired the urgent nine o'clock meeting. Terry wasn't there, and neither was Aysha Varma, the Deputy Medical Director (DMD) for Medicine with responsibility for the new Acute Receiving model, and my counterpart. I was sure she would have been an ally, but she was on holiday. I was puzzled that we were meeting without her. In hindsight, the layout of the room was not helpful and I regretted not getting there earlier. We were set up for confrontation from the outset. There was Jackie, myself and Ingrid, one of my consultant colleagues, the "Women's Services women", on one side of a long table, and a range of men on the other, including the young favourite from A&E, Chris Taylor.

Barry outlined the issue. The accommodation in the new hospital planned for Acute Receiving, incorporating A&E, was not going to be big enough. The logical solution was to expand into the adjoining area which just happened to be the gynaecology ward. This was the only reasonable solution and had to be agreed *now*, or it would risk missing all the deadlines for the planned move date of June next year. He said that Terry was fully supportive of the changes that needed to be agreed.

So, there it was. The bombshell. The hand grenade. The rug being pulled.

"Hang on a minute," I heard myself say in a shrill, belligerent tone, "When exactly was all this discussed and decided? This hasn't been agreed with us. What about the implications for our service?" It came out of my mouth without a moment's hesitation. It needed to be said and yet, looking back, I could have done better.

The men sitting opposite all looked down, shuffling their useless meeting papers.

"Well," said Barry, "we've had to think about what is best for the greater good, and yours is a very small service. There is no reason why your patients can't be managed in one of the new surgical wards. We think the 10 beds you'll need could be available. You'll be sharing with urology, ENT and vascular. I'm sure they will each be happy to give up a few beds."

I couldn't believe what I'd heard. What about our nurse-led service? How on earth would the junior doctors work safely between these distant clinical areas overnight? We had our own emergency gynaecology patients to consider; where would these women be seen? The thought of women with miscarriage or ectopic pregnancy being managed in a large Acute Receiving area filled me with dread. The skill and expertise our gynaecology nurses had developed over years would be lost. Their telephone triage and advice saved many admissions and was a great service to our women. Our cancer patients had direct access to the ward; what would happen to them? And I was absolutely certain that none of the other surgical specialties would happily give up their precious few beds!

These questions and fears crowded into my mind. I had a sense of cold dread close to despair.

Barry was keen to move on quickly: "One of the reasons for this meeting is to try and understand what you actually do, so that we can make sure this is all sorted out in good time for the move. I am sure it won't be a problem."

I looked at Barry in disbelief, "You're saying this has been decided before there is any understanding of the needs of our patients and our service. Before you know what we actually do!"

"Well, moving gynaecology is the only solution that will resolve the bigger issue." Barry looked anxiously across to Chris Taylor for some support. He obliged. "It seems to me this is the only answer. I'm sorry for your service but it isn't as if you have many sick patients and your nurses aren't exactly overworked."

Once again my service, the service for women, was being diminished, dismissed, seen of little consequence in comparison to the "real heroic work" of the hospital, saving "important" lives. Our patients were only women after all! I was livid. Would they have been so dismissive if Aysha Varma had been here?

Jackie, my General Manager, who had been very quiet up until this point, finally sprang to the defence of her nurses, arguing that the proposal would mean losing all the work that been done to develop the gynaecology nurses in extended roles, something which should have been happening across the whole hospital for the past decade. "All that will be lost if they are diluted in a 32-bedded ward," she said.

Chris looked at his watch, "I'm sorry, but I don't see why your women should have a Rolls Royce service and the rest of us just have to make do. Can we get this sorted out? I have work to do." He was an impatient man. He saw things in black and white. It seemed that his idea of leadership was about telling others what to do, about pushing his ideas forward. We were spiralling down into a very negative win-lose battle. Any hope of reasonable conversation and dialogue was disappearing in acrimony.

Ingrid had been listening with characteristic thoughtfulness throughout this exchange. "I'm wondering where you suggest our miscarriage and abortion service will be located?" She had played our trump cards, abortion and miscarriage. The undiscussables.

"Ah," said Barry, sheepishly, "we hadn't thought about that. I'm sure it can be resolved." He looked over to Jackie, imploring rescue, as if he had suddenly become the victim, not our patients. Ingrid and I had become his perse-cutors! He went on, "We must close now. The work of this group seems to be done. I don't think we need to meet again. Jackie, can you work out with the other general managers how the gynaecology nursing staff will be distributed across the other wards? Terry is anxious to know that it will all be tied up in good time. We have to get it through the Clinical Steering Group next week."

I could hear myself almost shouting, "This is not the end of it! It will not be safe for our patients. This dismantles the whole gynaecology service. And there are implications for maternity care as well. There has to be a solution we can all live with."

Then Ingrid repeated firmly, and far more calmly, "What about the miscar-riage and abortion service?"

The men sidled out, without seeking any further understanding of what we "actually do", leaving Ingrid, Jackie and me reeling from the tidal wave that had just swamped us.

Jackie broke our stunned silence, "I thought this would happen." I wondered how much she had known about it in advance. Was that why I couldn't find her the previous evening? Had she been having some back stage conversa-tions that might help us? Or had she colluded in this threat of destruction? She went on, "We might as well think about how we will make it work. It's going to happen anyway. If you consultants are called in more at night because the junior staff can't cover both areas safely, then perhaps, if we play our cards right, we'll get another consultant out of this."

I wasn't contemplating giving in, even if my General Manager was. "How is one extra consultant going to help?" I replied tersely. The proposed in-patient accommodation for gynaecology patients in the new building was about as far from the labour ward and the maternity in-patient areas as it could possibly be. The separation of the two arms of our service would be impossible to cover safely, particularly out of hours, with the same team of medical staff.

"And what about the miscarriage and abortion service?" Ingrid had that hot potato firmly grasped.

I was not going to acquiesce to this ill-thought out proposal. It was unacceptable and unsafe for women and staff. I was angry too at the way things had been handled, the lack of dialogue, the imposition of a top down solution, the apparent dismissal of all the improvement work we had done as a team over the last several years. It felt like a personal attack on my leadership integrity, as if we were being punished for being the standard-bearers of good practice. It was an attack on the service for women!

How was I going to challenge in a way that would be heard? I felt we were already on the back foot. Had I succeeded in getting us labelled as resistant and belligerent?

One of the most important things I had learnt early on in the GenerationQ programme was about the power of conversation. In the apparent chaos and complexity of organisational life, everything begins with someone talking to someone else. Now was the time for some serious conversation.

I headed over to Terry Murphy's office to see if I could speak to him, or at least get into his diary. He wasn't there. His PA wasn't hopeful, "He's very busy with the new hospital you know, and then he's off for Christmas." I said I would send an email.

Turning to the team and compromise

I needed to share the situation with the team. Jackie had reminded me that Terry had asked that the content of the nine o'clock meeting remained confidential. However, I felt betrayed that the issue had been considered for several months without discussion with my service and I wasn't willing to compound the betrayal by not sharing the news with the team. Ingrid and I called an emergency meeting at four thirty that afternoon, inviting the senior medical staff, the gynaecology ward sister and the service managers. Jackie couldn't be there.

It was hard to bring the meeting to order as my colleagues vented their shock, anger and fear. Fighting talk began to emerge, "We need to go to the press; this is an attack on services for women." We were in danger of becoming caught in the grip of the drama triangle and, whilst I empathised with their reactions (hadn't I played out such reactions in front of my senior colleagues?) I knew we must not become victims of our own emotional response. As strongly as we all felt, we had to find our Adult voices, just as Ingrid had done so well and to good effect.

I reminded everyone that going to the local press was dangerous. It would be very likely to backfire, triggering even more negative feelings and even retribution. I needed to keep the team together, focused on achieving our goal through clear, reasoned argument. I tried to steer the discussion round to thinking about our priorities for patients, what was non-negotiable and what we could give way on. At the meeting that morning there had been little evidence of any interest in a compromise, but it seemed to be our only hope of rescuing our service from disaster. We had to find a solution that both sides could live with. To my relief, two of the senior gynaecology nurses immediately started to think about practical ways forward.

Although I wasn't hopeful, I said that I had emailed Terry Murphy asking him to meet us. He could help us understand the wider issues and we could put forward our concerns. Ingrid and I recognised that we needed to be more politically savvy. We agreed who we were each going to speak with on behalf of the team. I volunteered to have a conversation with Terry Murphy and the Medical Director. I also considered contacting our Chairman and CEO. Now was the time to make the most of my good relationship with both. Could it do any harm?

People were leaving to collect children or to do the 5.30pm ward rounds. Back at my desk, an email from Jackie popped up on my screen. It was getting late and there was already a dusting of snow, with more to come. Should I open the email? I decided, yes.

Her angry message accused me of scaremongering, creating worry for staff who may ultimately lose their jobs, when they didn't need to know any of this yet, particularly before Christmas, telling me I should have kept quiet about the proposals.

On the point of closing the message, regretting that I had opened it, I was surprised to see an attachment outlining a proposal. Jackie had been thinking about other possible solutions too and she was suggesting taking this proposal to the Clinical Steering Committee the following week. I looked through it and had to admit, there was definitely something workable. For a fleeting moment I was able to reflect, to "catch myself" and to notice the possible impact of my gestures and responses: was I at risk of amplifying the drama, making it worse by assuming deliberate mal-intent, of pre-judging others? Was I rushing in, keen to be the hero and save the day?

My pager went off. I was surprised but pleased to hear the Medical Director on the other end of the phone. He was a good MD, a good listener, and had been a great support to me in the past. He was always fair, considered and had genuine integrity and honesty. I liked and respected him.

"I've just had Terry on the phone. He's asked me to speak to you about the proposed changes for the Acute Receiving area in the new hospital. I haven't been involved in the discussions until now. I gather there is a chance that Acute Receiving will expand into the gynaecology ward?" I launched into my tirade of why this would be dangerous, how it undermined all the changes in preparation for the move, how it wasn't fair and there had to be other options. My fleeting moment of reflection lost.

He listened patiently then said, "As you know, Chris Taylor has been working with the team, looking at flow and how we need to manage within the accommodation we will have at the new place. There is a big risk for all of us. We have to find a way forward." I was disappointed to learn that he wasn't going to be at the Clinical Steering Committee meeting and even more disappointed that he was giving me the message to "tone it down" and consider my "corporate responsibility".

Over the next few days a small group of us, including Jackie, went across to the almost finished new hospital. We looked at the ward area we had expected to move into, the colours we had chosen and the carefully planned layout. Our excitement and eager anticipation for the hospital move had certainly lost its shine. We paced the area, the stairs, the lift, the corridors. We went over to the surgical wards, to see the proposed alternative accommodation. We timed our walk back to the labour ward, the distance our junior doctors would have to walk, or run. It was easily eight minutes, even at a brisk pace. We sat down over a coffee and tried to work out the minimum accommodation feasible for our gynaecology service. We couldn't compromise on safety but there were other options, perhaps sharing some accommodation between the our two specialties, obstetrics and gynaecology. We would have to use our beds even more efficiently, further reducing length of stay for maternity and gynaecology patients. But there was a chance it could work. "I'll send our proposal to Terry for the meeting," said Jackie.

In the event, the Clinical Steering Committee didn't get much opportunity to discuss our proposal. The papers didn't go out until the morning of the meeting, very few of the clinical staff had read them. Terry, as the Chair, had decided our proposal wouldn't work. "Unless we agree the expansion of Acute Receiving into the gynaecology ward the whole move to the new hospital will be delayed. It will be a disaster. There is no credible alternative." The loss of the gynaecology service was rubber stamped without ceremony.

I'd had to choose between the Clinical Steering Committee and two days at Ashridge for GenerationQ. I felt torn. However, GenerationQ was what I needed. The time and space with my GenerationQ colleagues, with faculty and my action learning set helped me to keep my emotions in check and to prepare for a conversation with the CEO. She was always generous with her time as far as I was concerned, and later that week she and I took my issue out for a "walk and talk" in the cold, crisp December air. In spite of the prickly nature of what we were discussing, we enjoyed the opportunity to get muffled up and out into the winter daylight. "It's really an operational matter and the correct process has been followed. Terry is trying his best to resolve this." She had listened to my concerns, but was I picking up the hint there had already been some discussion with Terry? I asked her advice:

"What do you think I should do now?"

"I'll speak to Alan (Medical Director) and see if we can't get some fresh eyes on this. Assuming the proposal goes through there is still work to be done to mitigate the impact on your service." Indirectly, I felt that the advice she was giving me was, "keep going". This decision wasn't done and dusted yet!

A shocking moment

I was rushing back to the women and children's area when my pager went off. I was supposed to be taking over the overnight on-call in half an hour and there was so much to catch up on after being away for a couple of days at Ashridge. It was after 4.30pm and it was Jackie's extension. I had to answer. "Hi Jackie, you're looking for me?" Jackie sounded a bit frosty, "Can we have a word in my office?" Reluctantly I made my way along the corridor to her office, hoping that there was some emergency that would soon rescue me.

I was surprised to see Terry sitting in Jackie's office. There was a definite chill in the air of the small room, but the temperature was on the rise. With no time for pleasantries, Terry launched into a tirade, telling me about the damage I was doing to everyone, accusing me of holding up the decisions for the new build, "This is ridiculous. And it's all your fault!"

"We are all agreed that you are getting far too emotionally involved. It is clouding your judgement." His voice rose, and fingers were pointed.

"You are just rabble-rousing. Your job is to tell those colleagues of yours that this is going to happen, and they need to xxxxxx well get on with it. What's your problem?!"

Jackie then added to the tirade. Blame was being well and truly laid at my door.

To my great relief I was rescued by the pager. It was the labour ward. Having urgent clinical things to do seemed the most appropriate response to this barrage. I left, choosing not to reveal my discussion with the CEO.

I hadn't expected this attack, which felt personally directed and very emotional. I had never been spoken to like this in my entire professional career. It was unnerving but there was something inauthentic, almost comic about it. I was able to take a step back, distance myself, almost observing what was happening. What was really going on?

It brought to mind some of the GenerationQ discussions and reading. It seemed to me that Terry and Jackie were both projecting their own emotions onto me. I certainly felt passionately about my service and had been very emotional at the beginning, but now I was much more in Adult, knowing that staying calm and clear headed was the only way of finding a compromise. I was also able to reflect that their display of anger showed that they cared, that we were in this mess together, looking for a way forward. We were all taking this personally! That was OK. But right now there were far more important things to deal with on the labour ward, always the best reminder of why I was there and why I loved my job.

The Chairman listened to me with his usual courtesy and patience. He had been a public servant for the long haul, a very experienced and influential public-sector chairman well used to navigating the tricky waters of organisational territorial disputes. I made sure he knew that our concern with the proposal was that it would dismantle the gynaecology service, it would result in caring for vulnerable women in a mixed-sex ward, dispersing the team of gynaecology nurses that had looked after one of his relatives so expertly. As I knew he would, he asked, "What do you want me to do?" Although I'd thought a bit about this before our meeting, it wasn't until he asked that I was able to articulate an answer.

"We need the time to reach a solution that we can all live with. Anything you can do to influence that would be a great help." In spite of his influential position, I knew he wasn't going to wave a magic wand. He wasn't going to go against procedure or overtly undermine the executive officers. But he had been speaking to the CEO and knew of her suggestion to get the Medical Director and others involved. I left with a bit more hope to hang on to. But it would all have to wait until after the Christmas and New Year holidays.

Before we battened down the festive hatches, I updated colleagues on the suggestions from the CEO and the Chairman. I kept the exchange with Terry and Jackie to myself. There was hope.

Thank goodness for wisdom

Early in the New Year we met again as a group of colleagues. I had received an email that morning from the Medical Director's PA to arrange dates and times for an airing of the "gynaecology issue"! The CEO had been as good as her word – the Medical Director, Nursing Director and Director of Public Health were going to review the decision and the process, to try and find the common ground and a way forward. Fantastic! We reviewed our compromise proposal. What was needed to really make it work? Were there extra resources, extra staff, different ways of working? Who else did we need to draw in?

Jackie arrived, out of breath but looking pleased. She had some news herself, "I've managed to negotiate with Terry for additional resources when we agree the gynaecology ward changes. I think we will get another consultant salary. You need to know though, as we speak they are knocking the wall through from the Acute Receiving area and changing the electrics for the call bells. That's it, that ward isn't ours anymore."

Over the next two weeks the meetings went ahead. The medical, nursing and public health directors listened patiently to all sides of the argument. We took them to the new building, stepping over cables and floor protectors, navigating ladders and dangling wires, we walked the corridors. It helped their understanding of the practicalities of what we were being asked to do. As Lean theory suggests, there is no substitute for "go and see" to really understand. And as we reminded them, nobody had come up with any suggestion for alternative accommodation for the miscarriage and abortion service, or any of the in-patient gynaecology care.

The three directors were wise. They did not bring their own solution. They said they would facilitate finding a compromise, or at least find a way of mitigating the effects on the service for women. The issue stayed open and live. The meetings were facilitated by the leader of the Organisational Development team. We spent the first two sessions restating our respective positions, us tabling our proposal and them saying how it wouldn't work. It didn't seem as if we were getting anywhere, and we were hurtling towards deadlines for the planned hospital move. What was supposed to have been resolved in six weeks at the turn of the year was now dragging on into March.

Just before the third meeting our gynaecology ward sister, Linda, asked if she could invite her colleague, the ward sister appointed to the newly proposed Acute Receiving area. They had trained and worked together over the years and had often helped each other out. It struck me as strange; why hadn't we involved her at the outset? At this point I was beginning to lose hope, wondering if I would have to resign.

At the third meeting, the two ward sisters began to explain what they had been looking at together over the preceding few days. The main obstacles to our compromise proposal seemed to be sharing ward facilities between Acute Receiving and gynaecology. As leaders of their respective teams they had quietly got on and worked out a way of allocating clinical and office accommodation that could work. They pointed out how they could help each other, for example checking drugs at night, being flexible about the use of the beds where the ward areas joined. The miscarriage and abortion service would not have to move. The gynaecology nursing team would be preserved. The critical co-location with the labour ward could be preserved. And, Acute Receiving would have all but six of the bed spaces they wanted. The two colleagues who were also friends had the will, relationship and trust in each other to make it work.

The mood in the room changed in an instant. This new dynamic, a new voice, a new solution, brought light and hope. The discourse changed from negative to positive: how we could make it work rather than why it wouldn't. It was the final meeting of that group, its work done.

Terry reluctantly agreed to the proposal, and stated firmly that this was a temporary arrangement to avoid any delay of the hospital move. It would be reviewed after three months.

We hastily called a meeting of our medical, nursing and midwifery colleagues to share the good news. Of course, we were all delighted. The threat hanging over us had dispersed. There was a huge sense of relief. We still had a significant task ahead to find a way of working within our dramatically reduced in-patient bed numbers, but with the threat lifted the ideas came tumbling out. The energy and creativity were back. This was a real reminder for me of the importance of staying with uncertainty and creating space for the emergence of great ideas. Complexity-informed leadership in action! We were looking forward again, with great hope and expectation, to our new hospital accommodation. Having held the hot potato for long enough, Ingrid said, "And our miscarriage and abortion service is safe!" "Yes!" the collective cry went up!

Inevitably there were lots of challenges about sharing the ward accommodation in a way that it hadn't been designed for. We had to learn and improvise together. Terry's three-month review never happened. Acute Receiving continued to expand its territory beyond any interest in the paltry number of beds that the gynaecology accommodation had to offer. Terry Murphy hardly spoke to me again.

On the other hand, my leadership capital with clinical colleagues across the organisation grew. And as an O&G team, importantly including Jackie, we grew as a team. We came of age and were able to successfully deliver the subsequent change and improvements needed to work within our new accommodation and to provide safe care. As a leader, I think one of the most important aspects of what I did was to contribute towards keeping discussion and the decision open until a workable compromise was found. We did that by conversation. We talked to people who could influence the decision. I used my own power of influence and connection.

Personal reflections

But how had this all caught me so unawares? I knew other services were struggling with the huge rise in emergency attendance and admissions. We all were. But it didn't seem that there was anything I could do to help them. Did I ask?

Had we been a bit too smug about how well we were doing in the Women's Service? Had I been a bit of a sheep, naïve, rather than paying attention to organisational politics and different interest groups? When the news first broke, and I was so angry and upset, did I sound more like a donkey, outwitted and out-manoeuvred by cunning and clever foxes?

What I initially experienced was like a seismic shock to the core of my relationship with the organisation. The assumptions colleagues and I in our service had made about fairness, integrity, commitment to quality of patient care, respect for clinical opinion and knowledge of the service, had all been profoundly shaken. Throughout this difficult time I was always confident that I had the support of my great team of colleagues. There was a very strong sense of being in it together.

I had the invaluable support of my GenerationQ family, coach and action learning set. I had been naïve about organisational and corporate life and certainly about the emotions that can be unleashed when assumptions, interests and perhaps power bases collide. Am I learning to be a wise owl?

Almost three years after our move, Linda, our wonderful gynaecology ward sister who played such a pivotal role in the outcome of the story, called me to the ward. "There's something I think you'll be interested to see." When I went to the ward there was the electrician re-wiring the door entry and call-bell system to separate gynaecology from Acute Receiving. It had been a constant annoyance since the move that the rooms for gynaecology patients were still wired up for the Acute Receiving area, the argument being that gynaecology was "temporary". Linda and I shared a knowing smile as we watched the electrician at work. We weren't temporary anymore. Job done!

But what of the wider organisational perspective? It hadn't started well but we eventually arrived at the place where we needed to be. Had we briefly glimpsed a patient-centred, learning and collaborative culture in action? I hope so.

CHAPTER 15

Owning Our History – Changing the Story

The conversation

As I got into the car after finishing one of the GenerationQ workshops, I reflected on how amazing the last few days had been. Another Fellow in the group had described Ashridge, the location for all the GenerationQ workshops, as "Narnia". I knew what he meant. It was a place with beautiful gardens, delicious food, time to think, learn and reflect; an opportunity to have meaningful conversations with amazing guidance on hand. No mention of "special measures". No talk of failure. No haranguing about the lack of performance delivery. It felt such a world away from the hospital trust where I worked which was labelled "failing" by external regulators.

I was a manager with a wealth of experience and positive ideas, with desire and energy to shift the culture of my hospital. Back at work, however, I felt unnoticed, unable to have much of an impact, and powerless. Our local culture wasn't great and in fact I think we all felt under siege and under threat. In this culture, I found myself feeling far from great a lot of the time. The sole focus of the board seemed to be to get out of special measures. At Ashridge, the opportunities for personal and organisational change seemed real, but driving away, as the physical distance between Ashridge and me grew, I felt as though all my hopes for change and positive energy were slipping away, like a picture on the sand being washed away by time and tide.

At this particular workshop, everyone's GenerationQ sponsor had come along for the first day. I had felt quite anxious sharing my special space with James, my sponsor and a board member. I was concerned: what if he didn't appreciate the experience? What if he was dismissive about something I cared deeply about? It turned out that James was as affected by his visit to "Narnia" as me, but in a way that I was not expecting. We went for a "walk and talk" that afternoon, as did each of the Fellows with their sponsor. "An opportunity for a different conversation in different surroundings," said the faculty. I was not prepared for just how different it was going to be.

We strolled past the fabulous exuberance of the pink and orange rhododen- drons. I was half paying attention to them when I was suddenly pulled back to focus on James. He was talking fast and urgently. It was as if he wasn't breathing. Concerns about our Trust came tumbling out. He was unsure what to do for the best and he was frustrated with progress. He was suddenly opening up, confiding in me, in a completely uncharacteristic wave of self- disclosure. Perhaps James had been so holding in all his concerns, his responsibilities, that once he had started talking, his concerns came out in an almost unstoppable flood. In that moment, for me personally, it was too much. I felt overwhelmed.

I was so taken by surprise, I found it hard to respond. As part of GenerationQ, I had been reading about complexity thinking and the unexpected, yet being confronted with this outpouring completely floored me. Here was my board member telling me his worries. I'd always seen James as so resolutely in control, with not a crack of vulnerability. It felt like he was almost a different person. I can't remember what I said, if I said anything at all. Hopefully all that was needed was for me to listen.

The following day, when James and all the other sponsors had gone, I reflected on my shock with the help of several of my GenerationQ colleagues. I realised that I had put James on a pedestal because he was a senior exec. Because he was a senior and experienced member of the board, I assumed he was in control, in charge and all-powerful, with no room for doubt. Hence, when he shared so much I felt shaken. Confronted with his vulnera- bility, he was no longer the strong (perhaps heroic) leader who could save the Trust... or rescue me. It made me realise that of course he was human too and just how difficult it can be, as a leader, to share difficulties with others whilst not over sharing and unintentionally making others feel too vulnerable. I realised what a fine judgement line this is. I wondered how well I was keeping the balance with my team. Was I being authentic and showing I trusted them by sharing what I was thinking and feeling at different times? Was I stopping short of over sharing so that they could still have confidence in me?

Acknowledging the organisational patterns

A few weeks after leaving "Narnia", James and I had a meeting to discuss my Ambition into Practice, which was to introduce the practice of quality improvement (QI) into the organisation. Neither of us mentioned what had transpired during our "walk and talk" and yet I sensed a new willingness in him to listen to my ideas. Perhaps, even more importantly, I was now seeing him differently and therefore the power dynamic between us was different too. Using Transactional Analysis terms, I felt as if I had grown up a bit, no longer the Child in our relationship and more an Adult, with less of a cavernous power difference sitting between us. I was certainly less deferential and feeling more confident about sharing my own knowledge of QI, knowing that James had been impressed by what that he had experienced at Ashridge. We talked through different ideas and I could feel myself becoming more and more excited. Then there was a pause in the conversation. James seemed lost in thought, staring up at the ceiling. At last he spoke.

"I'm just not sure," he said. "Maybe we are getting overly ambitious here and taking on too much. Why don't we ask our neighbouring Trust to provide the quality improvement programme? I'm sure they'll know more than us."

I groaned inwardly. From my perspective, this was part of the stuck cultural pattern we had got into as a Trust – purchasing someone else's solution, bringing in an outside team, seeming to ignore and therefore diminish the possibility of our own people contributing. I also felt a twinge of annoyance – was I going to be again prevented from contributing myself? We'd been crawled over by so many external consultants, often duplicating each other's work. They were like wasps sucking at a rotting apple. It was time for me to speak up, to push back and stand my ground. Could I do it in a way that James would experience as supportive, and not critical?

I could feel my feet firmly placed on the floor and, even though I was seated, I sat tall. I explained why I felt strongly that people from our own organisation should and could lead the quality improvement projects. I reminded him of how important clinical engagement was going to be and that this was much more likely to happen if QI was something done with, rather than done to, the doctors. "Pull not push", I reminded him from one of the Ashridge sessions he had attended.

"You're sounding like Geraldine, the CEO at our next-door Trust. They have lots of these QI initiatives. I visited them recently and asked her how she gets buy-in for the QI programmes. She said she led the organisation's vision and QI programme herself. Well, I mean, that might work for her there, where people want to get involved. But here, really, I don't see why it should always be up to me to sort everything out. Why does nobody round here ever take the initiative to make things happen?" At that moment I really caught a glimpse of the leadership burden. The challenge of the demands being put on him and the rest of the board by the regulator seemed to be sitting heavily.

Despite my growing empathy, I felt my energy seeping away, along with the connection between us that had developed at Ashridge. All I could hear was that word, "but". I just wished he would use the word "and" instead! He was in the drama triangle in the place of victim, "Why do I have to do it all?" and blaming everybody else in a sweeping generalisation. I had learned that using words like "always" and "never" are often the tell-tale signs of someone not being in the Adult ego state. James had another meeting to go to. I was seeing my coach later but I knew that I needed to keep the subject of the conversation alive.

"Let me have a think and come back to you," I said, not at all sure what I would come back with, but also not wanting to allow this to fade as perhaps I would have done in the past. I had to keep this on the agenda at all costs, an important insight for me at the time.

The thinking I did with my coach was about me and the choices I had in terms of my next meeting with James. In the past, although I had found it flattering when he had asked my opinion, I had also been on the receiving end of dismissive comments when he didn't agree, as if he were, consciously or not, labelling me as a "resistor" to his views. This had once happened in a large meeting, which had made me want to retreat and crawl away. My coach reminded me this recent meeting had been different. It was a one-on-one meeting, back stage and not in public view, and that I was intentionally trying to shift repeated patterns of behaviour, rather than allowing past patterns to be reignited. I hadn't quite realised this at the time, but I was beginning to rewrite my own story of how I am as a leader. As the poet, Ben Okri writes, "A people are as healthy and confident as the stories they tell themselves. Sick storytellers can make nations sick. Without stories we would go mad. Life would lose its moorings or orientation. Stories can conquer fear, you know. They can make the heart larger." At that moment I was starting to tell myself a much healthier story about my own leadership.

With the help of my coach, I explored how to stay in an Adult ego state when I next met James. My intention was to try and shift the pattern of us descending into the drama triangle. We looked at the gestures I could make, how to start. Mental rehearsing was not something I would have done before GenerationQ, but I was realising that this type of preparation is really important for significant conversations.

A few days later I made another appointment to see James to discuss the next steps regarding QI, and the direction the organisation needed to take. James was interested in what I thought. He asked my opinion: should we look at the organisation's vision or just get on and do QI? I took a deep breath.

"I honestly think that until we, as an organisation, start setting the narrative about *who* we are, then we can't move forward. As an organisation we need to take back control of our own story! There is nothing motivating about waiting for the CQC results, or Monitor's feedback. We need to resist having others' narratives imposed upon us; we need to write our own story, use our own language. The senior clinical staff are disengaged, and getting a good CQC result is not a sufficiently meaningful focus for them. This doesn't mean the CQC results or Monitor's feedback are not important, they are, and yet they are not enough..."

There was a pause. Time for another breath.

"So, in summary, yes, I do think that the organisation needs to set its own vision, write its own strategy. It is the right thing to do. I wrote it as my conclusion in my last assignment."

James laughed at that.

"You should have let me read it, then we wouldn't have needed to spend time talking about it, and I agree with your thinking. I am really concerned that everything we do at the moment is related to the CQC action plan and the focus on turning all actions blue. (Blue was a new external measure of an objective being embedded into the organisation.) What will the organisation do after the CQC leave us? That is a really good question."

I replied, "Yes, I agree with you. The Trust needs to define and tell its own story, not just the regulator's one. What are we proud of, what is the healthy story we want to tell ourselves?"

James looked up at the ceiling again, "I find myself wondering why we haven't done this before."

I found my voice to support him: "We have been so completely focused on being placed in special measures that it feels as if we have lost our own identity, that we no longer feel responsible for ourselves. We doubt ourselves too much. We need the staff to be engaged and I don't think that they are engaged about being in special measures. It's too painful."

He was looking intently at me, interested, curious.

"Keep going," he said.

I offered my truth: "I feel that the organisation works on a four-monthly cycle. We are so keen for a new system, any system, to work and show improvement to justify removal of special measures that we wobble when a new system or initiative doesn't work immediately. We lose our nerve, and change to a new one."

I had caught James' attention, "I just struggle to understand why the organisation doesn't want to embed the changes we need to make in order to remove the regulation spotlight?"

By now, I was in flow: "I think it is because people can't relate to them. If you look at trusts that have been removed from special measures, they have focused their activities on things that are meaningful to staff. The other challenge is that our local initiatives are normally devised and imposed by external management consultants, which makes achieving ownership by our staff so much harder. This is a 'stuck pattern' for us as a trust."

"Am I part of this pattern?" He was looking me straight in the eye.

I hesitated. I appreciated his willingness to ask for feedback. I felt there was no need to say more, other than to suggest that we were all part of the pattern but that patterns can be shifted. I mentioned how I personally had been helped to shift my own patterns with the support of some coaching and reflection. James thanked me for my honest feedback and suggested that I call a firm of facilitators who would help us develop our own approach to QI, rather than imposing a solution on us. He also said he'd think about getting himself a coach.

I felt elated – and a little scared. This is what I had wanted. Could I do it, could I lead this well?

I commissioned a small firm, QINTA*, who are experienced in QI and yet have a facilitative approach. It was important to me, given that we were commissioning *yet another* firm of externals, that they had a different approach. They needed to model the shift in behavioural pattern we were seeking, and the process of change needed to be congruent with our desired change. They were to work with the board of directors, and I felt pleased at such a positive step. However, unbeknownst to me, other conversations were going on at the same time about hiring additional external consultants to do some board development work. This only came to light when I had organised some meetings for QINTA. This was not the first time that I reflected, after the event, that I need to be more politically aware. The other directors were angry and puzzled about why James had not discussed this

---

*   This is a pseudonym and any association with a registered organisation is accidental.

QI work with them and how it fitted with the other external companies. I did my best to explain and explore, listening to their concerns without blaming or rescuing James. I was feeling rather uncomfortable though. It was starting to all look a bit muddy.

Two days before QINTA's work was due to start James interrupted a meeting I was in, asking, rather too casually, "Would it cause you a personal problem if I cancelled the work with QINTA that you have arranged?"

Was this really a question or was it a statement in disguise, I thought, as I replied, "It won't cause me a personal problem, yet why would you want to do that?"

"It's not going down well with the other directors. They keep asking me why we need to do it, and how it differs from the board development work."

My previous default would have been to just say, "OK". This time, rather than letting James off the hook, I asked more questions, helping me understand the issues and hopefully helping him think through the options too; keeping the conversation alive. It turned out that James was under such pressure that he had been too busy to read the proposal from QINTA in full, so no wonder he hadn't been able to confidently answer the other directors' questions.

I took (yet another) deep breath.

"You *could* cancel the work, but how are you going to achieve the development of the board and setting of the organisation's vision and forward journey?"

He looked sheepish, "Well there is a range of different people on the board who could facilitate the process."

Feeling that this was my last chance, I kept challenging him, repeatedly asking him the same question: "How will you do it?" I kept reminding myself of the power of inquiry and the use of the "broken record technique" that I had discussed with my coach. I then shared with James that I was personally finding the board challenging to work with at that time, and that I felt outside facilitation would be essential. It took a lot of courage for me to hold this conversation. I concentrated on suppressing my personal driver to please others, to be liked, to shy away from challenge and potential conflict. I desperately tried to stay in Adult mode. I felt sick and worried afterwards, concerned that I might have somehow crossed a line of acceptable behaviour with James, yet he seemed calm and to be reflecting on the conversation. He ended by thanking me and stating that he would think about it.

James was out of the office the next day but left a message for me to continue the work with QINTA.

Following the inquiry interviews with the executives and senior staff, I worked with the QINTA facilitators to collate the themes that had emerged from the conversations.

A theme that I personally felt was the most powerful was *Culture of Compliance*. This felt such a strong statement to come from the executives, about not feeling in charge of the next steps for the organisation, of not being able to resist imposed change well. It resonated with how I personally felt about the past three years of waiting for the organisation to notice that I existed and could do more. Why were we all so compliant? Why am I so compliant? I pondered if it was the organisation that was my regulator, or perhaps it was my own internal voice telling me that I am not good enough. Perhaps in the past I too had been stuck in a drama triangle of my own, blaming others – the organisation, the CEO, anyone – for my own lack of influence, so persecuting them and at the same time feeling in Victim mode myself. Poor me, unnoticed and powerless!

I began to see that the tasks of organisational change and my own personal change were starting to merge. There was a clear parallel between my own experience and that of the Trust. In order to help the organisation, I also needed to start helping myself. If I was to help the Trust tell its own story, I had to begin to tell my own story with more confidence.

From deficit to appreciation

Alongside the work QINTA was doing, I decided to use a change approach called Appreciative Inquiry (Cooperrider 2005). The core idea is that what we pay attention to counts. If people only talk about the problems, and the things that are wrong, then people feel a sense of burden, despair and heaviness that can be overwhelming and de-energising. I know that's how I felt with all the talk of special measures and perhaps this, in part, explained how James felt too.

I decided to explore all the positive things people felt about working at the hospital, what the organisation did well and what we needed to continue to do in the future. It was a way of helping shift another dominant cultural pattern – that of deficit thinking. This time I wasn't trying to get those senior to me to do something. This time I was doing something more directly myself. I chose to speak to a representative range of staff: an executive director other than James, a nurse director, a surgeon, a medical secretary and a health care assistant.

I based my questions around the first three stages of the appreciative inquiry methodology which are called discovery, dream and design. In the *discovery* stage, I explored what the participants loved about coming to work at the hospital. As I asked the questions I was taken aback by how passionate the individuals were about the organisation. It was completely opposite to the normal daily grumblings: "Back again", "I hate this place", "Can't wait for the end of the day".

One of the members of staff described how he had worked at the Trust for the last 20 years and that it felt like a "second home". Someone else described feelings of pride when the hospital corridors were painted recently. I was astounded by this as the corridor had been painted grey, which I had personally felt was a bad choice of colour and made it look like an institution. It was a reminder how different people interpret artefacts differently. This individual remarked, "The walls being decorated gave me a spring in my step!"

Others described the pride of "being at the heart of a local community", "proud of the care we deliver, not a conveyor belt", and went on to mention the gifts they receive from patients. The surgeon described pride at patient outcomes being better than average, stating "We punch above our weight".

I was surprised how easy it was to enable positive spirals in the conversation. One of my fears had been that I might keep getting stuck in a pattern of having to pull the conversations back from negative aspects, yet it didn't happen.

Only one participant referred to special measures and said "I know things haven't been as good as they should be". It was striking how her body language changed when talking about this – her head dropped, she crossed her arms in a protective manner. I wanted to acknowledge this but at the same time didn't want to amplify the deficit talk and get drawn into the negative dialogue. I was worried we might lose the appreciative focus. Instead I chose to just smile my acknowledgement and touched her on the arm, explaining that I had found it difficult too.

In the second *dream* stage I focused on where they saw the organisation going and their hopes for the future. Everyone mentioned coming out of special measures, but more emotional words were used: "Hope people believe in us again", "People see we have done something well and helped the hospital", "Brighter outlook, with renewed energy".

The third set of questions focused on the *design* of how we could achieve the things we had surfaced in the dream phase. I had been worried about these questions, as I doubted whether people would know how they were going to get there, and if they didn't, how could I help? Did I know all the answers? I was again overwhelmed by their responses. My fears proved to be unfounded. Everyone readily produced positive answers that involved new pathways, departmental meetings planned out of hours to discuss different ventures, and embedding different teams into wards to improve patient care. The huge range of positive ideas and solutions overwhelmed me, but in a good way.

I started to see how my individual gestures had made a difference to these conversations, to the mood, to the local culture. This was complexity thinking in action. This was me leading by making some deliberate gestures to create positive dialogue across departments, specialties and levels. The communications department produced a video showcasing all the positive things the organisation does including the quote that I first heard on the *Vulnerability* TED TALK (Brown 2010) at Ashridge:

> When we deny the story, it defines us.
> When we own the story, we can write a brave new ending.
>
> Brené Brown

The Trust was beginning to feel different, or maybe I was beginning to feel different. The executives seemed to have a sense of renewed energy and spoke positively, using different language, about the board development day. I had more energy too. The relationships with external bodies and our commissioners were becoming more collaborative and less compliant.

I felt that I wanted to experiment with communicating in meetings in a different way, a way that was more informal, encouraged more dialogue and focused on what was going well. I discussed this with a colleague who suggested I start experimenting with this approach at one specific meeting. I didn't ask for permission to do this, I just gave it a go. It went so well that two other colleagues created a template for senior staff focusing on appreciate inquiry and positive behaviour in meetings.

To my amusement, my boss put it into practice the next week, not knowing I had been involved. She informed the attendees at the meeting that there was a new set of "rules" for meetings and no one was allowed to leave the meeting until they had thought of something positive to share! I reflected that it had started a shift in some form, even though not quite as I had intended.

The end of special measures

There were other signs that the Trust was starting to own its own future. The board commissioned a quality improvement programme, with training for a full range of staff, across disciplines and at different levels across the whole organisation.

The Trust exited special measures, with the CQC report citing changes in operational culture and climate, specifically:
- Board responded positively to CQC inspections
- Staff reported they felt more empowered and valued in their roles
- It was observed that staff felt comfortable raising concerns and challenging senior members of staff
- Staff were proud to work for the Trust.

Our CEO was to announce that we were being removed from special measures at an All- Welcome trust event, but suddenly stopped, unable to step forward onto the stage, saying "You make the announcement, I can't, I'm too emotional." A senior colleague was emphatic. "Go on up there; the staff need to see your emotion. It will show them how proud you are. You can do it. You have led this. It is your moment."

So our CEO stepped up and told the staff the good news, with a slightly wobbly voice. The staff were overjoyed by the news about special measures. I reflected that here was another senior leader showing their emotions and doing so in a way which moved others. I heard several people saying how pleased they were that we had a CEO who obviously cared so much and was so personally affected by the news. I can remember feeling so proud; proud of my organisation and our exec team who had guided us through. Perhaps I was beginning to feel just a little bit proud about myself too.

The dominant negative management discourse that pervaded the organisation previously began to change. This was especially apparent amongst the executives, with different words being used such as "bold", "deciding the solution for ourselves", "people to look to us for solutions", "development and talent management from within". All these phrases are now used in our normal everyday language. Shaw (2002) talks of change as the "art of organisational conversing" and, indeed, I think that as an organisation we now talk differently and that there is a marked shift in atmosphere and tenor throughout the Trust.

The power of story

The Trust now publishes stories of success and is having many positive responses from people wanting to learn more about them.

Before my participation in GenerationQ I would have dismissed the power of storytelling, being stuck in a mind-set that operational issues and systems trump everything else. The more I researched and reflected on the Trust, the more I believed in the positive potential of it being able to tell its own story. This belief has grown stronger the more developed the organisation's personal narrative has become, with tangible positive outcomes increasingly obvious. A key learning for me, as I reflect on my story and that of the Trust, is the powerful impact labels have on how we define ourselves as individuals and as institutions. I can remember how we all felt about "working in a special measures Trust", and the sense we each had that we must therefore be dreadful. Being labelled a special measures Trust is now part of our Trust's history, yet crucial to me has been our eventual response to regulatory action. We collectively owned our history and organisational story, which included being open and acknowledging that there were real problems that needed addressing. We didn't, however, collapse into despair or become victims to others' labels and others' solutions. I feel that we actively resisted, in a good way. I feel proud to have helped by having what were for me some brave conversations. I can never know exactly how much I personally contributed to the shift away from compliance, but that is the nature of working in a complex system.

I tried to identify the tipping point that made the cultural patterns in the organisation finally begin to shift. Initially, all the interventions had been focused on solving the problem, defined as "How do we get out of special measures?" The approaches chosen had mostly come from turn-around directors, newly appointed by external agencies, and were seen by staff as being "done to" them. Looking back, this problem-solving approach served to only further exacerbate the sense of oppression and hopelessness. The positive impact of the decision to appoint QINTA to facilitate shared conversations in order to develop the organisational story, and the use of appreciative inquiry throughout the organisation, seem to support the idea that shifts in conversation can be more effective in stimulating cultural shifts.

Change begins with the first question. Sustainability comes when people own what they create. Appreciative inquiry can work in crises as well as in situations where organisations are performing well.

My story as a leader

When I first started GenerationQ, I felt my career was at risk of losing its way. I felt I was invisible, not recognised in the Trust, which I found incredibly frustrating and diminishing. Deep down I knew I could do so much more, but didn't feel brave enough to apply for a bigger job because of self-doubt, and concerns about having to make compromises with family life. Being willing to keep in conversation with James, staying in Adult mode rather than joining in the drama triangle, recognising my own contribution and power rather than allowing myself to fade away at the first setback, these have all been important learnings in my changing story. At the start of this story, I labelled myself a middle manager. On reflection, I don't think that is the right way of describing who I became as a result of these experiences: senior leader with influence.

However, one other aspect of my learning remains to be shared. Watching the TED talk on *Vulnerability* by Brené Brown (2010) whilst at one of the GenerationQ workshops transformed my approach to my life. It was my own personal tipping point. I was struck by how much better my life would be, at home and at work, if I could accept the past and own my own story, both the successes and the failures. If I could accept that my story makes me who I am, and that "I am good enough", then I could move forward.

My first experiments with vulnerability and authentic leadership didn't quite work. I jumped in with two feet thinking that owning my story and being authentic meant telling everyone everything! People didn't know how to react, as indeed I hadn't when James revealed so much during our walk and talk at Ashridge. My coach helped me see that being authentic and owning the past includes owning how much you want to share, depending on the context. Once I had made this connection, I began to fully under-stand the personal strength and peace this can bring. A colleague on GenerationQ offered the metaphor of now being able to put my clothes back on. This description felt correct. I was in control of myself, and not exposed. This feeling is mirrored in the Trust, owning its story and vision. We have our clothes back on, we are no longer naked and being scrutinised by the regulators, but taking charge of our own destiny.

My tutor in my Masters' supervision group was the person who first raised with me the similarities between my own story and that of my organisation. Initially I was a little confused, but then could see the strong parallels in the way both the organisation and I were trying to explain away our current situations. Both are influenced by, and influence, the systems in which we exist. It is a process of mutual contagion. We cannot help but be shaped by the context and cultural patterns in which we operate, and we cannot help but influence the system. Thus, the boundaries between behaviour in different systems become blurred, and over time we see parallel process, where we "take on" or "mirror" the behaviour of another system.

Through the joint work and appreciative inquiry, both I and the organisation have begun to change, shifting the way we are, recognising the need to acknowledge the past and to pause and take time to work out how to write our futures.

> *When we deny the story it defines us.*
> *When we own the story, we can write a brave new ending.*

Brené Brown

Closing Reflections

Learning is personal and contextual

In the introduction to this book we wrote that the stories represent the Fellows' individual truths, their learning, their inner dialogue about what they thought and felt about what they did and why. With a similar sentiment, we hope and anticipate that each of you, having now read this book, will have found your own learning – ideas, possible actions, new ways of seeing situations and people. Some of what you have read perhaps resonated with you, affirming what you are already doing. Other aspects may have offered stimulation for alternative approaches, expanding your repertoire of options. We encourage you to make sense of what you have read for yourself, considering your own experience and your own unique context. The reflective questions we offered in the Introduction might be useful in this respect. As a reminder, they are:

- What has struck you as important or interesting?
- What has caught your attention or curiosity?
- What has challenged you or makes you want to disagree?
- What questions do the stories leave you with, for your own leadership?

Themes emerging from the stories

We believe strongly that learning is personal and contextual, and that it is more helpful to share *good* practice rather than advocate *best* practice. It would therefore be incongruent for us to try and "wrap the book up" by offering conclusions that aspire to have some universal truth, that are mandates or prescriptions about what you ought to do as a leader.

However, themes have emerged from the stories that seem pertinent for all leaders wishing to shift their local cultures to be more conducive to high-quality patient care, and they are the themes represented by each of the previous sections:

- The theme of Tempered Tenacity, where as a leader you know why you hold dear to certain beliefs, your moral compass, that enables you to *speak up*, to say your truth in a way that others can hear without either you or your idea being rejected.
- The theme of Bridging the Divides, where as a leader you choose to *reach out* to others, to have empathy and build working relationships, even if you don't always see eye to eye, so that co-operation and collaboration are possible.
- The theme of Constructive Resistance, where as a leader you choose to *stand firm*, to protect something that is valuable even if in the face of opposition, or mandate from those more senior in the hierarchy.

And, of course, these themes are closely linked. In choosing to reach out to others, or to stand firm in the face of opposition, tempered tenacity is required. As a senior colleague commented to us recently, tempered tenacity is a more meaningful descriptor than resilience for what is required to lead in health and social care right now. It speaks to an attitudinal and emotional state of being, to having purpose – almost a moral imperative – to having strong personal values and to having the courage to stand out from the crowd. It also speaks to acting with skill and judgement, knowing when and how to act and when to keep one's powder dry.

Further reflections

Beyond inviting personal reflection and reminding you of the themes emerging from the stories, we are tempted to offer just a few reflections of our own, drawing upon our experience of authoring this book and from coming to know the Fellows' stories in depth.

The impact of thinking differently

The first relates to just how impactful thinking differently has proven to be; how challenging leaders' assumptions about the nature of organisations, leadership and culture can make a positive difference to both their practice and experience of leadership.

In Chapter 3 we described how Fellows, when first exposed to complexity thinking, can throw their hands up in horror as their own sense of identity as a leader is challenged. And yet, how over time, it can liberate them from the burden of machine thinking, heroic leadership and trying to be in control.

As we read the stories, we are struck by just how liberated the Fellows have become, liberated to experiment with making small and yet significant gestures to shift their local cultures, to challenge and speak up, to reach out and to stand firm. The sense of burden often associated with heroic leadership appears to have been lifted, or perhaps become more bearable, as they lead with a sense of shared endeavour and shared responsibility. The task of leadership has become to act skilfully and with good intent, rather than to deliver pre-determined outcomes with certainty. Their confidence to lead appears to have grown and Imposter Syndrome (Clance and Imes 1978) seems to have been held at bay, with less looking over shoulders, waiting to be "found out". Accepting that "I am good enough" to lead seems to have become a reality for many, as has the possibility of experiencing leadership as personally fulfilling.

The importance of relational skills

We know that shifting cultures, working across organisational, professional and hierarchal boundaries takes finely tuned relational skills. It requires understanding of others, being aware of your own hooks and biases, being able to deeply listen and to create the conditions for genuine exchange.

And, even though we knew this at the outset, we are struck by just how significant relational skills are in each of the stories, whether that be knowing how to judge when to push and when to pull, knowing how to create the conditions for dialogue or how to contain anxiety (own and others') in the face of uncertainty. These are the skills we explored in brief in Chapter 4.

The need for political nous and savviness has also come to the fore, being comfortable and active with back stage as well as front stage conversations, being a wise owl rather than a naïve sheep or an awkward donkey. In the stories, the Fellows talk frequently of making choices, in the moment, about when to challenge and when to keep quiet, "walking the line versus toeing the line", being brave and taking calculated risks, without being fool-hardy or politically naïve. Politics, rather than being a dirty or manipulative word, has become a necessary enabler of change.

We are also struck by the unexpected that reaching out and developing relationships can bring. The delight of discovering that you have more in common with others than you perhaps assumed, the delight of discovering creativity and new possibilities for action.

The need for time, space and support

Fellows on the programme value having other, like-minded leaders to talk with – good colleagues, a coach, being a member of an action learning set. The energy and tenacity required to keep going can be draining, especially if the impact of your gestures can seem elusive or difficult to gauge. Reaching out to others rather than acting alone or keeping everything to yourself seems to be essential to thriving not just surviving as a leader, according to these accounts.

It is also striking that many of the accounts took place over a considerable period. These are not stories of quick fixes but of holding to a direction of travel, even if the exact route is unclear and winding. They are stories of leaders being willing to take advantage of what emerges and work with what is, as well as keeping sight of what is needed in the future. To lead in this way takes the gift of time and space, not just to reflect and to choose wisely, but to be trusted to "get on with the job" and to take the time needed to see it through well.

Generosity and hope

Finally, we want to turn again to generosity and hope. This book has taken many months to write and it has been a period of uncertainty for the key contributors who have offered their stories and contributions, not quite knowing where we are going but trusting that something good will come of it. We are struck by their generosity and willingness to "put themselves out there", their deeply felt desire to help others working in the system, and the degree of care they have shown. We are struck by their courage to "stay with it" during periods of uncertainty and know that this is as true in their work as it has been in this collaborative endeavour. All of us owe them our thanks.

And to close, what might be possible if more leaders in health and social care felt empowered to make a difference, to shift patterns of behaviour to make their local cultures more conducive to high-quality patient care? We are not denying that other big questions such as funding still need to be addressed, and yet our hope is that by reading this book, you feel better equipped and enabled to make the difference locally to improve the quality of patient care.

Suggested Further Reading

1. Binney, G., Wilke, G., and Williams, C. (2012). *Living Leadership: a practical guide for ordinary heroes.* 3rd Edition. Harlow: Pearson Education Limited
2. Wiggins, L. and Hunter, H. (2016). *Relational Change: The art and practice of changing organizations.* London: Bloomsbury Business
3. Stacey, R. (2012). *The Tools and Techniques of Leadership and Management: meeting the challenge of complexity.* London: Routledge
4. Isaacs, W. (1999). *Dialogue and the Art of Thinking Together.* New York: Doubleday
5. Lapworth, P. and Sills, C. (2011). *An Introduction to Transactional Analysis.* London: Sage
6. Oshry, B. (2008). *Seeing Systems: unlocking the mysteries of organizational life.* Oakland: Berrett-Koehler Publishers Inc.
7. Heron, J. (2009). 5th Edition. *Helping the Client: a creative practical guide.* London: Sage

References

Preface

Berwick, D. (2013). Letter accompanying the Berwick Report into safety in the NHS. [Online] https://www.gov.uk/government/uploads/system/uploads/attachment_data/file/226709/berwick_letter_to_NHS.PDF

Schien, E. (2009). *Helping – How to Offer, Give, and Receive Help.* San Francisco: Berrett-Koehler Publishers

Stacey, R. (2012). Responding to Complexity and Uncertainty: The Agile Organisation. [Online] https://complexityandmanagement.wordpress.com/2012/08/29/responding-to-complexity-and-uncertainty-the-agile-organisation/

West, M. (2016). [Online] https://www.kingsfund.org.uk/blog/2016/01/if-it%E2%80%99s-about-culture-it%E2%80%99s-about-leadership

Introduction

Keough, B. (2017). Key note address at Leaders on Healthcare Conference. Liverpool, 1st November 2017

Section 1: Framing
Chapter 1: Reframing Contexts

Ashforth, B. and Kreiner, G. (1999). How Can You Do It? Dirty work and the challenges of constructing a positive identity. *Academy of Management Review,* 24(3), pp. 413 – 434

Charlesworth, A., Thorlby R., Roberts, A. and Gershlick, B (2017). *Election Briefing: NHS and social care funding. Three unavoidable challenges.* London: The Health Foundation

Goffee, R. and Jones, G. (2015). *Why Should Anyone Be Led by You?* Boston: Harvard Business Review Publishing

Isaacs, W. (1999). *Dialogue and the Art of Thinking Together.* New York: Doubleday

Lafond, S., Charlesworth, A. and Roberts, A. (2016). *A Perfect Storm: an impossible climate for NHS providers' finances? An analysis of NHS finances and factors associated with financial performance.* London: The Health Foundation

Lapierre, L. (1989). Mourning, Potency, and Power in Management. *Human Resource Management,* 29(2), pp. 177-189

Scherer, J. (2009). *Five Questions that Change Everything: Life lessons at work.* Word Keepers Inc.

Stiehm, J. and Townsend, N. (2002). *The U.S. Army War College: military education in a democracy.* Philadelphia: Temple University Press

Chapter 2: Shifting Local Culture(s)

Brown, M. (1998). The Invisible Advantage. *The Ashridge Journal.* Nov 1998, p. 20

Isaacs, W. (1999). *Dialogue and the Art of Thinking Together.* New York: Doubleday

Schein, E. (2010). *Organizational Culture and Leadership.* 4th Edition. San Francisco: Jossey-Bass

Chapter 3: Thinking Differently About Organisations and Leadership

Binney, G., Wilke, G., and Williams, C. (2012). *Living Leadership: a practical guide for ordinary heroes.* 3rd Edition. Harlow: Pearson Education Limited

Clance, P. and Imes, S. (1978). The Imposter Phenomenon in High Achieving Women: dynamics and therapeutic interventions. *Psychotherapy: Theory, Research and Practice,* 15(3) pp. 241–247

Gladwell, M. (2002). *The Tipping Point: how little things can make a big difference.* Boston: Little, Brown and Company

Stacey, R. (2012). *The Tools and Techniques of Leadership and Management: meeting the challenge of complexity.* London: Routledge

Streatfield, P. (2001). *The Paradox of Control in Organisations.* London: Routledge

The Kings Fund (2011). *The future of leadership and management in the NHS. No more heroes.* Report from The King's Fund Commission on Leadership and Management in the NHS.

Weick, K. (1995). *Sensemaking in Organizations.* London: Sage

Chapter 4: Making Moves

Argyris, C. and Schon, D. (1995). *Organizational Learning II: theory, method and practice.* Reading, MA: Addison-Wesley

Baddeley, S. and James, K. (1987). Owl, Fox, Donkey, Sheep: political skills for managers. *Management Education and Development*, 18(1), pp. 3-19

Berne, E. (1968). *Games People Play: the psychology of human relationships* Harmondsworth: Penguin

Buchanan, D. and Boddy, D. (1992). *The Expertise of the Change Agent; Public Performance and Back Stage Activity.* London: Prentice Hall

Choy, A. (1990). The Winner's Triangle. *Transactional Analysis Journal*, 20(1), p. 40

Heron, J. (2009). *Helping the Client: a creative practical guide.* 5th Edition. London: Sage

Isaacs, W. (1999). *Dialogue and the Art of Thinking Together.* New York: Doubleday

Karpman, S. (2011). Fairy Tales and Script Drama Analysis. *Group Facilitation*, (11), p. 49

Section 2: Tempered Tenacity

Meyerson, D. and Scully, M. (1995). Tempered Radicalism and the Politics of Ambivalence and Change. *Organization*, 6(5), September–October

Chapter 5: Blocking the Door

Bromiley, M. (Producer) (2011). Just a routine operation. [Online video] Available at https://www.youtube.com/watch?v=JzlvgtPIof4.

Brown, B. (Producer). (2011). The Power of Vulnerability. [Online video] Available at https://www.youtube.com/watch?v=iCvmsMzlF7o.

Heifetz, R. and Linsky, M. (2002). *Leadership on the Line.* Boston: Harvard Business School Press

Kahane, A. (2010). *Power and Love: a theory and practice of social change.* 1st Edition. San Francisco: Berrett-Koehler Publishers Inc.

Scott, S. (2002). *Fierce Conversations: achieving success in work and in life, one conversation at a time.* London: Piatkus

Chapter 7: The Cycle Helmet and the Fire Starter

Baddeley, S. and James, K. (1987). Owl, Fox, Donkey, Sheep: political skills for managers. *Management Education and Development*, 18(1), pp. 3-19

Brown, B. (2010). The Power of Vulnerability. [Online] TED. Available at: https://www.ted.com/talks/brene_brown_on_vulnerability.

Deming, W. (2000). *Out of the Crisis.* Cambridge Ma: Center for Advanced Engineering Study, Massachusetts Institute of Technology

Fletcher, J. (2001). *Disappearing Acts: gender, power and relational practice at work.* Cambridge MA: MIT Press

Chapter 8: They'll All Die Anyway

Gowens, P. and Sinclair, N. (2017). *SAS Data Warehouse Ad-Hoc ROSC Report 2011-17.* [Online] http://www.scottishambulance.com/. Available at: http://SAS Data Warehouse

Chapter 9: Leading From the Heart

Burhouse, A., Rowland, M., Niman, H. et al (2015). Coaching for recovery: a quality improvement project in mental healthcare. *BMJ Open Quality.* [Online] http://bmjopenquality.bmj.com/content/4/1/u206576.w2641

Deming, W. (2000). *Out of the Crisis.* Cambridge Ma: Center for Advanced Engineering Study, Massachusetts Institute of Technology

Isaacs, W. (1999). *Dialogue and the Art of Thinking Together.* New York: Doubleday

Juran, J. and Godfrey, A.B. (1999), *Juran's Quality Handbook,* 5th Edition. New York: McGraw-Hill

Meddings, S., Byrne, D., Barnicoat, S., Campbell, E., and Locks, L. (2014a). Co-delivered and co-produced: Creating a Recovery College in Partnership. *The Journal of Mental Health Training, Education and Practice,* 9(1), pp. 16-2

Pattakos, A. (2007) *Prisoners of Our Thoughts: Viktor Frankl's principles for discovering meaning in life and work.* 2nd Edition. San Francisco: Berrett-Koehler Publishers Inc.

Perkins, R., Repper, J., Rinaldi, M. and Brown, H. (2012). Recovery Colleges Briefing. Centre for mental health. [Online] https://www.centreformentalhealth.org.uk/recovery-colleges-paper

Scully, Frank (1950). Scully's Scrapbook. *Variety* 1950 September 20. Published by Variety Inc., New York

Section 3: Bridging the Divides
Chapter 10: Seeing Through the Eyes of Another:

Oshry, B. (2008). *Seeing Systems: unlocking the mysteries of organizational life.* Oakland: Berrett-Koehler Publishers Inc.

Stacey, R. (2012). *Tools and Techniques of Leadership and Management: meeting the challenge of complexity.* London: Routledge

Whitney, D. and Trosten-Bloom, A. (2010). *The Power of Appreciative Inquiry: a practical guide to positive change.* 2nd Edition. San Francisco: Berrett-Koehler Publishers Inc

Chapter 11: Now for Something Completely Different

Stacey, R. (2011). *Strategic Management and Organisational Dynamics: the challenge of complexity.* 6th Edition. New Jersey: FT Press

Stacey, R. (2012). *The Tools and Techniques of Leadership and Management: meeting the challenge of complexity.* London: Routledge

Chapter 12: Choosing Wedlock Over Deadlock

Barrett, F. and Fry, R. (2005). *Appreciative Inquiry: a positive approach to building cooperative capacity.* Ohio: Taos Institute Publications

Binney, G., Wilke, G., and Williams, C. (2012). *Living Leadership: a practical guide for ordinary heroes.* 3rd Edition. Harlow: Pearson Education Limited

Buchanan, D. and Badham, R. (2008). *Power, Politics and Organizational Change: winning the turf game.* 2nd Edition. London: Sage

Cartwright, S. and Cooper, G. (1996). *Managing Mergers, Acquisitions & Strategic Alliances: integrating people and cultures.* 2nd Edition. Abingdon: Routledge

Cooperrider, D., Whitney, D. and Stavros, J. (2005). *Appreciative Inquiry Handbook: for leaders of change.* 2nd Edition. Ohio: Crown Custom Publishing Inc.

Heifetz, R. and Linsky, M. (2002). *Leadership on the Line.* Boston: Harvard Business School Press

Johnson, B. (1992). *Polarity Management, Identifying and Managing Unsolvable Problems.* Massachusetts: HRD Press Inc.

Karpman, S. (1968). Fairy Tales and Script Drama Analysis. *Transactional Analysis Bulletin,* 7(26), pp. 39-43

Lapworth, P. and Sills, C. (2011). *An Introduction to Transactional Analysis.* London: Sage

Stacey, R. (2010). *Complexity and Organizational Reality.* 2nd Edition. Abingdon: Routledge

Tajfel, H. (ed.) (1978). *Differentiation Between Social Groups: studies in the social psychology of intergroup relations.* London: Academic Press

Tajfel, H., Billing, M., Bundy, R.P. and Flament, C. (1971). Social Categorization and Intergroup Behaviour. *European Journal of Social Psychology,* 1, pp. 149-77

Chapter 13: Quietening the Wind

Binney, G., Wilke, G., and Williams, C. (2012). *Living Leadership: a practical guide for ordinary heroes.* 3rd Edition. Harlow: Pearson Education Limited

Section 4: Constructive Resistance
Chapter 14: Creating Space

Deming, W. (2000). *Out of the Crisis.* Cambridge Ma: Center for Advanced Engineering Study, Massachusetts Institute of Technology

Chapter 15: Owning Our History – Changing the Story

Brown, B. (Producer). (2011). The Power of Vulnerability. [Online video] Available at https://www.youtube.com/watch?v=iCvmsMzlF7o.
Cooperrider, D. and Whitney, D. (2005). *Appreciative Inquiry: a positive revolution in change.* San Francisco: Berrett-Koehler Publishers Inc
Okri, B. (n.d.) Available at: https://www.goodreads.com/quotes/239712-a-people-are-as-healthy-and-confident-as-the-stories
Shaw, P. (2002). *Changing Conversations in Organizations: a complexity approach to change.* London: Routledge

Closing Reflections

Clance, P. and Imes, S. (1978). The Imposter Phenomenon in High Achieving Women: dynamics and therapeutic interventions. *Psychotherapy: Theory, Research and Practice,* 15(3) pp. 241–247

About the Authors

The authors co-lead GenerationQ, a Master's programme in Leading for Quality Improvement for senior leaders in health, social care and health charities. The programme is sponsored by the Health Foundation and designed and delivered at Ashridge Executive Education, Hult Business School.

Liz Wiggins is Associate Professor of Change and Leadership and has over twenty-five years' experience of working with leaders in the US, Europe and Asia. She worked as a leader herself at Unilever and has two Masters degrees and a PhD in Organizational Psychology from Birkbeck College, University of London.

Janet Smallwood has also been involved with GenerationQ since the outset of the programme and has more than 20 years' experience as an OD consultant and leadership developer. She holds Masters Degrees in Natural Sciences and Chemical Engineering from Cambridge and the Ashridge Masters in Organization Consulting.

Brian Marshall is Academic Director and Discipline Lead for OD and Change at Ashridge Executive Education, part of the Hult International Business School and was formerly Strategy Director for Unipart and head of OD at the UK Civil Service. Brian has a first degree in English literature from London University, and a Master's degree in Organisational Change from Ashridge.

Contributors. The stories are written by senior leaders who participated in GenerationQ and they provide rarely heard, personal, "warts and all", accounts of what it is like to lead in practice, making moves to improve things for the better in their workplaces.